27th International Conference on Computational Linguistics (COLING 2018)

System Demonstrations

Santa Fe, New Mexico, USA
20 – 26 August 2018

ISBN: 978-1-5108-6905-9

Printed by Curran Associates, Inc. (2018)

For permission requests, please contact the Association for Computational Linguistics
at the address below.

Association for Computational Linguistics
209 N. Eighth Street
Stroudsburg, Pennsylvania 18360

Phone: 1-570-476-8006
Fax: 1-570-476-0860

acl@aclweb.org

Additional copies of this publication are available from:

Curran Associates, Inc.
57 Morehouse Lane
Red Hook, NY 12571 USA
Phone: 845-758-0400
Fax: 845-758-2633
Email: curran@proceedings.com
Web: www.proceedings.com

COLING 2018

The 27th International Conference on Computational Linguistics

Proceedings of System Demonstrations

August 20-26, 2018
Santa Fe, New Mexico, USA

Preface

This volume contains papers from the system demonstration session of the 27th International Conference on Computational Linguistics (COLING 2018) held in Santa Fe, New Mexico, USA. The conference will be held at the Santa Fe Community Convention Center from August 20th through 26th 2018, under the auspices of the International Committee on Computational Linguistics (ICCL).

The demonstration session complements the conference's presentation and poster sessions and is focused on working software systems that are the tangible outcomes of research on computational linguistics.

As a result of a rigorous review process, we accepted 35 papers out of 53 submissions. The program committee consisted of 36 members and one chair from both academia and industry. Each member evaluated 3-5 papers, which amounted to at least two reviews per paper. The acceptance criteria we followed during the selection process included the quality of work as well as the utility and demonstrability potential of the presented systems. Consequently, most of the accepted systems are user-interactive and feature rich graphical user interfaces.

First and foremost we would like to thank the program committee for their hard work and dedication to help make this event a success. Our special thanks also go to the people who made COLING 2018 and this volume possible. We thank General Chair, Dr. Pierre Isabelle (Principal Scientist of NCR), Program Chairs, Prof. Emily M. Bender (University of Washington) and Prof. Leon Derczynski (University of Sheffield), Local Arrangements Chair, Prof. Sergei Nirenburg (Rensselaer Polytechnic Institute), Proceedings Chairs, Prof. Xiaodan Zhu (Queen's University) and Prof. Zhiyuan Liu (Tsinghua University), and Webmaster Dr. Qian Chen (University of Science and Technology of China) and Christine Tang, for their tireless work.

Dongyan ZHAO

COLING 2018 Demonstration Program Chair

10 July 2018

Demonstration Chair

Dongyan Zhao, Peking University, China

Program Committee:

Daniel Bauer, Columbia University, USA
Yi Cai, South China University of Technology, China
Chen Chen, University of Texas at Dallas, USA
Liwei Chen, Peking University, China
Nancy Chen, A*START, Singapore
Zhumin Chen, Shandong University, China
Li Cheng, Xinjiang Technology Institute, CAS, China
Vincent Claveau, IRISA, France
Christos Doulopoulos, Carnegie Mellon University, USA
Chong Feng, Beijing Institute of Technology, China
Yang Feng, Institute of Computing, CAS, China
Yansong Feng, Peking University, China
Xianpei Han, Institute of Software, CAS, China
Tianyong Hao, Guangzhou Foreign Language University, China
Ben He, Institute of Software, CAS, China
Minlie Huang, Tsinghua University, China
Wenbin Jiang, Baidu Inc., China
Yuxuan Lai, Peking University, China
Phillippe Langlais, University of Montreal, Canada
Jun Liang, Alibaba Inc., Singapore
Xiao Ling, University of Washington, USA
Zhanyi Liu, Baidu Inc., China
Bingfeng Luo, Peking University, China
Yajuan Lv, Baidu Inc., China
Pascual Martínez-Gómez, AIST Tokyo, Japan
Xianling Mao, Beijing Institute of Technology, China
Hiroshi Noji, Nara Institute of Science and Technology, Japan
Jinsun Su, Xiamen University, China
Weiwei Sun, Peking University, China
Haofen Wang, Gowild Tech, China
Xiaojie Wang, Beijing University of Post and Telecommunication, China
Zheng Wang, Lancaster University, UK
Kun Xu, Tencent AI Lab, USA
Dongdong Zhang, Microsoft Research, China
Huaping Zhang, Beijing Institute of Technology, China
Hai Zhao, Shanghai Jiaotong University, China

Table of Contents

Conference Program

August 21

Demo Session 1

Abbreviation Expander - a Web-based System for Easy Reading of Technical Documents
Manuel Ciosici and Ira Assent

The INCEpTION Platform: Machine-Assisted and Knowledge-Oriented Interactive Annotation
Jan-Christoph Klie, Michael Bugert, Beto Boullosa, Richard Eckart de Castilho and Iryna Gurevych

JeSemE: Interleaving Semantics and Emotions in a Web Service for the Exploration of Language Change Phenomena
Johannes Hellrich, Sven Buechel and Udo Hahn

T-Know: a Knowledge Graph-based Question Answering and Infor-mation Retrieval System for Traditional Chinese Medicine
Ziqing Liu, Enwei Peng, Shixing Yan, Guozheng Li and Tianyong Hao

A Korean Knowledge Extraction System for Enriching a KBox
Sangha Nam, Eun-kyung Kim, Jiho Kim, Yoosung Jung, Kijong Han and KEY-SUN CHOI

Real-time Scholarly Retweeting Prediction System
Zhunchen Luo and Xiao Liu

Document Representation Learning for Patient History Visualization
Halid Ziya Yerebakan, Yoshihisa Shinagawa, Parmeet Bhatia and Yiqiang Zhan

HiDE: a Tool for Unrestricted Literature Based Discovery
Judita Preiss and Mark Stevenson

Active DOP: an Active Learning Constituency Treebank Annotation Tool
Andreas van Cranenburgh

Demo Session 2

CRST: a Claim Retrieval System in Twitter
Wenjia Ma, WenHan Chao, Zhunchen Luo and Xin Jiang

Utilizing Graph Measure to Deduce Omitted Entities in Paragraphs
Eun-kyung Kim, Kijong Han, Jiho Kim and KEY-SUN CHOI

Transparent, Efficient, and Robust Word Embedding Access with WOMBAT
Mark-Christoph Müller and Michael Strube

SetExpander: End-to-end Term Set Expansion Based on Multi-Context Term Embeddings
Jonathan Mamou, Oren Pereg, Moshe Wasserblat, Ido Dagan, Yoav Goldberg, Alon Eirew, Yael Green, Shira Guskin, Peter Izsak and Daniel Korat

Detecting Heavy Rain Disaster from Social and Physical Sensor
Tomoya Iwakura, Seiji Okajima, Nobuyuki Igata, Kunihiro Takeda, Yuzuru Yamakage and Naoshi Morita

Simulating Language Evolution: a Tool for Historical Linguistics
Alina Maria Ciobanu and Liviu P. Dinu

A Unified RvNN Framework for End-to-End Chinese Discourse Parsing
Lin Chuan-An, Hen-Hsen Huang, Zi-Yuan Chen and Hsin-Hsi Chen

A Web-based Framework for Collecting and Assessing Highlighted Sentences in a Document
Sasha Spala, Franck Dernoncourt, Walter Chang and Carl Dockhorn

Cool English: a Grammatical Error Correction System Based on Large Learner Corpora
Yu-Chun Lo, Jhih-Jie Chen, Chingyu Yang and Jason Chang

Demo Session 3

Appraise Evaluation Framework for Machine Translation
Christian Federmann

KIT Lecture Translator: Multilingual Speech Translation with One-Shot Learning
Florian Dessloch, Thanh-Le Ha, Markus Müller, Jan Niehues, Thai Son Nguyen, Ngoc-Quan Pham, Elizabeth Salesky, Matthias Sperber, Sebastian Stüker, Thomas Zenkel and Alexander Waibel

Graphene: a Context-Preserving Open Information Extraction System
Matthias Cetto, Christina Niklaus, André Freitas and Siegfried Handschuh

LanguageNet: Learning to Find Sense Relevant Example Sentences
Shang-Chien Cheng, Jhih-Jie Chen, Chingyu Yang and Jason Chang

Automatic Curation and Visualization of Crime Related Information from Incrementally Crawled Multi-source News Reports
Tirthankar Dasgupta, Lipika Dey, Rupsa Saha and Abir Naskar

Lingke: a Fine-grained Multi-turn Chatbot for Customer Service
Pengfei Zhu, Zhuosheng Zhang, Jiangtong Li, Yafang Huang and Hai Zhao

Writing Mentor: Self-Regulated Writing Feedback for Struggling Writers
Nitin Madnani, Jill Burstein, Norbert Elliot, Beata Beigman Klebanov, Diane Napolitano, Slava Andreyev and Maxwell Schwartz

NLATool: an Application for Enhanced Deep Text Understanding
Markus Gärtner, Sven Mayer, Valentin Schwind, Eric Hämmerle, Emine Turcan, Florin Rheinwald, Gustav Murawski, Lars Lischke and Jonas Kuhn

Sensala: a Dynamic Semantics System for Natural Language Processing
Daniyar Itegulov, Ekaterina Lebedeva and Bruno Woltzenlogel Paleo

Demo Session 4

Abbreviation Expander -
A web-based system for easy reading of technical documents

Manuel R. Ciosici
UNSILO A/S and
Aarhus University
Aarhus, Denmark
manuel@cs.au.dk

Ira Assent
Department of Computer Science
Aarhus University
Aarhus, Denmark
ira@cs.au.dk

Abstract

Abbreviations and acronyms are a part of textual communication in most domains. However, abbreviations are not necessarily defined in documents that employ them. Understanding all abbreviations used in a given document often requires extensive knowledge of the target domain and the ability to disambiguate based on context. This creates considerable entry barriers to newcomers and difficulties in automated document processing. Existing abbreviation expansion systems or tools require substantial technical knowledge for set up or make strong assumptions which limit their use in practice. Here, we present Abbreviation Expander, a system that builds on state of the art methods for identification of abbreviations, acronyms and their definitions and a novel disambiguator for abbreviation expansion in an easily accessible web-based solution.

1   Introduction

Abbreviations and acronyms are often used in text documents and denote typically long, often domain-specific, concepts that authors need to refer to multiple times. However, the use of abbreviations and acronyms can make reading and understanding difficult for people new to a specific field, can lead to confusion, and make automated text processing challenging, for example, in indexing text documents. Unfortunately, expanding abbreviations is a complex task. The meaning of some abbreviations and acronyms (e.g. DNA meaning *deoxyribonucleic acid* in biology-related domains) is often considered well-known, and is rarely defined in documents using them. Other abbreviations and acronyms can denote multiple concepts, depending on their context (e.g. PCB can refer to a number of distinct concepts[1]).

Available abbreviation expansion systems are limited in their usefulness either due to requiring technical knowledge on the user side or by relying on simple, dictionary-based methods which cannot be applied to ambiguous abbreviations that have more than one meaning. We present a system that automatically expands abbreviations and acronyms in a user provided document. Our system is a web-based application that does not require that users have experience setting up pipelines for Natural Language Processing. We build on state-of-the-art Natural Language Processing techniques and a novel disambiguation method based on unsupervised learning.

2   System Architecture

By building a web application, we aim to make users oblivious to the technical complexities of processing natural language. From a user's point of view, they upload a text file to the system and immediately see the file's content with all abbreviations and acronyms expanded.

Figure 1 shows the architecture of Abbreviation Expander's back-end. Text is first tokenized and split into sentences, after which a number of abbreviation expanders are used. Finally, their results are combined. The biggest part of our system is composed of the processing pipeline. We use the *UIMA*[2] framework as the basis for our system because it provides mature support for construction of processing

---

[1] https://en.wikipedia.org/wiki/PCB

[2] https://uima.apache.org

Proceedings of the 27th International Conference on Computational Linguistics: System Demonstrations, pages 1–4
Santa Fe, New Mexico, USA, August 20-26, 2018.

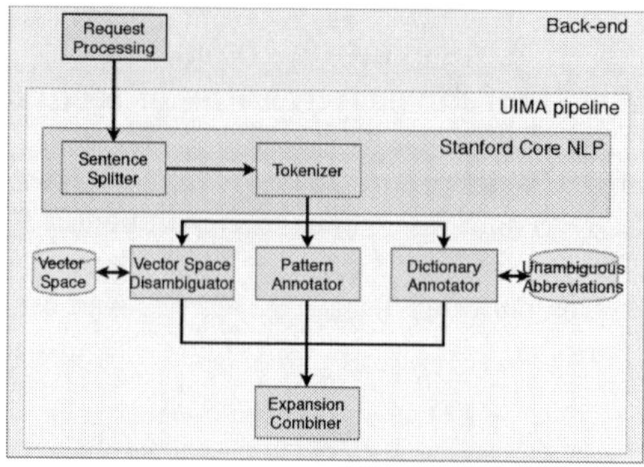

Figure 1: System architecture: input text is split and tokenized, defined abbreviations are extracted and expanded (Pattern Annotator), a dictionary resolves unambiguous cases (Dictionary Annotator), ambiguous cases are expanded using context (Vector Space Disambiguator); possible conflicts are resolved in the Expansion Combiner.

pipelines and benefits from a wide-array of external NLP libraries. The wide support for libraries allows us to employ established tools for pre-processing steps such as tokenization and sentence splitting for which we use the Stanford Core NLP library (Manning et al., 2014). We separate the abbreviation and acronym expansion into four different components: three components that perform expansion and one that combines their outputs in order to achieve consistency.

Before we describe the various components in detail, we establish some definitions. An *unambiguous abbreviation or acronym* is one that never expands into more than a single long-form. This corresponds to a one-to-one mapping. For example, in all of English Wikipedia we could only find one meaning for the acronym *SSRMS*, meaning *Space Station Remote Manipulator System*, popularly referred to as *Canadarm2*. An *ambiguous abbreviation or acronym* is one that can expand to multiple long-forms and the correct expansion is dependent on the context. However, *an unambiguous use* of an ambiguous abbreviation or acronym is one where an ambiguous abbreviation or acronym is used in such a way that the correct expansion is obvious. One such case is the definition of an abbreviation, such as *The Mobile Servicing System (MSS), is a robotic system on board the International Space Station*[3]. Because of the definition, it is clear which expansion is intended by the author.

The *Pattern Annotator* component is a re-implementation of the rules presented by Schwartz and Hearst (2003). It uses linguistic patterns to identify definitions of abbreviations and acronyms. More specifically, it looks for either the pattern *text (<short-form>)*, or the reverse *<short-form>(text)*. For each identified instance, it attempts to find a long-form expansion in the text preceding the parenthesis or contained in the parenthesis, respectively. This component can thus identify abbreviations and acronyms defined directly in the user-provided text. Our implementation differs from that of BADREX (Gooch, 2011) by the fact that it more closely follows the extraction rules defined in Schwartz and Hearst (2003). At the same time, we provide added support for various edge cases. For example, the original method does not support mapping of long-forms to short-forms when the long form contains two words at the beginning that start with the same letter (for example, *OAS* meaning *Organization of American States* is wrongly mapped to *of American States*). Our system solves this by a combination of looking ahead and a small set of stop-words not to be considered for the first word in a long-form (e.g. which, where, at, on, . . .).

The *Dictionary Annotator* component uses a dictionary of unambiguous abbreviations and acronyms, that we automatically extracted from English Wikipedia. We pre-processed English Wikipedia using only our Pattern Annotator in order to extract all abbreviations and acronyms that are unambiguous. Unambiguous abbreviations and acronyms have a one-to-one mapping between long-forms and short-forms. This annotator gives our system the ability to expand abbreviations and acronyms that are not

---

[3]https://en.wikipedia.org/wiki/Mobile_Servicing_System

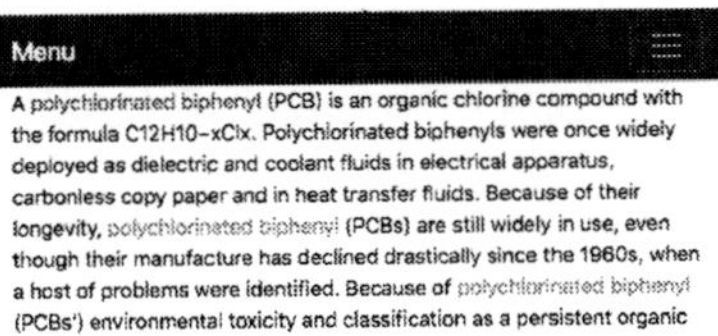

Figure 2: Screenshot of text with highlighted definition and added expansion of short forms to long forms

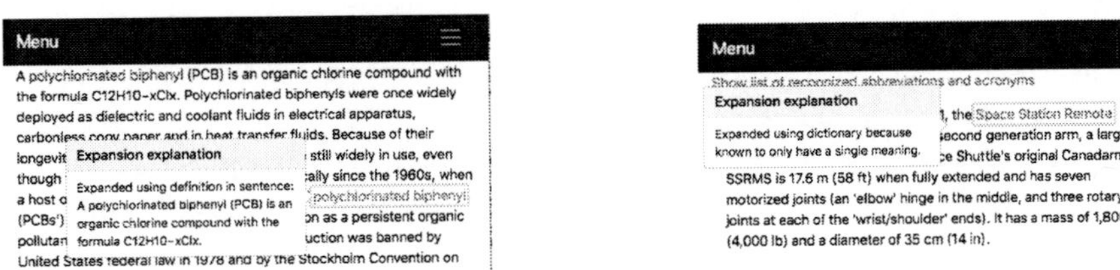

Figure 3: Screenshot of explanation information on long form source annotation that users can review.

defined in the text, but are known to only ever mean one thing. By focusing exclusively on unambiguous abbreviations and acronyms, this annotator avoids the pitfalls of dictionary based systems described in Section 3, i.e., the annotator avoids creating wrong expansions for abbreviations which can mean multiple things by working exclusively with abbreviations known to be unambiguous.

The third component that performs expansions, the *Vector Space Annotator* deals exclusively with ambiguous abbreviations and acronyms. It uses the context surrounding a short-form and a pre-computed vector space in order to disambiguate the abbreviation. The vector space is based on sentences from English Wikipedia containing ambiguous abbreviations (meaning abbreviations containing a one-to-many mapping between short-forms and long-forms) that are used in an unambiguous way (meaning that we already know which one of the multiple expansions is the correct one). We extracted these sentences using our *Pattern Annotator*. The *Vector Space Annotator* can thus expand abbreviations and acronyms that can have multiple meanings and whose definitions do not appear in the user provided text.

Finally, the *Expansion Combiner* uses the annotations from the previous components and combines them into consistent overall expansions. Please note that it is possible that two annotators expand an abbreviation to different long-forms. For example, the user provided text might introduce a new meaning for an abbreviation that we know as unambiguous and so, the *Pattern Annotator* and *Dictionary Annotator* might disagree. Similarly, the *Pattern Annotator* and *Vector Space Annotator* might arrive at different expansions if the author uses a new meaning for a known ambiguous abbreviation, or if the *Vector Space Annotator* should output an incorrect expansion. Finally, since the *Vector Space Annotator* works on one sentence at a time, it is possible that it disambiguates the same abbreviation to different long-forms in different sentences, thus leading to inconsistencies. The *Expansion Combiner* addresses these cases by implementing a priority system and, for the *Vector Space Annotator* specifically, a voting system.

Figure 2 shows a screenshot from the Abbreviation Expander system. In the example text, the original definition given in the text is marked and all subsequent uses of the short-form are preceded by the abbreviation's expansion. Users can verify how the system arrived at a specific expansion by clicking on the inserted expanded form, see Figure 3. The system features a menu where users can input or open some pre-loaded text files.

3 Related Work

BADREX (Gooch, 2011) is a plugin for the GATE (Cunningham et al., 2013) text analysis framework. It performs abbreviation expansion using dynamic regular expressions based on linguistic patterns for their definition (Schwartz and Hearst, 2003). The system requires an installation of GATE and familiarity with establishing GATE pipelines and loading plugins. It can identify abbreviation and acronym definitions in text and can then co-reference other instances of the identified short-forms to the found definition.

BADREX cannot perform abbreviation disambiguation, i.e., it cannot handle ambiguous cases as it relies exclusively on the definitions present in the document.

Web browser-based systems, like ABBREX (ABBREX, 2018), can be installed in a browser and expand abbreviations found on web pages. The expansion is based on stored dictionaries of abbreviations and lists of web pages they apply to. Thus, they cannot pick up definitions in text, or perform disambiguation. Being a dictionary-based expander, ABBREX assumes a one-to-one mapping between abbreviations and their long-forms, which means that in the case of ambiguous abbreviations, it has no other alternative, but to expand to whichever long-form is stored in the dictionary.

Another type of system, found e.g. in commercial software (Bartels Media, 2018; SmileOnMyMac, 2018), tries to expand user-defined abbreviations at writing time. This kind of software targets a different use case and cannot be applied to already written text.

The problem of matching abbreviations and acronyms with their long-forms has also been studied in research such as (Wu et al., 2015; Moon et al., 2015). However, they assume supervised learning settings, where a large amount of human effort has to go into providing ground truth examples. Also, they generally focus on methods, and do not provide (online) systems that users can easily use.

Abbreviation Expander presents a working web-based solution that does not require supervised ground truth information, and that can handle both unambiguous and ambiguous cases.

4 Conclusion

We present Abbreviation Expander, a web-based system that allows users to expand abbreviations and acronyms in text documents. Our system builds on state of the art methods for identification of abbreviations, acronyms and their definitions and our novel disambiguator based on word vector spaces. The *Vector Space Annotator* is still under active research and will be described in detail in a research paper in the near future. Abbreviation Expander requires no technical knowledge on part of its users and reliably expands both unambiguous and ambiguous abbreviations, improving text understanding and access in practice. In the future we plan to include feedback features into the system so that users can reject wrong expansions.

References

[ABBREX2018] ABBREX. 2018. ABBREX - The Abbreviation Expander. http://abbrex.com.

[Bartels Media2018] GmbH Bartels Media. 2018. WordExpander. http://www.wordexpander.net.

[Cunningham et al.2013] Hamish Cunningham, Valentin Tablan, Angus Roberts, and Kalina Bontcheva. 2013. Getting more out of biomedical documents with gate's full lifecycle open source text analytics. *PLoS computational biology*.

[Gooch2011] Phil Gooch. 2011. BADREX: In situ expansion and coreference of biomedical abbreviations using dynamic regular expressions. https://github.s3.amazonaws.com/downloads/philgooch/BADREX-Biomedical-Abbreviation-Expander/Gooch_BADREX_biomedical_abbreviation_expansion_2012.pdf".

[Manning et al.2014] Christopher D. Manning, Mihai Surdeanu, John Bauer, Jenny Finkel, Steven J. Bethard, and David McClosky. 2014. The Stanford CoreNLP natural language processing toolkit. In *Association for Computational Linguistics (ACL) System Demonstrations*, pages 55–60.

[Moon et al.2015] Sungrim Moon, Bridget McInnes, and Genevieve B Melton. 2015. Challenges and practical approaches with word sense disambiguation of acronyms and abbreviations in the clinical domain. *Healthcare inform. research*, 21(1):35–42.

[Schwartz and Hearst2003] A Schwartz and M Hearst. 2003. A simple algorithm for identifying abbreviation definitions in biomedical text. *Pacific Symp. Biocomp.*, 8.

[SmileOnMyMac2018] LLC SmileOnMyMac. 2018. TextExpander. https://textexpander.com/.

[Wu et al.2015] Yonghui Wu, Jun Xu, Yaoyun Zhang, and Hua Xu. 2015. Clinical abbreviation disambiguation using neural word embeddings. In *Proceedings of the 2015 Workshop on Biomedical Natural Language Processing (BioNLP)*, pages 171–176.

The INCEpTION Platform:
Machine-Assisted and Knowledge-Oriented Interactive Annotation

Jan-Christoph Klie   Michael Bugert   Beto Boullosa
Richard Eckart de Castilho   Iryna Gurevych
Ubiquitous Knowledge Processing Lab, Technische Universität Darmstadt, Germany
https://www.ukp.tu-darmstadt.de

Abstract

We introduce INCEpTION, a new annotation platform for tasks including interactive and semantic annotation (e.g., concept linking, fact linking, knowledge base population, semantic frame annotation). These tasks are very time consuming and demanding for annotators, especially when knowledge bases are used. We address these issues by developing an annotation platform that incorporates machine learning capabilities which actively assist and guide annotators. The platform is both generic and modular. It targets a range of research domains in need of semantic annotation, such as digital humanities, bioinformatics, or linguistics. INCEpTION is publicly available as open-source software.[1]

1   Introduction

Due to the success of natural language processing (NLP), there is a large interest to apply NLP methods in a wide range of new application domains, for instance to scale textual data analysis or to explore textual data. This requires being able to quickly bootstrap new annotated corpora in these domains. As target users, we consider for instance data scientists who train and evaluate machine learning algorithms as well as researchers who to wish to cross-reference and disambiguate text collections for better exploration and discovery. Furthermore, every application domain uses specific semantics and vocabularies which need to be modeled, making entity linking one of the most important annotation tasks. Thus, we identify three requirements that annotation tools must meet in order to address today's demands:

Annotation assistance. Creating annotated corpora is challenging and requires experts who are highly familiar with the annotation schemes in order to reach high inter-annotator agreement as well as high quality annotations. For semantic annotations, it is even more difficult: tasks such as entity and fact linking are very time intensive and often require an in-depth familiarity with the inventory of the resource. To improve the efficiency of these tasks, it is necessary to create an environment in which the computer can learn from the human and use this knowledge to support the human annotator.

Knowledge management. Semantic resources for new domains typically do not exist from the start. Instead, they are constructed and expanded as part of the annotation task. Thus, while some annotation tools already support entity linking against existing large-scale general knowledge bases (KB) such as Wikidata or DBPedia, it is also necessary that domain specific knowledge can be collected and modeled directly in the annotation tool.

Customizability and extensibility. Every annotation project has specific requirements that go beyond the basic task requirements, e.g. due to the data formats, knowledge resources, or text genres involved. Therefore, it is important that the tool can be customized, extended, and adapted to novel tasks.

INCEpTION addresses these requirements in several ways. To improve the efficiency of (semantic) annotation tasks, so-called *recommenders* are implemented which provide users with suggestions for possible labels. To navigate the annotation suggestions, an *active learning mode* can be enabled which

---

[1] https://inception-project.github.io ; software is licensed under the Apache License 2.0

Proceedings of the 27th International Conference on Computational Linguistics: System Demonstrations, pages 5–9
Santa Fe, New Mexico, USA, August 20-26, 2018.

guides the annotator in an efficient and effective manner. *Knowledge management* is fully integrated; knowledge bases can be created and edited, *entity and fact linking* is supported. The *modular architecture* of INCEpTION enables users to augment their instance with custom machine learning algorithms, data formats, knowledge bases, annotation types, visualizations and more.

2   Related Work

In recent years, several knowledge management and annotation tools have been developed, but none of them offer an integrated environment addressing all of the mentioned requirements.

Several tools, e.g. GATE Teamware (Bontcheva et al., 2013) implement support for automatically pre-annotating text. These are then corrected by the annotator in the next step. In contrast to that, INCEpTION allows recommenders to give suggestions at any time during the annotation process and learns from the user interactions (new annotations, rejections, etc.).

WebAnno (Yimam et al., 2014) integrates an automation mode in which the system can learn from annotations made by the user and provide suggestions. However, retraining has to be triggered manually by an administrator. Also, it uses a non-modular backend that provides only one machine learning algorithm and does not support active learning. WebAnno presents the document to be annotated and the recommended annotations separately in a split-screen mode which makes it tedious to relate recommendations to already existing annotations.

The general approach described by Emanuele Pianta and Zanoli (2008) who integrate an active learning process with an existing annotation tool and the ability to call out to different machine learning backends for recommendations as well as *Prodi.gy*[2] are similar to our approach. However, they focus strongly on the active learning aspect and force the user to follow the lead of the active learning module, restricting the user's workflow. In INCEpTION, the active learning algorithm highlights a particular recommendation to be judged by the user, but does not prevent the user from making other annotations.

The web-based tool AlvisAE (Papazian et al., 2012) supports both linking entity mentions to a knowledge base and editing knowledge bases (with limitations), but it does not support recommendations or active learning. Knowtator (Ogren, 2006) is another instance of a desktop application which ships as an annotation plugin for an ontology building tool. However, single-user tools like the ones above do not meet today's demand for collaboration-oriented annotation tools.

3   INCEpTION – System Overview

INCEpTION offers a number of functionalities expected from a generic annotation platform: a versatile and yet intuitive user interface, flexible configuration of the annotation schema, the ability to run multiple annotation projects concurrently for multiple users and workflow-support with annotation and adjudication stages, etc. With respect to these basic functionalities, we build on our previous work in the context of WebAnno (Yimam et al., 2014) and UIMA (Ferrucci et al., 2009), and therefore refer the interested readers to these projects.

In this paper, we focus specifically on INCEpTION's unique features, in particular on annotation assistance via *recommenders* and *active learning*, the *knowledge management capabilities* and its options for *customizations and extensions*.

Annotation User Interface   The annotation scheme used by INCEpTION organizes annotations into layers which define the set of attributes that an annotation may carry. Users can define an arbitrary number of layers that are each either spans or relations between spans. Each layer can have an arbitrary number of features which can be strings, numbers booleans, concept references, or references to other annotations.

The annotation user interface (Figure 1) displays the document text in the central part (1). Marking a span of text here creates a new annotation on the layer that is selected in the right sidebar (2) (e.g. named entity). Span annotations are displayed as bubbles above the text.

When an annotation is created or an existing annotation is selected, its features are shown in the right sidebar and can be edited there (3)(4). Depending on the feature type, a specialized editor is shown. For

---

[2]https://prodi.gy

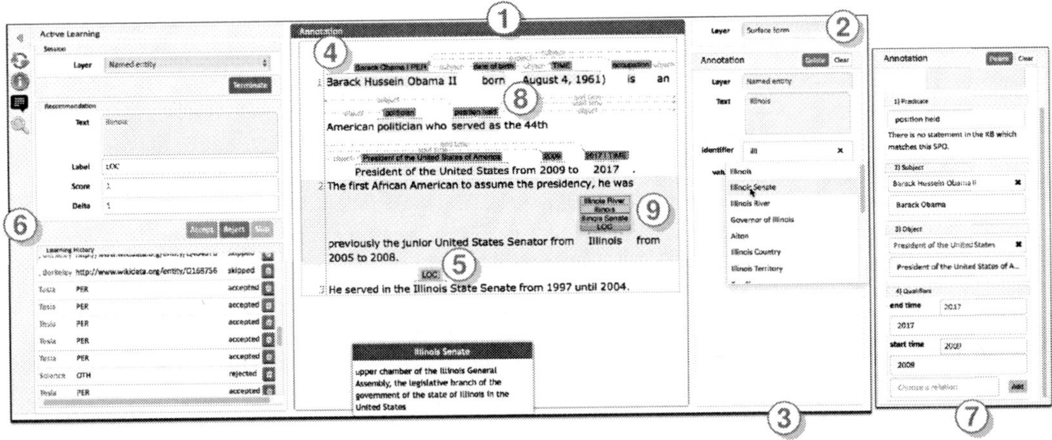

Figure 1: INCEpTION annotation editor: (1) annotation area, (2) annotation layer selection, (3) entity linking feature editor, (4) named entity linked to Wikidata, (5) entity mention suggestion, (6) active learning sidebar, (7) fact linking editor, (8) annotated fact, (9) entity linking recommendations.

instance, the editor to assign concepts from a knowledge base is an auto-complete input field which shows entities from the knowledge base that match the users' input. The left sidebar provides access to further functionalities, in particular to the active learning mode.

Recommenders To improve annotation efficiency, INCEpTION offers *recommenders*. These are algorithms that make use of machine learning and/or knowledge resources to provide annotation suggestions; they are displayed to the user alongside already made annotations in a different color (5). The user may accept a suggestion by clicking on it. This turns the suggestion into a proper annotation which can then be further edited if desired. The user may also reject the suggestion by double-clicking on it.

The recommender subsystem is designed to continuously monitor the users' actions, to update/retrain the recommendation models, and to provide always up-to-date suggestions. Multiple recommenders can be used simultaneously, e.g. high-precision/low-recall recommenders (e.g. using a dynamic dictionary) which are useful during early annotation stages, and context sensitive recall-oriented classifiers (e.g. sequence classifiers) for later stages. To avoid classifiers providing too many wrong suggestions during bootstrapping, a quality threshold can be configured per recommender.

INCEpTION supports two types of recommenders: internal and external. Internal recommenders are directly integrated into the platform by implementing a Java interface, while external recommenders use a simple, HTTP-based protocol to exchange UIMA CAS XMI (a XML representation of UIMA annotations). External recommenders allow users to leverage already existing and pre-trained machine learning models or libraries from other programming languages.

Active learning The goal of active learning (AL) is to quickly reach a good quality of annotation suggestions by soliciting feedback from the user that is expected to be most informative to the underlying machine learning algorithm. Presently, we use the uncertainty sampling strategy (Lewis and Gale, 1994) to drive the AL as it only requires that the recommenders produce a confidence score for each suggestion. The AL mode (6) works for one layer at a time to avoid confusion. After the layer has been selected, the system highlights the suggestion it seeks input for in the annotation area and displays its details in the AL sidebar. The user can then accept, reject or skip the suggestion. Skipped suggestions are presented again to the user when there are no more suggestions to accept or reject. The choices are stored in the learning history where the user can review and undo them if necessary. When the AL mode is enabled, the user can still deviate from its guidance and arbitrarily create and modify annotations. All changes made through the AL sidebar or in the main editor are immediately picked up by the recommenders causing the suggestions as well as the AL guidance to be updated.

Knowledge Management   For knowledge management, INCEpTION supports RDF-based knowledge bases. While internal KBs can be used for small domain-specific knowledge, large external (remote) knowledge bases can be accessed via SPARQL. A flexible configuration mechanism is used to support different knowledge representations, such as Wikidata, DBPedia, OWL, CIDOC-CRM, SKOS, etc. INCEpTION has notions of classes, instances, properties and qualifiers (for KBs using reification). However, it does not aspire to offer full support for advanced features of schemes such as OWL.

Knowledge bases enable the user to perform knowledge-driven annotations, e.g. annotating mentions of knowledge base entities in documents (entity linking ③) or creating new knowledge bases by annotating subjects, predicates and objects in text (fact linking ⑦⑧). Users can also explore and edit the knowledge base contents within INCEpTION.

To facilitate the entity linking process, INCEpTION can optionally take into account the context of the entity mention in order to provide the user with a ranked list of potential candidates. The same approach is used to drive an entity linking recommender which displays high-ranking candidates as annotation suggestions ⑨ in the annotation area where the user can accept them with a single click.

Customizability and extensibility   There are two approaches to customize and extend INCEpTION:

Internal extensions. The dependency injection and event mechanisms of Spring Boot[3] are used to internally modularize INCEpTION. Extension points make it possible to register new types of annotation properties, new editors or new internal recommenders. Modules can coordinate their tasks with each other through events. As an example, the main annotation area issues an event when an annotation has been created or changed. The recommenders and the AL mode react to this event in order to update themselves. Functionality can thereby not only be added but also removed to create custom branded versions of INCEpTION. The event-driven modular approach also enables the system to comprehensively log user and system actions. This data can for instance be used by annotation project managers in order to evaluate the performance of their annotators.

External extensions. Currently supported are external recommenders and knowledge bases. Benefits of using external services include increased stability (failing services do not crash the entire platform), scalability (deploy resource-hungry services on different machines) and the free choice of programming language (e.g. most deep learning frameworks are not implemented in Java).

Additionally, INCEpTION uses (de-facto) standards such as UIMA for annotations and RDF, OWL and SPARQL for knowledge bases to achieve a high level of interoperability with existing tools and resources.

4   Use cases

To ensure that INCEpTION remains generic, we collaborate with multiple use cases:

FAMULUS. Schulz et al. (2017) use INCEpTION to annotate medical case study reports with argument components. These are used to train a machine learning model which evaluates the diagnostic competence of aspiring doctors. A pre-trained deep learning model is integrated as an external recommender and is used during annotation. The annotators that use INCEpTION in conjunction with the recommenders report the usefulness and improvement in annotation speed and quality.

EDoHa. Stahlhut et al. (2018) have created a hypothesis validation tool using INCEpTION. It features a hypothesis/evidence editor which allows users to create hypotheses and link evidence in the form of text paragraphs to it.

Knowledge-driven rntity ranking. In order to support users during entity linking, the re-ranking approach described in (Sorokin and Gurevych, 2018) was adapted and integrated into INCEpTION. It is used as a recommender and in the auto-suggestion box for the named entity layer.

As part of the collaborations with the above use-cases, INCEpTION logs the users' actions in order to investigate for instance which assistive features (i.e. recommenders) work best for the respective tasks, whether they introduce a bias in the annotator's results, and how to improve the user interface for an improved user experience.

---

[3]Spring Boot: `https://projects.spring.io/spring-boot/`

5   Conclusion and Future Work

In this paper, we have presented INCEpTION which –to the best of our knowledge– is the first modular annotation platform which seamlessly incorporates recommendations, active learning, entity linking and knowledge management. Our approach provides a number of advantages over current state-of-the-art annotation tools. Recommenders giving suggestions on-line allow users to annotate texts more quickly and accurately. External recommenders can be added to leverage already existing machine learning models and bootstrap the annotation for new domains. Knowledge management is directly integrated which allows entity- and fact linking together with building the knowledge base on the fly. The modular approach used by INCEpTION provides users with the possibility to tailor the platform according to their needs, for instance by adding new machine learning algorithms, annotation editors or knowledge bases.

INCEpTION is publicly available as open source-software. We welcome early adopters and encourage feedback for a continued alignment of the platform with the needs of the community. Several collaborations are on the way to develop and improve features that are useful to researchers and annotators, e.g. corpus search, recommenders that check the plausibility of annotations or fully custom user interfaces.

Acknowledgements

We thank Wei Ding, Peter Jiang and Marcel de Boer and Naveen Kumar for their valuable contributions and Teresa Botschen and Yevgeniy Puzikov for their helpful comments. This work was supported by the German Research Foundation under grant No. EC 503/1-1 and GU 798/21-1 (INCEpTION).

References

Kalina Bontcheva, Hamish Cunningham, Ian Roberts, Angus Roberts, Valentin Tablan, Niraj Aswani, and Genevieve Gorrell. 2013. GATE Teamware: A Web-based Collaborative Text Annotation Framework. *Language Resources and Evaluation*, 47(4):1007–1029.

Christian Girardi Emanuele Pianta and Roberto Zanoli. 2008. The TextPro Tool Suite. In *Proceedings of the Sixth International Conference on Language Resources and Evaluation (LREC'08)*, pages 2603–2607.

David Ferrucci, Adam Lally, Karin Verspoor, and Eric Nyberg. 2009. Unstructured information management architecture (UIMA) version 1.0. OASIS Standard.

David D. Lewis and William A. Gale. 1994. A Sequential Algorithm for Training Text Classifiers. In *Proceedings of the 17th Annual International ACM SIGIR Conference on Research and Development in Information Retrieval*, pages 3–12.

Philip V. Ogren. 2006. Knowtator: A Protégé plug-in for annotated corpus construction. In *Proceedings of the Human Language Technology Conference of the NAACL, Companion Volume: Demonstrations*, pages 273–275.

Frédéric Papazian, Robert Bossy, and Claire Nédellec. 2012. AlvisAE: a collaborative Web text annotation editor for knowledge acquisition. In *Proceedings of the Sixth Linguistic Annotation Workshop*, pages 149–152. Association for Computational Linguistics.

Claudia Schulz, Michael Sailer, Jan Kiesewetter, Christian M. Meyer, Iryna Gurevych, Frank Fischer, and Martin R. Fischer. 2017. Fallsimulationen und automatisches adaptives Feedback mittels Künstlicher Intelligenz in digitalen Lernumgebungen. *e-teaching.org Themenspecial "Was macht Lernen mit digitalen Medien erfolgreich?"*, pages 1–14.

Daniil Sorokin and Iryna Gurevych. 2018. Mixing context granularities for improved entity linking on question answering data across entity categories. In *Proceedings of the Seventh Joint Conference on Lexical and Computational Semantics (*SEM)*, pages 65–75.

Chris Stahlhut, Christian Stab, and Iryna Gurevych. 2018. Pilot experiments of hypothesis validation through evidence detection for historians. In *Proceedings of Design of Experimental Search & Information REtrieval Systems (DESIRES)*. (in press).

Seid Muhie Yimam, Chris Biemann, Richard Eckart de Castilho, and Iryna Gurevych. 2014. Automatic Annotation Suggestions and Custom Annotation Layers in WebAnno. In *Proceedings of 52nd Annual Meeting of the Association for Computational Linguistics: System Demonstrations*, pages 91–96.

JeSemE: A Website for Exploring Diachronic Changes in Word Meaning and Emotion

Johannes Hellrich[1,2] **Sven Buechel**[2] **Udo Hahn**[2]

[1] Graduate School 'The Romantic Model'
`modellromantik.uni-jena.de`

[2] Jena University Language & Information Engineering (JULIE) Lab
`julielab.de`

Friedrich-Schiller-Universität Jena, Jena, Germany

Abstract

We here introduce a substantially extended version of JeSemE, an interactive website for visually exploring computationally derived time-variant information on word meanings and lexical emotions assembled from five large diachronic text corpora. JeSemE is designed for scholars in the (digital) humanities as an alternative to consulting manually compiled, printed dictionaries for such information (if available at all). This tool uniquely combines state-of-the-art distributional semantics with a nuanced model of human emotions, two information streams we deem beneficial for a data-driven interpretation of texts in the humanities.

1 Introduction

Historical, manually compiled dictionaries are central to many kinds of studies in the humanities, since they provide scholars with information about the lexical meaning of terms in former time periods. Yet, this traditional approach is limited in many ways, coverage being perhaps the most pressing issue: Is a dictionary for the specific time period a scholar is investigating really available and, if so, does it cover all of the lexical items of interest?

Word embeddings have been proposed as a technical vehicle to increase lexical coverage (Kim et al., 2014). However, they require locally installed software and time-consuming calculations, thus being ill-suited for mostly non-technical users in the humanities. As an alternative, we here present an extended version of JeSemE, a user-friendly open source website[1] for accessing embedding-derived diachronic information on lexical meaning and emotion. The first release of JeSemE (Hellrich and Hahn, 2017b) mainly provided time-variant diachronic lexical semantic information. Its second version, the focus of this paper, excels with the unique capability to additionally track the diachronic *emotional* connotation of words in parallel with their lexical semantics. Such a functionality is widely considered beneficial for the data-driven interpretation of literary text genres (Kim et al., 2017).

Measuring affective information on the lexical level is an active field of research in computational linguistics (Liu, 2015). Yet, most contributions focus on contemporary language and are limited to shallow representations of human emotions, mainly distinguishing between *positive* and *negative* feelings. Current research in sentiment analysis either starts to include historical trends in word polarity (Hamilton et al., 2016a) or incorporates more nuanced models of emotions, such as Valence-Arousal-Dominance (Buechel and Hahn, 2018). This contribution integrates both lines of work in a unique way based on our prior research activities (Buechel et al., 2016; Buechel et al., 2017). To the best of our knowledge, only few systems share similarities with JeSemE. Alternative websites for tracking diachronic word meaning yet offer far less diverse collections of corpora compared to JeSemE and neither of them incorporates emotion values attached to lexical entries. For example, Arendt and Volkova (2017) provide only short term trends in word similarity in two social media corpora in their ESTEEM system.[2] The system[3] by

---

[1] Website available at: `jeseme.org`; sources available at: `github.com/JULIELab/JeSemE`
[2] `esteem.labworks.org/`
[3] `embvis.flovis.net/s/neighborhoods.html`

Proceedings of the 27th International Conference on Computational Linguistics: System Demonstrations, pages 10–14
Santa Fe, New Mexico, USA, August 20-26, 2018.

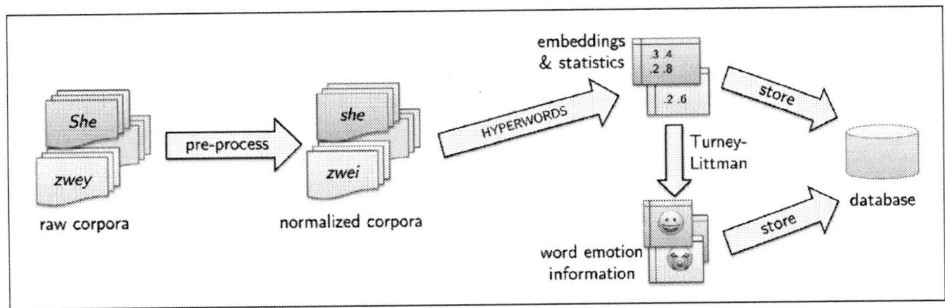

Figure 1: JeSemE's text processing pipeline.

Heimerl and Gleicher (2018) is intended as a mere showcase for a novel visualization technique and re-uses SGNS embeddings trained on the English Google Books corpus by Hamilton et al. (2016b). The Diachronic Explorer[4] which uses sparse vector representations instead of word embeddings to calculate lexical similarity is limited to the Spanish Google Books corpus (Gamallo et al., 2018).

2 Architecture and Website

JeSemE uses five diachronic corpora: the Google Books N-Gram Corpus for German and its English fiction register (Michel et al., 2011), the Corpus of Historical American English (COHA; Davies (2012)), the Deutsches Textarchiv ['German Text Archive'] (Geyken, 2013) and the Royal Society Corpus (Kermes et al., 2016). To ensure high embedding quality, these corpora are divided into temporal slices of similar size covering between 10 to 50 years each.

JeSemE's processing pipeline is depicted in Figure 1. It starts with orthographically normalizing the corpus slices, i.e., lower casing only for English and a historical spelling-aware lemmatization for German (Jurish, 2013). We then use a modified version of Hyperwords[5] to calculate slice-specific

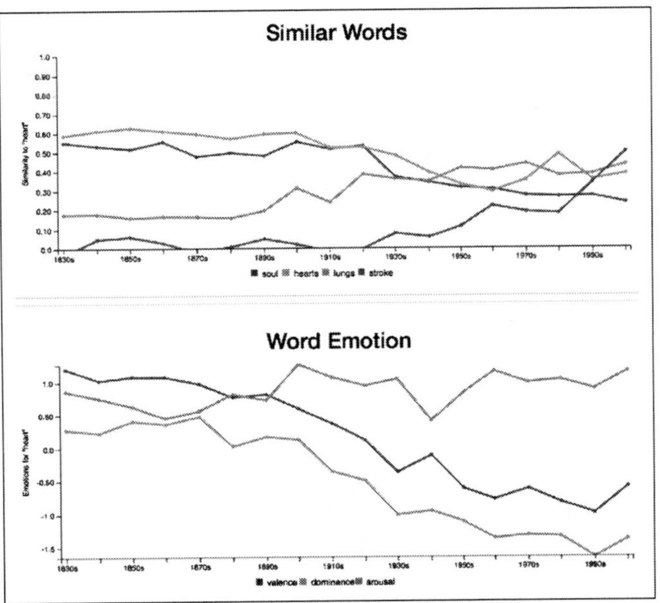

Figure 2: JeSemE in operation I: Meaning change of "heart" relative to reference words since the 1830s in the COHA.

embedding models with SVD_{PPMI} (Levy et al., 2015). This algorithm was chosen for its superior reliability which is essential for interpreting local neighborhoods in embedding spaces as is done in the remainder of this paper (Hellrich and Hahn, 2016; Hellrich and Hahn, 2017a). Apart from word vectors, we also calculate word-based co-occurrence statistics, frequency information and emotion values for each slice (see Section 3). All this information is stored in a relational database. Compared to Hellrich and Hahn (2017b), our current version also reduces the database size from approximately 120GB to 40GB. This is achieved by storing word vectors instead of pre-computed similarity scores. Unlike the previous version, semantic similarity between most words will be computed on the fly. Only the most

---

[4]tec.citius.usc.es/explorador-diacronico
[5]github.com/hellrich/hyperwords

similar ones for each word (automatically picked as references) are cached for fast retrieval.

JeSeme's website prompts a search form for selecting the word under scrutiny as well as one of the five corpora we supply. Its result page then provides graphs depicting the development of semantic similarity to automatically chosen reference words over time as an indicator for semantic change, as well as information on diachronic affective meaning (see Figure 2). These two main sources of information are complemented with information on word co-occurrence and relative frequency, thus providing scholars with additional information to increase interpretability and rule out measurement artifacts. Users may also add further reference words to the analysis on demand. Besides this graphical interface JeSeme also offers a REST API.[6]

3 Representing and Computing Emotions

We represent emotions following the Valence-Arousal-Dominance (VAD) scheme (Bradley and Lang, 1994), one of the major models of emotion in psychology (for an illustration, see Figure 3). The VAD model describes affective states relative to three dimensions, namely, Valence (degree of displeasure vs. pleasure), Arousal (degree of calmness vs. excitement) and Dominance (degree of perceived control in a social situation).

We used a modified version of the emotion induction algorithm by Turney and Littman (2003) based on evidence that it outperforms alternative methods for historical emotion lexicon creation (Buechel et al., 2017; Hellrich et al., 2018). In this work, each word's predicted emotion value $\hat{e}(w)$ is calculated by averaging the emotion values $e(s)$ for each member s of a seed set S, with $sim(w, s)$, the similarity between w and s, serving as a weight:

$$\hat{e}(w) := \frac{\sum_{s \in S} sim(w, s) \times e(s)}{\sum_{s \in S} sim(w, s)}$$

For the emotion scores stored in JeSeme, we used the emotion lexicons by Warriner et al. (2013) and Schmidtke et al. (2014) as seed sets for English and German corpora, respectively. Word emotions were induced independently for each temporal corpus slice, using the respective embedding model to retrieve similarity scores. Hence, the similarity between the seed words and the target word reflects word usage at a given language stage, thereby infusing historical emotion information into the resulting emotion ratings (Buechel et al., 2017).

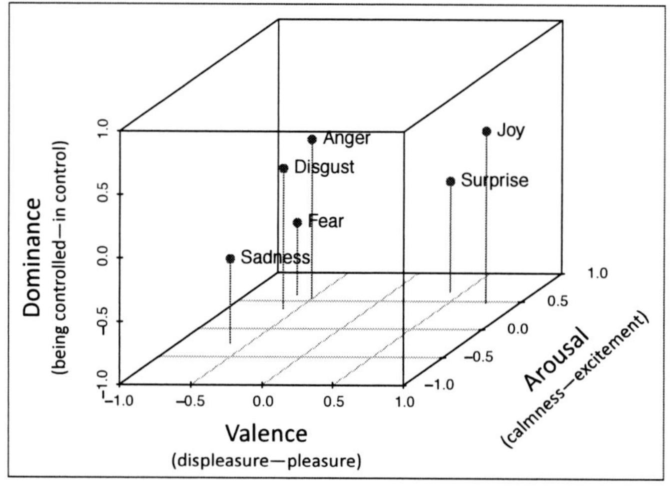

Figure 3: Affective space spanned by the Valence-Arousal-Dominance (VAD) model, together with the position of six basic emotion categories. Adapted from Buechel and Hahn (2016).

4 Examples

The new insights provided by diachronic emotion models can be demonstrated by re-visiting the example of "heart" we used in Hellrich and Hahn (2017b) as shown in Figure 2. This lexeme is often used metaphorically or metonymically despite the fact that the heart's anatomical function was already known for a long time. Results for our novel emotion tracking functionality match a move from metaphorical to anatomical usage we previously observed in the genre-balanced COHA. Around 1900, the similarity of "heart" to words such as "stroke" increases, while Dominance and Valence ratings drop sharply in

---

[6]See online documentation: `jeseme.org/help.html#api`

tandem (see Figure 2; y-axis values are centered and scaled). This simultaneous drop seems plausible, since we can "change our heart" in a metaphorical sense, yet have little control over our anatomical heart. Also, with its increasing anatomical usage, "heart" becomes less positive, since we are under mortal threat by cardiovascular diseases such as a "stroke".

Changes in emotion can also be traced for items with a more constant meaning, e.g., for "woman" as shown in Figure 4. Here similarity scores for the most similar words—"man" and "girl"—remain rather static. Yet, emotion values are highly dynamic and seem to match turning points in women's rights movement, e.g., women's suffrage in the US is connected with an increase in all VAD dimensions for the 1920s.

5 Conclusion

We introduced a substantially extended version of JeSemE, an interactive website for tracking diachronic changes in word meaning and, as a novel and unique feature, word emotion. To the best of our knowledge, no other system combines these two traits. JeSemE allows users with a limited technical background to interactively explore semantic evolution based on

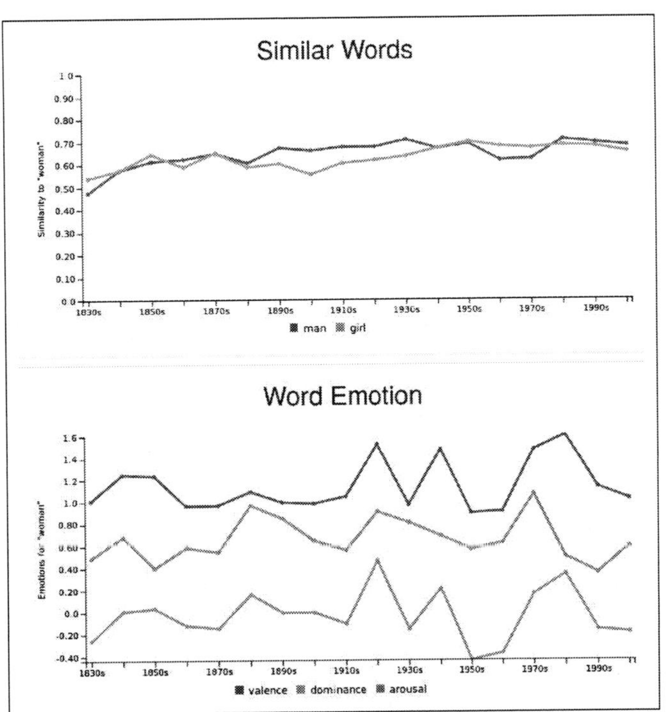

Figure 4: JeSemE in operation II: Meaning of "woman" since the 1830s in the COHA.

five large diachronic corpora for two languages, German and English. We believe that JeSemE will be most useful for diachronic linguists and scholars within the digital humanities. We see two major applications: First, it can be used to generate hypotheses by querying words of interest to get a first impression of their semantic evolution. Second, scholars can first shape a hypothesis using traditional means and then query JeSemE for testing its plausibility based on diachronic statistical evidence.

Acknowledgements

This research was partially funded by grant GRK 2041/1 from *Deutsche Forschungsgemeinschaft* within the Graduate School *"The Romantic Model. Variation–Scope–Relevance"*.

References

Dustin Arendt and Svitlana Volkova. 2017. ESTEEM: A novel framework for qualitatively evaluating and visualizing spatiotemporal embeddings in social media. In *ACL 2017: System Demonstrations*, pages 25–30.

Margaret M. Bradley and Peter J. Lang. 1994. Measuring emotion: The self-assessment manikin and the semantic differential. *Journal of Behavior Therapy and Experimental Psychiatry*, 25(1):49–59.

Sven Buechel and Udo Hahn. 2016. Emotion analysis as a regression problem—Dimensional models and their implications on emotion representation and metrical evaluation. In *ECAI 2016*, pages 1114–1122.

Sven Buechel and Udo Hahn. 2018. Word emotion induction for multiple languages as a deep multi-task learning problem. In *NAACL 2018: Long Papers*, pages 1907–1918.

Sven Buechel, Johannes Hellrich, and Udo Hahn. 2016. Feelings from the past: Adapting affective lexicons for historical emotion analysis. In *LT4DH @ COLING 2016*, pages 54–61.

Sven Buechel, Johannes Hellrich, and Udo Hahn. 2017. The course of emotion in three centuries of German text: A methodological framework. In *Digital Humanities 2017*, pages 176–179.

Mark Davies. 2012. Expanding horizons in historical linguistics with the 400-million word Corpus of Historical American English. *Corpora*, 7:121–157.

Pablo Gamallo, Iván Rodríguez-Torres, and Marcos Garcia. 2018. Distributional semantics for diachronic search. *Computers & Electrical Engineering*, 65:438–448.

Alexander Geyken. 2013. Wege zu einem historischen Referenzkorpus des Deutschen: Das Projekt Deutsches Textarchiv. In Ingelore Hafemann, editor, *Perspektiven einer corpusbasierten historischen Linguistik und Philologie*, pages 221–234.

William L. Hamilton, Kevin Clark, Jure Leskovec, and Dan Jurafsky. 2016a. Inducing domain-specific sentiment lexicons from unlabeled corpora. In *EMNLP 2016*, pages 595–605.

William L. Hamilton, Jure Leskovec, and Daniel Jurafsky. 2016b. Diachronic word embeddings reveal statistical laws of semantic change. In *ACL 2016: Long Papers*, pages 1489–1501.

F. Heimerl and M. Gleicher. 2018. Interactive analysis of word vector embeddings. In *EuroVis 2018 — Eurographics Conference on Visualization*. [to appear]. Preprint: `graphics.cs.wisc.edu/Papers/2018/HG18`.

Johannes Hellrich and Udo Hahn. 2016. Bad company—Neighborhoods in neural embedding spaces considered harmful. In *COLING 2016: Technical Papers*, pages 2785–2796.

Johannes Hellrich and Udo Hahn. 2017a. Don't get fooled by word embeddings: Better watch their neighborhood. In *Digital Humanities 2017*, pages 250–252.

Johannes Hellrich and Udo Hahn. 2017b. Exploring diachronic lexical semantics with JESEME. In *ACL 2017: System Demonstrations*, pages 31–36.

Johannes Hellrich, Sven Buechel, and Udo Hahn. 2018. Inducing affective lexical semantics in historical language. `arxiv.org/abs/1806.08115`.

Bryan Jurish. 2013. Canonicalizing the Deutsches Textarchiv. In Ingelore Hafemann, editor, *Perspektiven einer corpusbasierten historischen Linguistik und Philologie*, pages 235–244.

Hannah Kermes, Stefania Degaetano-Ortlieb, Ashraf Khamis, Jörg Knappen, and Elke Teich. 2016. The Royal Society Corpus: From uncharted data to corpus. In *LREC 2016*, pages 1928–1931.

Yoon Kim, Yi-I Chiu, Kentaro Hanaki, Darshan Hegde, and Slav Petrov. 2014. Temporal analysis of language through neural language models. In *LT-CSS 2014 @ ACL 2014*, pages 61–65.

Evgeny Kim, Sebastian Padó, and Roman Klinger. 2017. Investigating the relationship between literary genres and emotional plot development. In *LaTeCH-CLfL 2017 @ ACL 2017*, pages 17–26.

Omer Levy, Yoav Goldberg, and Ido Dagan. 2015. Improving distributional similarity with lessons learned from word embeddings. *Transactions of the Association of Computational Linguistics*, 3:211–225.

Bing Liu. 2015. *Sentiment Analysis: Mining Opinions, Sentiments, and Emotions*. Cambridge University Press.

Jean-Baptiste Michel, Yuan Kui Shen, Aviva Presser Aiden, Adrian Veres, Matthew K. Gray, The Google Books Team, Joseph P. Pickett, Dale Hoiberg, Dan Clancy, Peter Norvig, Jon Orwant, Steven Pinker, Martin A. Nowak, and Erez Lieberman Aiden. 2011. Quantitative analysis of culture using millions of digitized books. *Science*, 331(6014):176–182.

David S. Schmidtke, Tobias Schröder, Arthur M. Jacobs, and Markus Conrad. 2014. ANGST: Affective norms for German sentiment terms, derived from the affective norms for English words. *Behavior Research Methods*, 46(4):1108–1118.

Peter D. Turney and Michael L. Littman. 2003. Measuring praise and criticism: Inference of semantic orientation from association. *ACM Transactions on Information Systems*, 21(4):315–346.

Amy Beth Warriner, Victor Kuperman, and Marc Brysbært. 2013. Norms of valence, arousal, and dominance for 13,915 English lemmas. *Behavior Research Methods*, 45(4):1191–1207.

T-Know: A Knowledge Graph-based Question Answering and Information Retrieval System for Traditional Chinese Medicine

Ziqing Liu[1], Enwei Peng[2], Shixing Yan[2], Guozheng Li[3✉], Tianyong Hao[4✉]

[1]Second School of Clinic Medicine, Guangzhou University of Chinese Medicine, Guangzhou, China emma.liu_el@hotmail.com

[2]AI Center, Green Valley, Shanghai, China pengenwei@jindengtai.cn, yanshixing@green-valley.com

[3]Data Center of Traditional Chinese Medicine, China Academy of Chinese Medical Science, Beijing, China gzli@ndctcm.cn

[4]School of Computer, South China Normal University, Guangzhou, China haoty@126.com

Abstract

T-Know is a knowledge service system based on the constructed knowledge graph of Traditional Chinese Medicine (TCM). Using authorized and anonymized clinical records, medicine clinical guidelines, teaching materials, classic medical books, academic publications, etc., as data resources, the system extracts triples from free texts to build a TCM knowledge graph by our developed natural language processing methods. On the basis of the knowledge graph, a deep learning algorithm is implemented for single-round question understanding and multiple-round dialogue. In addition, the TCM knowledge graph also is used to support human-computer interactive knowledge retrieval by normalizing search keywords to medical terminology.

1 Introduction

Traditional Chinese Medicine (TCM) is one of precious intangible cultural heritages of the Chinese nation. After thousands of years of development, it has been evolved as a distinct and unique theoretical medical system. Compared with disease treatment only, TCM pays more attention to living conditions and advocates timely adjustment of diet and rest to deal with physical discomforts. This philosophy has an advantage in dealing with sub-health status and chronic disease management (Wang, et al., 2007). With the increasing attention of health from public, the demands of reliable and convenient TCM knowledge services are increasing.

In recent years, there are great progresses being made in domain-specific knowledge graph construction. On TCM, a number of literature databases have been established. These digital resources containing rich TCM knowledge can be utilized to capture knowledge elements to serve public and benefit health management (Gao, et al., 2012). There are several existing TCM knowledge service platforms, such as TCMKS (Yu, et al., 2014). However, most of the systems target for medical professionals rather than public. A typical situation is that, their search functions allow formal TCM terms only, causing common users without TCM background difficulties to obtain required information without rich TCM background. Therefore, how to utilizing natural language methods to analyze informal or even vague queries for more convenient public services is an essential issue (Xu, et al., 2016).

To that end, we propose the T-Know, a user-friendly knowledge service system based on a TCM knowledge graph. The overall system architecture is shown as Figure 1.The system has two major modules: a question answering module and a knowledge retrieval module. The TCM knowledge graph integrates diversified data to enrich knowledge search and usage. The question answering module utilizes deep learning models to understand questions by analyzing question intents. The question answering module provides an interface for common users in both single-round question answering and multi-round dialogue ways. The knowledge retrieval module integrates TCM terminology and synonym dictionaries to extend search keywords semantically. The module can also navigate common users to use the TCM knowledge retrieval in an interactive way.

Proceedings of the 27th International Conference on Computational Linguistics: System Demonstrations, pages 15–19
Santa Fe, New Mexico, USA, August 20-26, 2018.

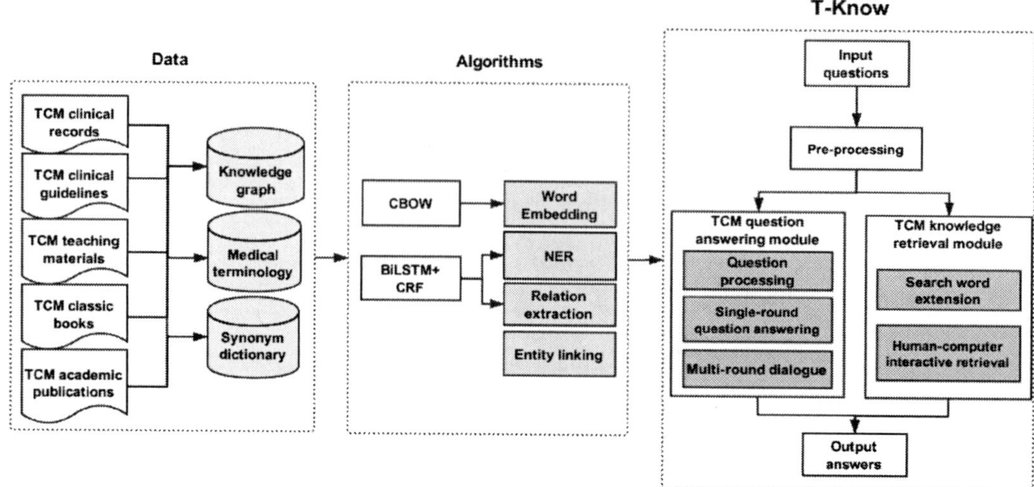

Figure 1: The overall system architecture of the T-Know system

2 The TCM Knowledge Graph

In order to construct the TCM knowledge graph, authorized and anonymized clinical records, clinical guidelines, teaching materials, classic medical books, and academic publications are collected as data resources. The unstructured texts were preprocessed including Chinese word segmentation, stop word removal and word semantic labelling. After that, medical named entity recognition and relation extraction were implemented using a Bi-LSTM+CRF algorithm to obtain *<Entity, Relation, Entity>* triples. Finally, the knowledge graph was verified and automatically constructed from the extracted triples.

The constructed TCM knowledge graph mainly contains five types of nodes: Diseases, Symptoms, Syndromes, Prescriptions and Chinese Herbals. There are diversified logical relations among the nodes. We also integrate a reasoning function besides the TCM knowledge graph to support entity or relation deduction through of the reasoning of logical relations among entity nodes. The constructed TCM knowledge graph contains more than 10,000 nodes and 220,000 relations currently.

3 The TCM Question Answering Module

1) Question Processing

Medical Named Entity Reorganization: We use a Bi-LSTM+CRF model to achieve named entity recognition, as reported in (Huang, et al., 2015), on different types of TCM texts. In the Bi-LSTM+CRF model, the first layer is a look-up layer, in which each word in a question sentence can be presented as a vector by using a pre-trained or randomly initialized word embedding matrix. The second layer is a bi-directional LSTM, which automatically extracts the characteristics of the sentence. Thus, the word embedding sequence of each word in the sentence can be the input of the bi-directional LSTM. It then splices implicit state sequence output by a forward LSTM in terms of locations to obtain a complete implicit state sequence. The third layer is a CRF layer, which labels sentence-level sequences.

Relation Extraction: Multi-channel convolutional neural networks (CNNs) are utilized to determine the relations between a pair of entities in a given free question (Xu, et al., 2016). Specifically, two CNNs channels are used. One is used to capture syntax information and the other is to capture context information. The convolutional layer of each channel accepts an input of variable length, while returns a vector of fixed length using the Maximum Sampling method. These fixed-length vectors are combined together to form the input of final softmax classifier, whose output vector dimension equals to the total number of relation categories and the value of each dimension equals to the degree of confidence mapped to the corresponding predicates in the knowledge graph.

2) Single-round Question Answering

Entity Linking: Entity linking plays a vital role in the TCM concept association and normalization (Liu, et al., 2016). After medical named entity identification, an entity linking tool named as S-MART is used to obtain associated entities in the TCM knowledge graph.

Joint Disambiguation of Entities and Relations: Under normal circumstances, both named entity recognition and entity relation extraction are independently predicted. The errors generated in the processes are usually difficult to avoid. We use a joint optimization model to select a globally optimal 'entity-relation' configuration from the candidate results of entity linking and relation extraction. The process of optimizing the globally configuration can be treated as a sorting problem in essence. To find 'reasonable' entity- relation configuration, TCM knowledge is applied to sort entity-relations, that is, the 'reasonable' entity-relation configuration should be more common in the TCM knowledge graph so as to efficiently locate answers to users' questions using the TCM knowledge graph.

3) Multi-round Dialogue

Multi-round dialogue refers to the management of multiple-round interactions while keeping context linkage. It contains entity linking for recognizing entities and joint disambiguation, through which, a topic and the certain slot are resolved and then stored. After that, the scope of the topic is identified. Given a new question, the system judges whether it follows the previous topic. If it follows, the question is regarded as in the same dialogue. Otherwise, it is treated as a new multi-round dialogue.

Forward facing centers strategy was adopted for anaphora resolution. When context information is insufficient to identify specific entity, a ranked list of discourse entities will be displayed to users along with inquiry. User's input straight after this list will be preferentially considered as the decision of entity assignment. If none of listed candidates is mentioned, then the entity of input question will be treated as constrain of last question to joint next round disambiguates. The screen snapshots of the whole TCM question answering module is presented as Figure 2.

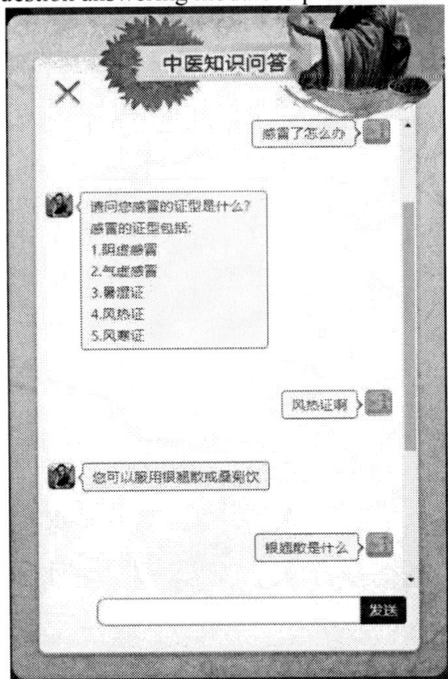
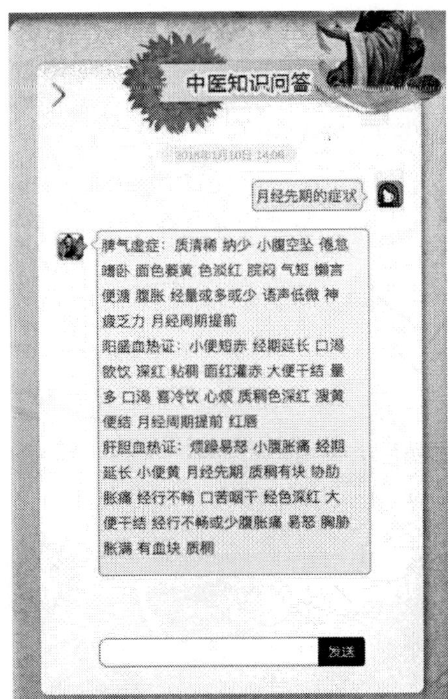

Figure 2: The screen snapshots of the TCM question answering module (left: the multi-round dialogue; right: the single-round question answering)

4   The TCM Knowledge Retrieval Module

1) Search Word Extension

Search word extension provides users with a guided retrieval, that is, the entity node in the knowledge graph can be located according to search words and corresponding entity attributes can be returned as a retrieval guide. For example, if a user asking about a specific disease, the module returns with disease interpretation, the disease property and other relevant information. In addition to retrieving entities, the user can also retrieve relations. For example, if the user asking a syndrome of a specific disease, all the associated syndromes of the disease are regarded as relevant information and are returned. Moreover, to assistant common users in the usage of the module, a list of TCM terminology and synonym dictionaries are integrated. The module will display matched synonyms of search words when a user simply type an informal medical term as a search word. The search word extension function is demonstrated as Figure 3.

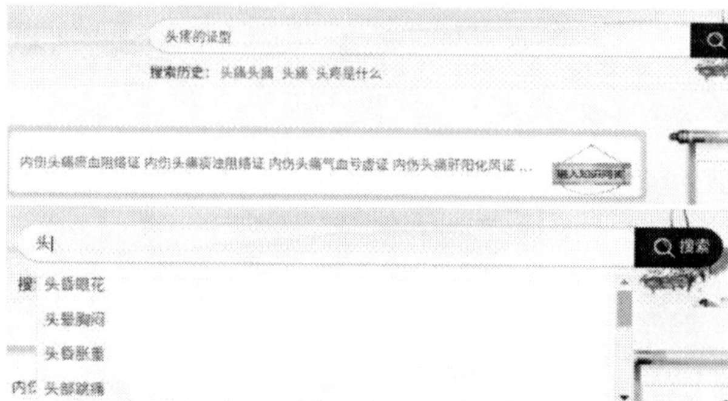

Figure 3: An example of search word extension of TCM syndromes of headache

2) Human-computer Interactive Retrieval

The Human-computer interactive retrieval module consists of entity-relation visualization, relevant illustration and knowledge association. The entity-relation visualization assists common users to view all associated entities and relations for a specific entity. When a user clicks an entity node, the module automatically presents related entities whose distances below a specific threshold. The relations between the nodes also are displayed. When a node or link is clicked, related knowledge information will be extracted and be displayed as the detailed explanation of the node to users as relevant illustration. The knowledge association provides users with relevant knowledge to search content according to the classical TCM logic of 'Theory-Approach-Prescription-Medicine'. From the expertise, contents are associated to different categories. For instance, associated contents are similar disease or frequently co-occurrence disease when search content is a disease, and the associated contents are co-occurrence Chinese herbal or same efficacy Chinese herbal when search content is a Chinese herbal. Through this TCM association, the interactive retrieval module can serve common and professional users who has partial knowledge about TCM better. The interactive retrieval module is shown as Figure 4

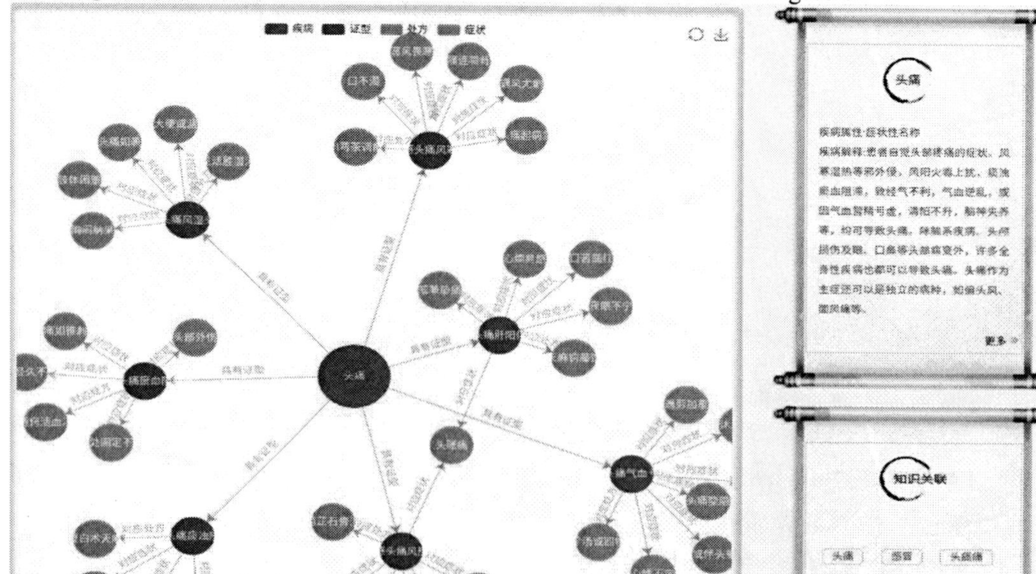

Figure 4: A knowledge graph about headache including TCM symptoms, syndromes, and prescriptions visualized by the human-computer interactive retrieval module

5 Summary

Aiming at improving the accessibility of TCM knowledge for general public. We proposed a knowledge based TCM question answering and information retrieval system named T-Know. Using heterogeneous medical texts as data resources, a TCM knowledge graph was automatically built. Based on the knowledge graph, T-Know delivers TCM question answering and knowledge retrieval services for public users via http://zhishi.jindengtai.cn:9999 .

Reference

Bo Gao, Meng Cui, Shuo Yang, Lirong Jia, Yan Dong, and Ling Zhu. 2012. Knowledge Services of TCM Based on Data. *Library and Information Service*, 56(9):5-9.

Kun Xu, Siva Reddy, Yansong Feng, Songfang Huang and Dongyan Zhao. 2016. Qustion answering on freebase via relation Extraction and textual evidence. *In Processing of the 54th Annual Meeting of the Association for Computational Linguistics*, (pp. 2326-2336).

Tong Yu, Daming Su, Renfang Yin, Zhulv Zhang, and Ye Tian. 2014. Research on the Construction of Knowledge Services Platforms for Traditional Chinese Medicine. *Medical Innovation of China*, 11(15):120-123.

Yanhui Wang, and Kuanqi He. 2007. Advantages of Traditional Chinese Medicine in Diagnosis and Treatment of Subhealth State. *China Journal of Traditional Chinese Medicine and Pharmacy*, 22(7):473-475.

Zhiheng Huang, Wei Xu, and Kai Yu. 2015. Bidirectional LSTM-CRF models for sequence tagging. arXiv preprint arXiv:1508.01991.

Zhiyuan Liu, Maosong Sun, Yankai Lin, and Ruobing Xie. 2016. Knowledge Representation Learning: A Review. *Journal of Computer Research and Development*, 53(2):247-261.

A Korean Knowledge Extraction System for Enriching a KBox

Sangha Nam, Eun-kyung Kim, Jiho Kim, Yoosung Jung, Kijong Han, Key-Sun Choi
KAIST / The Republic of Korea
`{nam.sangha, kekeeo, hogajiho, wjd1004109, han0ah, kschoi}@kaist.ac.kr`

Abstract

The increased demand for structured knowledge has created considerable interest in knowledge extraction from natural language sentences. This study presents a new Korean knowledge extraction system and web interface for enriching KBox, a knowledge base that expands based on the Korean DBpedia. We aim to create an endpoint where knowledge can be extracted and added to KBox anytime and anywhere.

1 Introduction

Information extraction (IE) is an important task in the natural language processing (NLP) field. Various large-scale knowledge bases (KBs) such as Freebase(Bollacker et al., 2008), DBpedia(Auer et al., 2007), and YAGO(Suchanek et al., 2007) are widely used in many NLP tasks. These KBs store knowledge in the form of a triple; for example, (`Les Miserables, author, Victor Hugo`). However, because even large-scale KBs do not contain all the possible knowledge, the knowledge completion task remains crucial in the NLP field. Various approaches can be used for constructing knowledge completion systems, such as knowledge reasoning and extraction. Among them, the task of extracting factual knowledge from unstructured text, such as natural language sentences, is important.

In addition, (Lin et al., 2017) mentioned that certain knowledge is described only in a certain language. For example, the Korean Wikipedia contains much information about Korean culture; similarly, the English Wikipedia contains information about English culture. Moreover, as far as we know, no knowledge extraction system is available for all languages. In addition, building a KB for a specific language requires an ontology schema definition and a knowledge extraction system that is appropriate for that language, as if creating a WordNet (Miller et al., 1990) for each language.

This paper describes a work-in-progress (demo) for building a Korean knowledge extraction system[1] for enriching a KBox[2] knowledge base. The final goal of our research is to build an iterative knowledge learning and extraction system. This web interface plays an important role in accepting new text at anytime and anywhere. Then, knowledge can be extracted from the input text through the web interface and can be accumulated directly in KBox. By doing so, the key modules for knowledge extraction, entity linking and relation extraction (RE), can later learn and improve using this steadily accumulated knowledge. This study makes the following contributions: (1) the first open Korean knowledge extraction system with a web interface and (2) immediately accumulate knowledge that extracted from the proposed system in KBox.

2 System Description

Figure 1 shows the architecture of the proposed demo system. This system has three main parts: Pre-processing, Relation Extraction, and Post-processing. Through the web interface, text is processed se-

---

[1] http://wisekb.kaist.ac.kr
[2] http://kbox.kaist.ac.kr

Proceedings of the 27th International Conference on Computational Linguistics: System Demonstrations, pages 20–24
Santa Fe, New Mexico, USA, August 20-26, 2018.

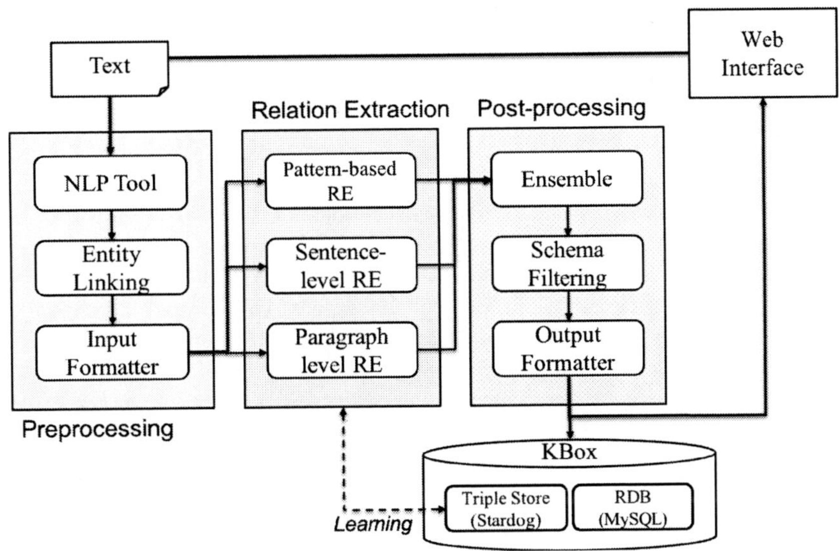

Figure 1: Architecture of the proposed demo system.

quentially by each main parts to extract knowledge and this knowledge is stored in KBox immediately. Details of each part are as follows.

2.1 Preprocessing

Preprocessing involves the following three steps in sequence. **NLP Tool** extracts features such as part-of-speech (POS) tags, dependency parsing, and named entity of input text. **Entity Linking** (Kim and Choi, 2015) links entity mentions in the text with their corresponding entities in KBox. This entity linking system consists of two modules: the entity boundary detection module finds out entity candidates from the text using a bidirectional long-short term memory (LSTM) model with inside-outside-beginning (IBO) and POS tags as features, and the entity disambiguation module takes entity candidates extracted from the entity boundary detection module and selects the most appropriate entity candidate. The system uses a support vector machine (SVM) with entity boundary information and semantic relations between entity candidates, such as entity popularity and inter-entity relations, as features. Korean has an entity made up of single character. Almost all single character entities have different meanings in the same representation, but features that distinguish these different meanings are not enough. Therefore, in our entity linking system, single character entity is not treated as candidate entity mention. **Input Formatter** prepares the input data for each RE model. Because the rule-based RE model use all features generated by the NLP tools, the JSON format was used to effectively deliver this data. Other RE models use the entity-linked text, and a paragraph-level model takes information to distinguish paragraphs using a new-line character.

2.2 Relation Extraction

RE is a task to classify ontological relations between two entities mentioned in a text, and it is a essential for extracting knowledge from natural language sentences. However, even a state-of-the-art RE model (Lin et al., 2017) shows low performance (F-scores 40%–50%). Because it cannot achieve satisfactory performance with just one RE module, we have configured an ensemble with multiple RE models. In the relation extraction step, our system considers not only the entities provided by the entity linking system but also the results of named entity recognition (NER) module as the entity. A new entity that does not exist in KBox cannot be identified by entity linking system, therefore we consider the result of NER as a new entity. Of the many types of NER, only three types of Person, Location, and Organization are considered to be new entities.

The **Pattern-based RE** model (Choi et al., 2016) aims to extract knowledge with high reliability. Human annotators use this model to generate patterns using lexical and syntactic features such as POS, dependency tree, and named entity recognition. This model shows a high precision but low recall, and therefore, scalability is a problem.

Sentence-level RE consists of both convolutional neural network (CNN) (Nam et al., 2018) and LSTM models to address scalability issues and increase recall. These models use distant supervision (Mintz et al., 2009) as a way to collect training data. Distant supervision assumes to collect all the sentences that contain both entities of a triple. Thus, it is widely used as an effective way to automatically create labeled data between a large-scale KB and a corpus. Both CNN and LSTM models use entity-embedded Korean word embedding as input vectors; the CNN model additionally uses vectors for position and POS. The sentence-level RE model is used to reveal the relation between two entities in a sentence; therefore, it is weak at extracting facts that can be found across sentences (paragraph).

One of the differences between Korean and English is the zero anaphora. In Korean, repeated subjects are frequently omitted in the latter sentence. To address this problem, the **Paragraph-level RE** model (Kim and Choi, 2018), which is useful for estimating omitted subjects and predicting relations, explores the incorporation of global contexts derived from paragraph-into-sentence embedding as a means of compensating for the shortage of training data in distantly supervised RE. This model specifically performs zero subject resolution through entity-relation-based graph analysis to find a central entity. The central entities are selected from each paragraph by calculating the out-degree centrality based on the network model of the entity graph using the knowledge base triples. This allows us to learn RE models for informal sentences and has the advantage of compensating for a shortage of training data in the DS-based approach to null subject languages.

2.3 Post-processing

Rather than independently determining the knowledge extracted from each RE module, it is important to combine the results of all modules. We have created an **Ensemble** module based on two concepts: (1) knowledge with high score from one module and (2) same knowledge extracted in multiple modules. A KB should be built based on an ontology schema. Unfortunately, automatically extracted knowledge includes some errors, many of which do not fit the ontology schema. **Schema Filtering** identifies invalid triples and filters them out using domain and range definition of each relation(property) based on two concepts: (1) If the domain or range of relation and subject or object entity types do not match, the triple will be filtered. (2) If the type of entity is not defined, the triple will pass with low calibrated score. **Output Formatter** produces two types of output data. The first is the JSON format for the web interface, and the second is the tab-separated values format that includes triple, triple score, source module, and source sentence for adding to KBox. Through this series of processes, knowledge is extracted and accumulate continuously in KBox.

2.4 KBox

KBox is a new KB that expands Korean DBpedia[3]. KBox consists of two types of storage: One keeps track of both candidate and reliable triples by MySQL, and the other stores only the reliable triples in the former storage by Stardog, a type of a triple store. All the information about all the triples, such as triple scores, the source module, and the source sentence, are stored by MySQL. The reliable triples consist of (1) the initial triples extracted from the Wikipedia infobox (DBpedia) and (2) the automatically extracted triples using the proposed system with a score above 0.9. The expansion of KBOX in Korean DBpedia is three-fold. First, the class hierarchy follows that used in DBpedia[4], but property definitions are revised and strengthened. The domain and range of each property are defined to be common to each language; however, we examined the triples in the Korean DBpedia and found that the schema can be defined more precisely or need to be modified. We then revised the KBox schema by performing instance-based domain range inference. Second, KBox has improved on the triple compared to Korean

---

[3]http://ko.dbpedia.org/
[4]http://mappings.dbpedia.org/server/ontology/classes/

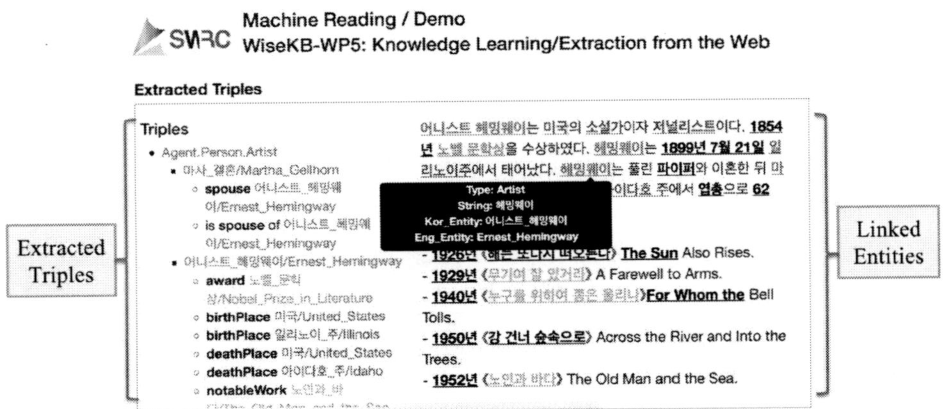

Figure 2: Screenshot of an extracted knowledge from a sample input

DBpedia. First, we defined 763,974 types for 81,991 entities based on the `sameAs` link information of the English DBpedia and Wikidata more than Korean DBpedia. Second, we converted local properties into ontological properties using a mapping table which was manually created by three expert annotators. As a result, 1,678,163 triples represented by Korean local properties were converted, for example, `prop-ko:chul-saeng-ji` to `dbo:birthPlace`. This makes it possible to express a triple represented by a different relation name for the same knowledge in one unified relation. Third, automatically extracted triples are added from this proposed demo and other batch processes in our own server.

3   Demonstration

Figure 2 shows a screenshot of the proposed demo system. Our demo system basically uses Korean natural language sentences as an input. The extracted knowledge is presented to the user in two forms. First, the entity linking results are displayed in color and underline on the input text. When you move the mouse over an entity, the entity type, lexical mention, and Korean and English entity names are displayed. Second, the triples are displayed sorted and rolled up by entity. To demonstrate effectively to users who do not use Korean as a native language, English entities corresponding to Korean entities are displayed together. The source code for our demonstration system has been released[5] under a CC BY-NC-SA license.

4   Conclusion

This study develops a new Korean knowledge extraction system for enriching a KBox. The main contribution is to improve the user accessibility through a web interface, and to provide a Korean knowledge extraction system. Furthermore, new knowledge extracted from the web interface is continuously accumulated in KBox. The core knowledge extraction core modules such as entity linking and RE have laid the foundation for improving the learning model based on the enhanced KBox.

References

Sören Auer, Christian Bizer, Georgi Kobilarov, Jens Lehmann, Richard Cyganiak, and Zachary Ives. 2007. Dbpedia: A nucleus for a web of open data. In *The semantic web*, pages 722–735. Springer.

Kurt Bollacker, Colin Evans, Praveen Paritosh, Tim Sturge, and Jamie Taylor. 2008. Freebase: a collaboratively created graph database for structuring human knowledge. In *Proceedings of the 2008 ACM SIGMOD international conference on Management of data*, pages 1247–1250. AcM.

---

[5]https://github.com/machinereading/wisekb-demo

GyuHyeon Choi, Sangha Nam, Dongho Choi, and Key-Sun Choi. 2016. Filling a knowledge graph with a crowd. In *Proceedings of the Open Knowledge Base and Question Answering Workshop (OKBQA 2016)*, pages 67–71.

Youngsik Kim and Key-Sun Choi. 2015. Entity linking korean text: An unsupervised learning approach using semantic relations. In *Proceedings of the Nineteenth Conference on Computational Natural Language Learning*, pages 132–141.

Eun-kyung Kim and Key-Sun Choi. 2018. Incorporating global contexts into sentence embedding for relational extraction at the paragraph level with distant supervision. In *LREC*.

Yankai Lin, Zhiyuan Liu, and Maosong Sun. 2017. Neural relation extraction with multi-lingual attention. In *Proceedings of the 55th Annual Meeting of the Association for Computational Linguistics (Volume 1: Long Papers)*, volume 1, pages 34–43.

George A Miller, Richard Beckwith, Christiane Fellbaum, Derek Gross, and Katherine J Miller. 1990. Introduction to wordnet: An on-line lexical database. *International journal of lexicography*, 3(4):235–244.

Mike Mintz, Steven Bills, Rion Snow, and Dan Jurafsky. 2009. Distant supervision for relation extraction without labeled data. In *Proceedings of the Joint Conference of the 47th Annual Meeting of the ACL and the 4th International Joint Conference on Natural Language Processing of the AFNLP: Volume 2-Volume 2*, pages 1003–1011. Association for Computational Linguistics.

Sangha Nam, Kijong Han, Eun-kyung Kim, and Key-Sun Choi. 2018. Distant supervision for relation extraction with multi-sense word embedding. *Global Wordnet Conference, Workshops on Wordnets and Word Embeddings*.

Fabian M Suchanek, Gjergji Kasneci, and Gerhard Weikum. 2007. Yago: a core of semantic knowledge. In *Proceedings of the 16th international conference on World Wide Web*, pages 697–706. ACM.

Real-time Scholarly Retweeting Prediction System

Zhunchen Luo[†*] and **Xiao Liu**[‡*]

[†]Information Research Center of Military Science, PLA Academy of Military Science
100142 Beijing, China
zhunchenluo@gmail.com
[‡]School of Computer Science and Technology, Beijing Institute of Technology
100081 Beijing, China
xiaoliu@bit.edu.cn

Abstract

Twitter has become one of the most import channels to spread latest scholarly information because of its fast information spread speed. How to predict whether a scholarly tweet will be retweeted is a key task in understanding the message propagation within large user communities. Hence, we present the real-time scholarly retweeting prediction system that retrieves scholarly tweets which will be retweeted. First, we filter scholarly tweets from tracking a tweet stream. Then, we extract Tweet Scholar Blocks indicating metadata of papers. At last, we combine scholarly features with the Tweet Scholar Blocks to predict whether a scholarly tweet will be retweeted. Our system outperforms chosen baseline systems. Additionally, our system has the potential to predict scientific impact in real-time.

1 Introduction

The volume of information about scientific papers is enormous on Twitter, and most data is real-time, even before the paper content is published and shortly after the notifications of acceptance. Besides, lots of scholars post tweets to express their excitement when their papers got accepted (Priem and Costello, 2010). We call the tweets that imply accepted papers scholarly tweets (*STs*) and the rest non-scholarly tweets (*NSTs*). Retweeting is an action of reposting others' tweet by using the *retweet* button on Twitter or other mechanism. To help understand the message propagation within large user communities, we develop a real-time scholarly retweeting prediction system.

Our task is to predict whether a *ST* will be retweeted. The problem of retweeting prediction has attracted more and more attention. Zhang et al. (2016) propose a deep learning method to predict retweeting. However, due to the special and structural ways using combinations of different Tweet Scholar Blocks (*TSBs*) encoding scholarly information about papers, venues, and authors, different methods should be explored to solve our task.

In this work, we propose a real-time scholarly retweeting prediction system by exploiting *TSBs* and scholarly features. We only focus on retweets made using the *retweet* button in Twitter. Under this circumstance, the tweet-retweet connection is unambiguously and can be retrieved directly by Twitter's API. At first, we trace a data stream by tracking "paper accepted" in Twitter using the Twitter API, but there are some *NSTs* in the data stream, so we build a classification model to filter *ST* tweets. It is investigated that most *STs* consist of text blocks called *Twitter Scholar Blocks* (*TSBs*) indicating meta data, and we build a sequence tagger to extract *TSBs* to gather metadata information. At last, we build a binary classification model by combining *TSBs* with scholarly information in Twitter to predict whether the *ST* will be retweeted. Experimental results show that our system outperforms chosen baseline systems and has the potential to predict scientific impact in real-time.

Proceedings of the 27th International Conference on Computational Linguistics: System Demonstrations, pages 25–29
Santa Fe, New Mexico, USA, August 20-26, 2018.

2 Real-time Scholarly Retweeting Prediction System

2.1 System Overview

Given a tweet t, our goal is first to learn a function STF that estimate the likelihood of whether t is a scholarly tweet, then learn a function RP to estimate the probability of whether t will be retweeted. By incorporating with the *TSBs* and scholarly features, we use the system to predict whether the *STs* will be retweeted. The framework of our approach is shown in Figure 1.

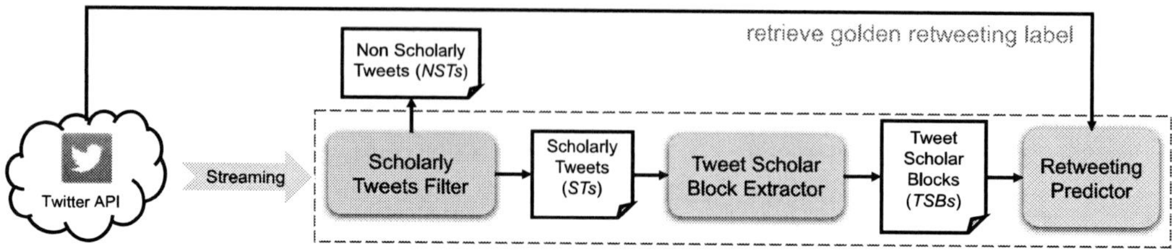

Figure 1: Framework of Our Approach

2.2 Scholarly Tweets Filter

We regard filtering *STs* from the data stream as a classification problem. In our scholarly tweets filter (*STF*) module, we build a classification model based on support vector machine.

To capture the information in social networks, we design a feature **user's scholarly membership of academic institutions** by examining whether user descriptions contain one of the high-frequency words of academic institution names in Wikipedia (we choose top sixty words in experiments). Additionally, we design **bag of words, words with trending symbols and length of the tweet** as features. We also find that almost no one would hide happiness if her paper were accepted, and we use a tweet-specified sentiment analysis API[1] to generate **sentiment labels** for tweets.

2.3 Tweet Scholar Block Extractor

Inspired by previous works on structuring tweets (Luo et al., 2012; Luo et al., 2015), we investigate that researchers post *STs* in structural ways using combinations of different Tweet Scholar Blocks (*TSBs*) encoding scholarly information about papers, venues, and authors. In this work, we propose six types of *TSBs*: **Author**, the names of authors; **Title**, the title of the paper; **Venue**, the short or entire name of the venue; **Time**, the time when the venue will be held; **Place**, the place where the venue will be held; **Other**, the rest part of tweet text. An example of extracted *TSBs* of a tweet is given in Figure 2.

In our tweet scholar block extractor (*TSBE*) module, we build a sequence tagger based on conditional random fields with BIO schema. We use **tokens starting with "@", surrounded by pairwise symbols, capitalized, trending symbols, POS-Tagging labels and NER labels** as our features. Tokens starting with "@" in *STs* are often mentioned co-authors. Besides, the paper titles usually occupy up to 40% text content which is often surrounded by pairwise symbols or all capitalized to show different formats.

2.4 Retweeting Predictor

In our retweeting predictor (*RP*) module, we build a classification model based on support vector machine (*SVM*). Apart from using text information generated from the extracted *TSBs* as our features, we take scholarly features from social networks information in Twitter into account. Apart from extracted *TSBs*, we categorize the rest scholarly features into following two categories:

Author Social Features: Previous work shows that the overall impact of all co-authors should have the potential to influence a paper's quality and popularity (Dong et al., 2015). We use extracted *Author* type of *TSBs* to find the authors in *ST tweets*. We think the influence of an individual is related to her **friend's**

---

[1] https://dev.exploreyourdata.com/index.html

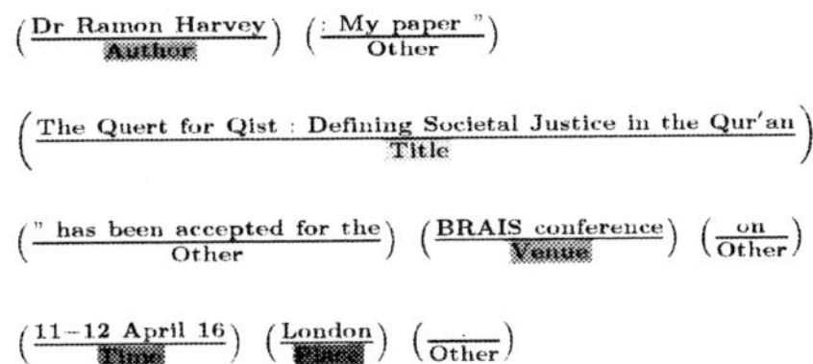

Figure 2: An Example of Extracted Tweet Scholar Blocks

number, followers number, and statuses quantity. To show the influence of a group, we calculate the **sum, maximum value, minimum value and average value** of influences of all participants in that group. In spite of these, we design a binary feature indicating **whether a user is verified**as verification is used by Twitter mostly to confirm the authenticity of celebrity accounts.

Venue Popularity Features: Different venues have large differences in their influences. Since the well-respected venues are better platforms for researchers to publish their work or results, our intuition is that better sites help scholars spread their scientific impact more. Scholars often use Twitter as a note-taking tool (Mapes, 2016) during venues, so **the number of statuses in the venue topic** may reflect the popularity and influence of the site. Considering the developments and the trends of the venues, we also take **the total historical quantity of statuses** into account.

3 Experiments

Predicted	Golden	User	Tweet
not	not	@Neonatal_Brain	New ultrasound marker for #brain growth. Paper is accepted. Nice and easy for both fetal and neonatal measurements. https://t.co/W17Wcnqv4L
yes	yes	@danieldekok	\o/. ACL short paper by me and Erhard Hinrichs on dependency parsing with topological fields (and BiDi LSTMs) accepted.
yes	not	@manaalfar	Short paper on non-distributional word vectors accepted at ACL 2015 #chinacl2015 #acl2015 #nlproc
not	yes	@dimazest	finally I got an email from emnlp and it's positive, the paper got accepted!

Table 1: Examples of predicted scholarly tweets and the golden labels of whether they will be retweeted

3.1 Data Preparation and Experiment Settings

To evaluate our system, we first track a tweets stream posted from Jan. 2012 to Apr. 2018 by tracking the key phrase "paper accepted" using Twitter API. randomly crawl 6,500 tweets Then we randomly sample 6,500 tweets and manually label them as *STs* and *NSTs* for training scholarly tweets filter. Next, we choose 1,400 original *STs* out of them by checking their "retweeted_status" attributes are empty from Twitter API. We use tweet-specific annotators (Owoputi et al., 2013; Ritter et al., 2011) to tokenize those tweets and get pos-tagging and NER labels, then manually label *TSBs* in BIO schema for training our tweet scholar block extractor. Last but not least, we get the golden labels of whether an original *ST* will be retweeted by finding the corresponding retweets. Additionally, five-fold cross-validation is used in our experiments and accuracy is used as the evaluation metric.

3.2 Baseline Comparison and Feature Selection

We choose two baselines, the one is random prediction (*Random*), the other is an CNN model (Zhang et al., 2016) (*SUA-ACNN*). Then we compare the result of using *TSBE* and golden *TSBs* with *RP* (*TSBE+RP* and *Golden+RP* respectively). To find the best feature conjunction, we use a greedy feature selection method in which we first choose the best feature set out of several randomly generated sets and then iteratively append features that yield better performance. The setting of using best feature set is called

TSBE+RP_Best and *Golden+RP_Best* respectively. Results are shown in Table 2. Besides, Table 1 demonstrates some predicted examples of our *TSBE+RP_Best* system.

Approach	Accuracy
Random	62.43%
SUA-ACNN	76.29%
RP	90.36%
TSBE+RP	87.43%
RP_Best	94.50%
TSBE+RP_Best	90.57%

Table 2: Comparing With Baselines and the Best Feature Conjunction

Overall, our system outperforms the baseline, and it is feasible to predict scientific impact in Twitter in real time. Moreover, the performance of *TSBE+RP* is lower than the performance of *RP* on manually labeled TSBs, because the errors produced in *TSBE* might affect the performance of *RP*. Besides, the best feature conjunction consisted of *Sum Friends Count*, *Sum Followers Count*, *Max Followers Count*.

3.3 Ablation Study

To find the effectiveness of each feature and which features are in particular highly valued by *RP_Best*, we also removed each feature from *RP_Best* and *TSBE+RP_Best* respectively to evaluate the effectiveness of each feature by the decrement of accuracy.

By comparing the results shown in Table 3, we can see that *Sum Followers Count* is very effective to our *RP_Best*. The reason might be that *Sum Followers Count* is more suitable to stand for the influence of the authors' group.

Approach	Accuracy
RP_Best	94.50%
RP_Best-Sum Friends Count	89.57%
RP_Best-Sum Followers Count	88.93%
RP_Best-Max Followers Count	89.14%
TSBE+RP_Best	90.57%
TSBE+RP_Best-Sum Friends Count	86.71%
TSBE+RP_Best-Sum Followers Count	85.14%
TSBE+RP_Best-Max Followers Count	86.43%

Table 3: Comparing Results by Decaying Every Feature One by One

4 Conclusion

In this paper, we propose our real-time scholarly retweeting prediction system which solves the scholarly tweets retweeting prediction problem. We introduce the three modules in our system: scholarly tweets filter, tweet scholar block extractor and retweeting predictor. In addition, our system has the potential to predict scientific impact in real-time. Sufficient experimental results demonstrate that our model outperforms the baseline systems. Hope our system can help researchers to stand on the shoulders of right giants.

Acknowledgement

We thank the anonymous reviewers for their helpful comments. We also thank our annotators for giving suggestions when accomplishing the dataset and holding helpful discussions. This work is supported by National Natural Science Foundation of China (No. 61602490).

References

Yuxiao Dong, Reid A. Johnson, and Nitesh V. Chawla. 2015. Will this paper increase your h-index?: Scientific impact prediction. In *Proceedings of the WSDM 2015*, pages 149–158.

Zhunchen Luo, Miles Osborne, Sasa Petrovic, and Ting Wang. 2012. Improving twitter retrieval by exploiting structural information. In *Proceedings of the AAAI 2012*, pages 648–654.

Zhunchen Luo, Yang Yu, Miles Osborne, and Ting Wang. 2015. Structuring tweets for improving twitter search. *JASIST*, 66(12):2522–2539.

Kristen Mapes. 2016. A qualitative content analysis of 19, 000 medieval studies conference tweets. In *Proceedings of the SIGDOC 2016*, page 48.

Olutobi Owoputi, Brendan O'Connor, Chris Dyer, Kevin Gimpel, Nathan Schneider, and Noah A. Smith. 2013. Improved part-of-speech tagging for online conversational text with word clusters. In *Proceedings of the NAACL-HLT 2013*, pages 380–390.

Jason Priem and Kaitlin Light Costello. 2010. How and why scholars cite on twitter. *Proceedings of The Asist Annual Meeting*, 47(1):1–4.

Alan Ritter, Sam Clark, Mausam, and Oren Etzioni. 2011. Named entity recognition in tweets: An experimental study. In *Proceedings of the EMNLP 2011*, pages 1524–1534.

Qi Zhang, Yeyun Gong, Jindou Wu, Haoran Huang, and Xuanjing Huang. 2016. Retweet prediction with attention-based deep neural network. In *Proceedings of the CIKM 2016*, pages 75–84.

Document Representation Learning For Patient History Visualization

Halid Ziya Yerebakan, Yoshihisa Shinagawa, Parmeet Bhatia
Siemens Medical Solutions USA / Malvern, PA
`halid.yerebakan@siemens-healthineers.com`
`yoshihisa.shinagawa@siemens-healthineers.com`
`parmeet.bhatia@siemens-healthineers.com`

Yiqiang Zhan
Shanghai Jiao Tong University / Shanghai, China
`yiqiang@gmail.com`

Abstract

We tackle the problem of generating a diagrammatic summary of a set of documents each of which pertains to loosely related topics. In particular, we aim at visualizing the medical histories of patients. In medicine, choosing relevant reports from a patient's past exams for comparison provide valuable information for precise treatment planning. Manually finding the relevant reports for comparison studies from a large database is time-consuming, which could result overlooking of some critical information. This task can be automated by defining similarity among documents which is a nontrivial task since these documents are often stored in an unstructured text format. To facilitate this, we have used a representation learning algorithm that creates a semantic representation space for documents where the clinically related documents lie close to each other. We have utilized referral information to weakly supervise a LSTM network to learn this semantic space. The abstract representations within this semantic space are not only useful to visualize disease progressions corresponding to the relevant report groups of a patient, but are also beneficial to analyze diseases at the population level. The proposed key tool here is clustering of documents based on the document similarity whose metric is learned from corpora.

1 Introduction

In medicine, examination of a patient's diseases is described in many reports in multiple specialties. Each report specializes in a specific aspect of the diseases, such as the chest, head and bones. For precise treatments, understanding the holistic picture of the patient's clinical history is critical. Unstructured text formats that are widely used further complicates the problem. Usually, relevant report retrieval and comparison are labor-intensive, particularly with patients having crowded clinical histories. As a result, important information may be overlooked due to time limitations.

Automatic matching of reports is not trivial since the reports are generally kept in unstructured text format in electronic health record (EHR) database. Exact keyword matching is not directly useful since the same entities could be written in different forms such as 'cardiac' and 'heart'. Additionally, acronyms are very common in these reports and many irrelevant reports may share same keywords. Semantic understanding of the text is necessary to find relevant report groups that experts consider as clinically similar which we named as *disease lines*.

This paper presents a representation learning algorithm and a visualization mechanism to enable clinicians to have holistic views of patients' history. In order to ensure the clinically meaningful similarity measure for the reports, we have utilized weak label information encoded in previous comparison studies conducted by radiologists.

2 Weakly Supervised Siamese LSTM

Among many alternative approaches for representation learning we decided to utilize siamese LSTM neural network architecture similar to (Mueller and Thyagarajan, 2016) on radiology reports. We de-

Proceedings of the 27th International Conference on Computational Linguistics: System Demonstrations, pages 30–33
Santa Fe, New Mexico, USA, August 20-26, 2018.

rived new insights from extracted continuous space representations of text documents. We applied two different clustering algorithms to analyze extracted representations in patient and population level.

A radiology report often refers to a previous report to understand and compare patient's disease progression. These referrals are used to construct positive ground truth labels for document pairs in order to learn representation space such that clinically similar documents lie close to each other. For a given pair of documents, the label is positive if the reports are directly or indirectly referring to the other report. All the report that do not refer to each other may be considered as negative pairs. However, since the positive labels for all possible pairs is not complete we added additional modality and anatomy constraints using Apache cTakes(Savova et al., 2010) for negative labels.

Similar to (Mueller and Thyagarajan, 2016) we utilized LSTM to reduce variable length documents to space with fixed dimension. The LSTM network can be effectively used to learn very long-term dependencies with a sequence of words which turns out to be useful mechanism for relatively long medical reports. In this network, Siamese structure ensures that both the documents in given pair are represented in same Euclidean space. Another alternative is obtaining document representations using doc2vec. However, unlike *doc2vec* (Le and Mikolov, 2014), our method learns the metric based on ground truth labels because medical reports can be relevant even when the sentences are very different among them. The difficulty of creating a large labeled corpus is tackled in a weakly supervised manner.

We have used word embeddings trained on Pubmed central biomedical articles using word2vec(Mikolov et al., 2013) model for the embedding layer of LSTM network. We kept the learned word embeddings fixed during training of siamese LSTM network since changing their weights did not improve results in our experiments.

We have utilized generalized logistic loss as our objective function given in Equation 1(Hu et al., 2014) to train siamese LSTM network. Minimization of such loss essentially reduces the distance between positive pair of document while at the same time increases the distance between negative pairs. In this formula, β and τ are the hyper parameters and y denotes label information. Distance d is selected as Euclidean norm.

$$F(d, y) = \frac{1}{\beta} log(1 + e^{\beta(\frac{3}{2} - y(\tau - d))}) \tag{1}$$

3 Data and Preprocessing

We collected a corpus of radiology reports containing 100,000 de-identified radiology reports including studies on chest x-rays, abdominal CTs, and brain MRIs. The maximum number of reports per patient is 74. There are 25,546 unique patients with 12,677 of them being one time admission only;i.e, these patients have only one report entry in the database. More than 97% of reports are shorter than 250 words. Thus, we decided to limit the maximum number of the words to 250. Furthermore, as a result of data generation step explained in previous section, we have total of 32,000 positive pairs and 91,000 negative pairs among the 165,000 possible pairs of reports. Note that we only considered intra-patient pair of documents to construct our training and test data sets.

For data preprocesing, we applied stemming and lowercase to all the words in documents for normalization. We have removed punctuation marks and numbers as well. For tokenization, we have used NLTK word tokenizer. We used cTAKES to obtain tags such as pathology, anatomies, symptoms and negation from the radiology reports.

4 Results

In this section, we evaluate the quality of the representations learned by the siamese LSTM network.

In the experiments, the hyper-parameters are chosen as follows: τ=0.25 , separation = 1, β=2. Network width is selected as 32. We have trained the network for 10 epochs with batch size of 200.

4.1 Performance Evaluation

After creating a split of training and test pairs at the patient level, the documents are converted into integer word IDs and are passed through the network. As a result, we have obtained 32-dimensional

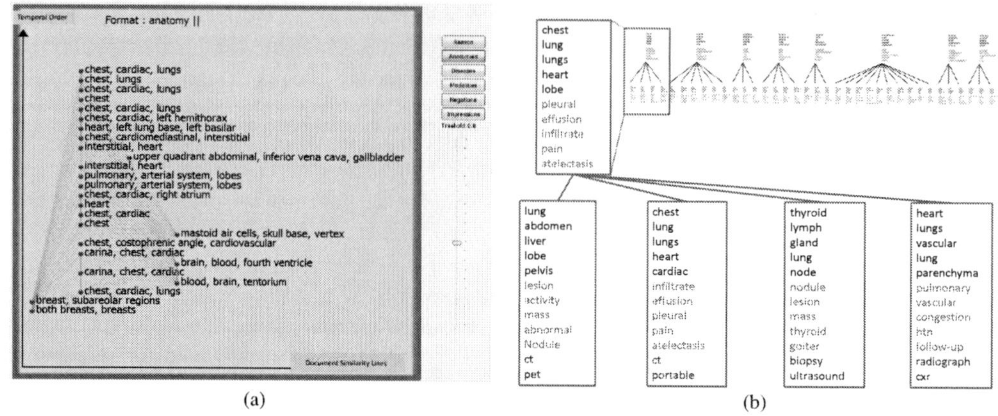

Figure 1: Patient level visualization system and population level analysis.

floating point representation for each report. There can be multiple alternatives to define a metric in this space to differentiate positive pairs from negative ones. We have chosen Euclidean norm as our metric that indicate similarity of documents. A pair of documents is considered as positive if the distance between their floating point representations is less than 0.5. With this threshold, we obtain 0.976 $F1$ score on the test set.

We further established baseline using bag-of-words model with support vector machines and logistic regression. These baselines gives 0.823 and 0.820 $F1$ scores, respectively. This clearly suggests that LSTM network can learn semantic relationship among words that bring positive pair of documents close to each other, whereas classical algorithms like bag-of-words fails to do so effectively.

4.2 Clustering Patient Lines

The learned representations captures the intrinsic comparison information given in referral of reports. In order to obtain meaningful report groups we further utilize connected component based clustering algorithm. The algorithm first calculates the distance matrix and then applies a threshold to the distance matrix, followed by calculation of connected components on the binarized distance matrix. Each connected component represents one cluster. This system allows to have different threshold levels which could change the granularity of obtained clusters. Other clustering algorithms could be used as well, however this approach provides a non parametric clustering with an interactive interface.

Using relevant reports groups, we have developed a 2-dimensional visualization methodology to get an overview of the patient's history. The reports in a cluster are given a unique y-coordinate and are aligned on a temporal line parallel to y axis according to their temporal order. Different clusters are represented by the lines at different x-coordinates. In this way, every cluster is represented by a distinct temporal line. Thus, the progression of diseases can be easily followed along the y-axis for a particular group (cluster) of reports. In order to qualitatively understand the performance of system, we have created a visualization where in we connected all the pairs with positive ground truth label with green lines and all negative pairs with blue lines as shown in Figure 1a. Ideally, there should be no green line across clusters and vice-versa for blue lines which is indeed the case as can be seen in Figure 1a.

Furthermore, our system facilitates visualization of patient's history in multiple perspectives such as anatomies, modalities and negations. The tagging system allows to extract the informative tags in the reports such as anatomies, modalities, and negations and these tags can be used to highlight particular perspective on visualization dashboard based on selection made by the medical practitioner. In this way, our system provides an interactive and holistic view of overall patient's history.

As it could be seen in the Figure 1a, the patient's reports are clustered into four groups, which match the ground truth labels shown in green lines. This patient first visited the hospital for breast screening, which is represented by the left most disease line. At one point, however, there was bleeding in the brain and the patient had CT exams, which is represented by right-most disease line. The patient was intubated and closely monitored, which is represented by the 2nd disease line from the left.

4.3 Population Level Analysis

Relationships in a large corpus of cross-patient radiology reports can help to understand disease patterns and their possible treatments. Manually analyzing such large radiology corpora is impractical for most clinically relevant applications. Thus, clustering algorithms could be used to visualize the patterns. However, basic clustering algorithms do not consider the hierarchical relations that exist in medical reports. Exploration of such structure within clinical data will further facilitate to understand the correlations across different diseases and sub-types. We choose the two-layer clustering algorithm named I2GMM (Yerebakan et al., 2014) that not only perform clustering but also extract sub-clusters for all the clusters.

We obtained representations of all the reports using shared LSTM network from the learned siamese network and applied I2GMM clustering algorithm on these representations. In order to understand the details of each cluster we extracted tags from each cluster. Most frequent tags are shown in Figure 1b. Zoomed cluster consist of different chest studies. The four sub-clusters from left to right in this cluster could be differentiated as malignant neoplasms, lung pathologies, neck related problems and vessel problems, respectively. In this figure, we used black color for anatomy tags, red for symptom or pathology tags, and purple for modalities. This result indicates that the learned document representations provide population level groups and sub-groups to relate patients at more abstract level. Such visualization could potentially be used to obtain information about different pathways of various diseases in more detail.

5 Conclusion

In this paper, we have presented a visualization system displaying a summary of the medical history of individual patients. The summary is obtained via clustering algorithm on top of the learned representations of documents encoding prior comparison information. Later, we have used these representations to analyze the whole corpus at population level by extracting clusters and sub-clusters.

For future studies combining image data with the corresponding free text information to focus on specific anatomical regions in images could facilitate the overall navigation of patient history.

References

Junlin Hu, Jiwen Lu, and Yap-Peng Tan. 2014. Discriminative deep metric learning for face verification in the wild. In *Proceedings of the IEEE Conference on Computer Vision and Pattern Recognition*, pages 1875–1882.

Quoc Le and Tomas Mikolov. 2014. Distributed representations of sentences and documents. In *International Conference on Machine Learning*, pages 1188–1196.

Tomas Mikolov, Ilya Sutskever, Kai Chen, Greg S Corrado, and Jeff Dean. 2013. Distributed representations of words and phrases and their compositionality. In *Advances in neural information processing systems*, pages 3111–3119.

Jonas Mueller and Aditya Thyagarajan. 2016. Siamese recurrent architectures for learning sentence similarity. In *AAAI*, pages 2786–2792.

Guergana K Savova, James J Masanz, Philip V Ogren, Jiaping Zheng, Sunghwan Sohn, Karin C Kipper-Schuler, and Christopher G Chute. 2010. Mayo clinical text analysis and knowledge extraction system (ctakes): architecture, component evaluation and applications. *Journal of the American Medical Informatics Association*, 17(5):507–513.

Halid Z Yerebakan, Bartek Rajwa, and Murat Dundar. 2014. The infinite mixture of infinite gaussian mixtures. In *Advances in neural information processing systems*, pages 28–36.

HiDE: A Tool for Unrestricted Literature Based Discovery

Judita Preiss
University of Salford
The School of Computing, Science & Engineering
Newton Building, Salford
Greater Manchester M5 4WT
J.Preiss@salford.ac.uk

Mark Stevenson
Department of Computer Science
University of Sheffield
211 Portobello
Sheffield S1 4DP
Mark.Stevenson@sheffield.ac.uk

Abstract

As the quantity of publications increases daily, researchers are forced to narrow their attention to their own specialism and are therefore less likely to make new connections with other areas. Literature based discovery (LBD) supports the identification of such connections. A number of LBD tools are available, however, they often suffer from limitations such as constraining possible searches or not producing results in real-time.

We introduce HiDE (Hidden Discovery Explorer), an online knowledge browsing tool which allows fast access to hidden knowledge generated from all abstracts in Medline. HiDE is fast enough to allow users to explore the full range of hidden connections generated by an LBD system. The tool employs a novel combination of two approaches to LBD: a graph-based approach which allows hidden knowledge to be generated on a large scale and an inference algorithm to identify the most promising (most likely to be non trivial) information.

Available at https://skye.shef.ac.uk/kdisc

1   Introduction

Literature based discovery (LBD) is an automatic technique addressing the ever increasing volume of research literature by inferring as yet unobserved connections. The approach was pioneered by Swanson (1986) who hypothesised a (hidden) connection between *Raynaud phenomenon* and *fish oil*, despite the fact that the two were not mentioned together in any publications. Swanson noticed that one publication linked *Raynaud phenomenon* to *blood viscosity* and another linked *blood viscosity* to *fish oil*, suggesting the trial of administering fish oil to Raynaud disease patients. LBD can be executed in one of two modes: closed or open discovery. In closed discovery, both A, the source term, and C, the target term, are specified, and only the linking terms (with relationships to both A and C) are sought, while open discovery explores a much larger space with only the source term being specified and all relationships being pursued (see Figure 1).

LBD has a range of applications including identification of potential treatments, drug repurposing and drug side effect prediction. However, in its general form LBD generates a vast number of hidden connections and the usefulness of existing open discovery systems, such as **Arrowsmith** (Swanson and Smalheiser, 1999), **Bitola**'s (Hristovski et al., 2006), **FACTA+** (Tsuruoka et al., 2008) or **Literome** (Poon et al., 2014), is often limited by heavy restrictions on the input, linking terms and output and/or time required to generate results.

2   Approach

HiDE combines two LBD approaches. To ensure a usable (rather than excessive) quantity of quality hidden knowledge, we combine: (1) the widely used *A-B-C model* introduced by Swanson (1986) which starts from a term, A, finds all terms B_i to which A is related, repeats the process to find all terms C_{ij} related to each B_i, and proposes any previously unconnected $A - C_{ij}$ as hidden knowledge, and (2) a

Proceedings of the 27th International Conference on Computational Linguistics: System Demonstrations, pages 34–37
Santa Fe, New Mexico, USA, August 20-26, 2018.

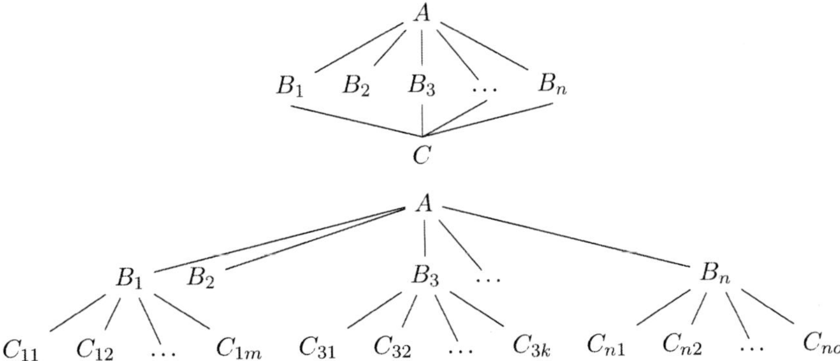

Figure 1: Closed discovery, both A and C specified (top), and open discovery, only A specified (bottom)

novel (to LBD) approach based on work in knowledge base completion which generates new connections by performing random walks through a knowledge base graph.

The *A-B-C model* is a useful approach for LBD but it can generate vast amounts of hidden knowledge potentially leading to the need for restrictions on the B/C terms and/or slow processing times. Exploiting techniques from graph theory (West, 2007), our LBD system (Preiss et al., 2015) uses the adjacency matrix M describing the graph formed from the connections between terms in a document collection: entry m_{ij} is a positive integer if a relation R is detected between terms t_i and t_j. If t_i and t_j are not related anywhere in the document collection, m_{ij} will be zero. Hidden knowledge in the document collection can then be identified by looking for non zero terms in the matrix generated by $\mathrm{norm}(M^2) - \mathrm{norm}(M)$ where norm converts m_{ij} to 1 if $m_{ij} > 0$ and leaves it as 0 otherwise. This generates hidden knowledge connected via a single linking step and allows large amounts of hidden knowledge to be pre-computed.

The *graph model* is an inference system due to Lao et al (2011) based on the Path Ranking Algorithm, which performs random walks through a knowledge base graph. In our case, the knowledge base is constructed from the manually created triples (such as *X may treat Y*) listed in the Unified Medical Language System (UMLS) Metathesaurus. The system generates path up to length 2, and uses logistic regression to combine the paths to yield new connections.

Both LBD systems are applied to all PubMed abstracts published up to 30 April 2016: the linguistically motivated *subject-relation-object* triples (such as *X-treats-Y* or *X-affects-Y*) are extracted from a SemRep (Rindflesch and Fiszman, 2003) annotated 2016 version of PubMed (available as semmed-VER26 download created using regular SemRep version 1.7 and UMLS 2016AA[1]) and used for the *A-B-C model*. UMLS 2016AA was used to obtain the manually created triples for the *graph model*. A range of filtering approaches are applied to reduce the volume of hidden knowledge (Preiss, 2014). Individually, the *A-B-C model* generated a total of 2,947,874,564 pairs of hidden knowledge, while the *graph model* yielded 198,295,133 pairs. The intersection of hidden knowledge pairs, 6,471,922 pairs, is presented within the interface, and the hidden knowledge pairs are ranked by the weights output by the *graph model*.

3 Online System

The approach described in Section 2 is implemented as a publicly available tool, HiDE (Hidden Discovery Explorer), which allows a user to interactively explore the hidden knowledge generated by an LBD system.

Interaction with HiDE begins with the user specifying a term of interest. HiDE then generates a list of potentially relevant UMLS CUIs from which the user selects one. The hidden knowledge available is grouped by UMLS Medical Subject Headings (MeSH) terms which provides types such as *disease*,

---

[1] https://semrep.nlm.nih.gov/

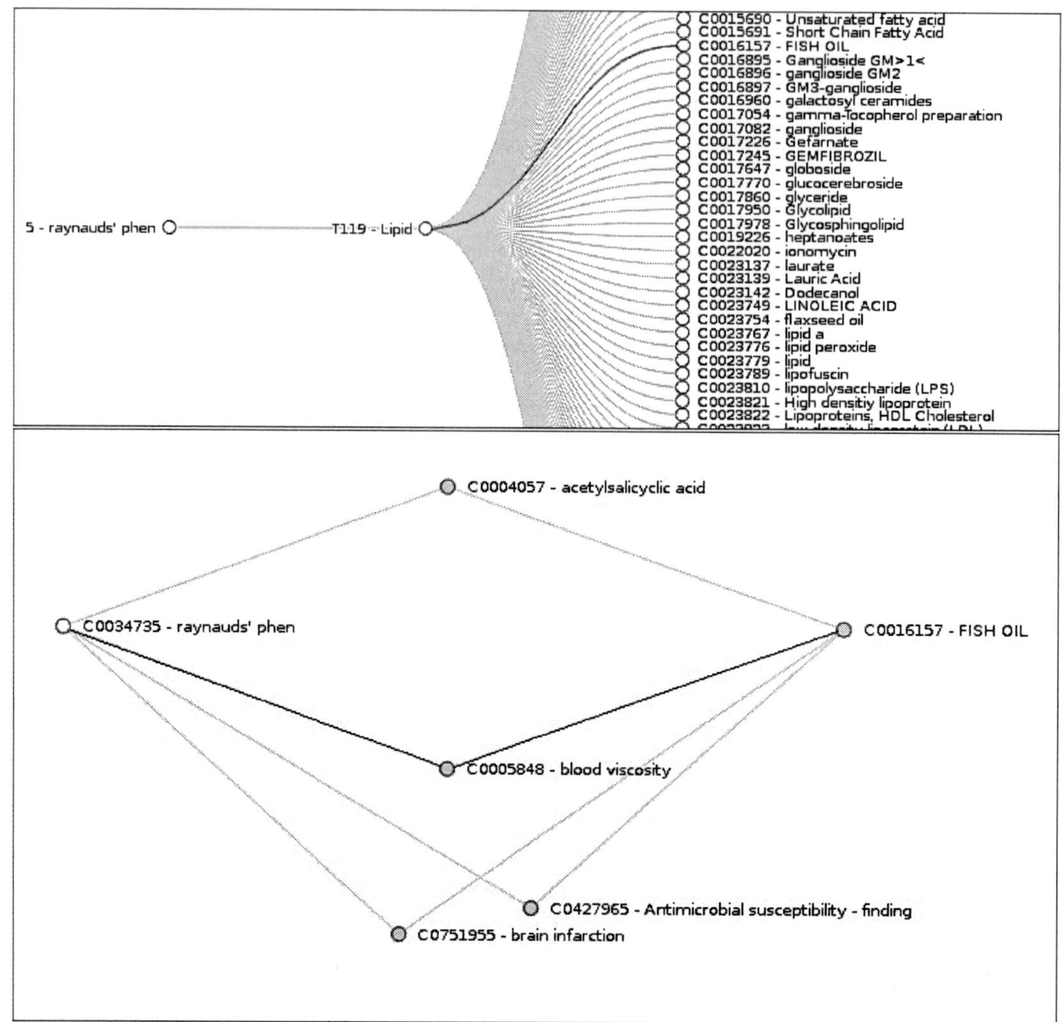

Figure 2: Raynaud phenomenon open discovery: **top** shows the first page of *lipid* hidden knowledge from *C0034735 – Raynaud Phenomenon* generated from publications between 1960 and 1985 highlighting Swanson's fish oil connection, **bottom** the linking terms between *C0034735 – Raynaud Phenomenon* and *C0016157 - fish oil* with the highly cited *blood viscosity* link highlighted

enzyme and *gene*. The user selects a MeSH term, which allows them to filter the result set to MeSH terms of relevant to them while also reducing the number of results returned, and the hidden knowledge generated from the original CUI is presented. Users can view hidden knowledge in increments of 100 pairs and linking terms in increments of 50.

3.1 Implementation Details

HiDE is a web-based system in which all rendering is achieved using the D3 JavaScript library. Hidden knowledge is generated offline and stored in a MySQL database which the interface accesses using PHP. Linking terms for a selected pair of CUIs are computed in real time. All results are cached to ensure subsequent access for the same knowledge pair will be virtually instant.

4   Example

Figure 2 presents the output of HiDE when replicating the connection between *Raynaud* and *fish oil* (Swanson, 1986) from 1960-8 Medline publications using the matrix method only (as the inference method would require a UMLS from 1968 which does not exist). The top portion of Figure 2 shows a zoomed in section of the hidden knowledge generated by HiDE by entering the search term *raynaud*, selecting the CUI *C0034735 – Raynaud Phenomenon* and then the MeSH term *lipid*. The figure shows that the link to the *C* term *fish oil* is found by HiDE (this link is highlighted). Selecting this CUI reveals the *B* term(s) via which the hidden knowledge was established; the bottom of Figure 2 shows the linking terms between *Raynaud* and *fish oil*, demonstrating that HiDE finds the frequently cited link via *blood viscosity* (highlighted).

5   Conclusion

We present HiDE, an LBD tool suitable for exploring hidden knowledge generated by an LBD system including linking terms. Rather than imposing a filtering by design, HiDE does not restrict the hidden knowledge presented to the user while allowing them to quickly drill down to MeSH terms of interest and thus carry out their own 'filtering'. Using a novel combination of two LBD approaches – a graph-based approach and an inference algorithm – the most promising information is computed off line, thereby enabling fast response times to queries and allowing users to fully explore the information generated.

Acknowledgements

The work described in this paper was funded by the Engineering and Physical Sciences Research Council (EP/J008427/1).

References

Dimitar Hristovski, Carol Friedman, Thomas C. Rindflesch, and Borut Peterlin. 2006. Exploiting semantic relations for literature-based discovery. In *Proceedings of the 2006 AMIA Annual Symposium*, pages 349–353.

Ni Lao, Tom M. Mitchell, and William W. Cohen. 2011. Random walk inference and learning in a large scale knowledge base. In *Proceedings of the Conference on Empirical Methods in Natural Language Processing*, pages 529–539.

US National Library of Medicine. Semantic knowledge representation. https://semrep.nlm.nih.gov/. Accessed: 31-07-2017.

Hoifung Poon, Chris Quirk, Charlie DeZiel, and David Heckerman. 2014. Literome: PubMed-scale genomic knowledge base in the cloud. *Bioinformatics*, 30(19):2840–2842.

Judita Preiss, Mark Stevenson, and Robert Gaizauskas. 2015. Exploring relation types for literature-based discovery. *Journal of the American Medical Informatics Association*, 22:987–992.

Judita Preiss. 2014. Seeking informativeness in literature based discovery. In *Proceedings of BioNLP 2014*, pages 112–117.

Thomas C. Rindflesch and Marcelo Fiszman. 2003. The interaction of domain knowledge and linguistic structure in natural language processing: interpreting hypernymic propositions in biomedical text. *Journal of Biomedical Informatics*, 36(6):462–477.

Don R. Swanson and Neil R. Smalheiser. 1999. Link analysis of MEDLINE titles as an aid to scientific discovery: Using Arrowsmith as an aid to scientific discovery. *Library Trends*, 48:48–59.

Don R. Swanson. 1986. Fish oil, Raynaud's syndrome, and undiscovered public knowledge. *Perspectives in Biology and Medicine*, 30:7–18.

Y. Tsuruoka, J. Tsujii, and S. Ananiadou. 2008. Facta: a text search engine for finding associated biomedical concepts. *Bioinformatics*, 24(21):2559–2560.

Douglas B. West. 2007. *Introduction to Graph Theory*. Prentice Hall.

Active DOP: A constituency treebank annotation tool with online learning

Andreas van Cranenburgh
Heinrich Heine University of Düsseldorf
Universitätsstraße 1, 40225 Düsseldorf, Germany
`cranenburgh@phil.hhu.de`

Abstract

We present a language-independent treebank annotation tool supporting rich annotations with discontinuous constituents and function tags. Candidate analyses are generated by an exemplar-based parsing model that immediately learns from each new annotated sentence during annotation. This makes it suitable for situations in which only a limited seed treebank is available, or a radically different domain is being annotated. The tool offers the possibility to experiment with and evaluate active learning methods to speed up annotation in a naturalistic setting, i.e., measuring actual annotation costs and tracking specific user interactions. The code is made available under the GNU GPL license at `https://github.com/andreasvc/activedop`.

1 Introduction

Treebank annotation is a labor-intensive manual task with various opportunities for automation. This is typically done with bespoke annotation tools (e.g., PTB, FTB, Negra, Tiger) that provide some form of semi-automatic annotation. The Penn treebank was annotated with the help of a rule-based deterministic parser (Marcus et al., 1993). This parser only provided a partial parse with constituents that it was certain about. A similar process was used for the French Treebank (Abeillé et al., 2003). The German Tiger treebank uses a more elaborate approach with two parsers providing candidate analyses (Brants et al., 2002). The first is a cascaded Markov model that provides interactive annotation and can be retrained on user feedback; the second is based on a precision grammar (HPSG) which is not retrained but has the advantage of always being consistent.

Compared to other treebank annotation tools, we believe our tool offers the following advantages:

- Applicable to any constituency treebank without feature engineering or handwritten rules. Discontinuous constituents and function tags are included in the annotation and suggested parses (ignored by most statistical parsers).

- Online learning: updating the grammar is fast and can therefore be done after every sentence instead of only after a larger batch, which makes the tool suitable for low resource settings and rapidly adapting the grammar to a new domain.

- The possibility to explore active learning methods in a naturalistic setting, i.e., measuring actual annotation cost instead of in synthetic simulations.

2 The Parser

Our system is based on the parser presented in van Cranenburgh et al. (2016), a constituency parser supporting discontinuous constituents and function tags. POS tagging and unknown word handling is integrated in the parser. The parser is based on the Data-Oriented Parsing framework (Scha, 1990; Bod, 1992), which views the treebank as a set of exemplars of which arbitrary fragments can be identified as

Proceedings of the 27th International Conference on Computational Linguistics: System Demonstrations, pages 38–42
Santa Fe, New Mexico, USA, August 20-26, 2018.

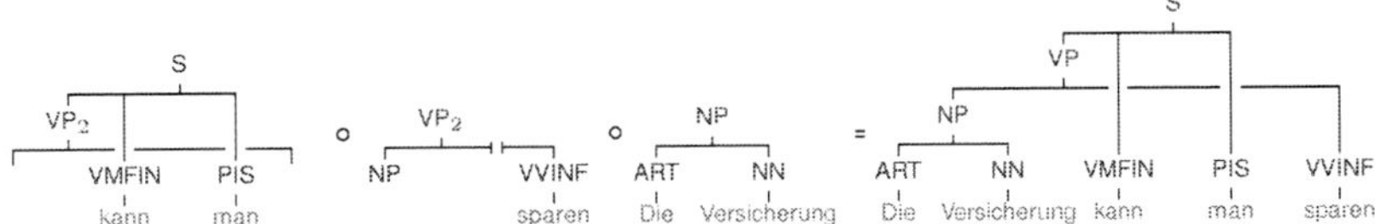

Figure 1: A DOP derivation with discontinuous constituents. Translation: *The insurance one can save.*

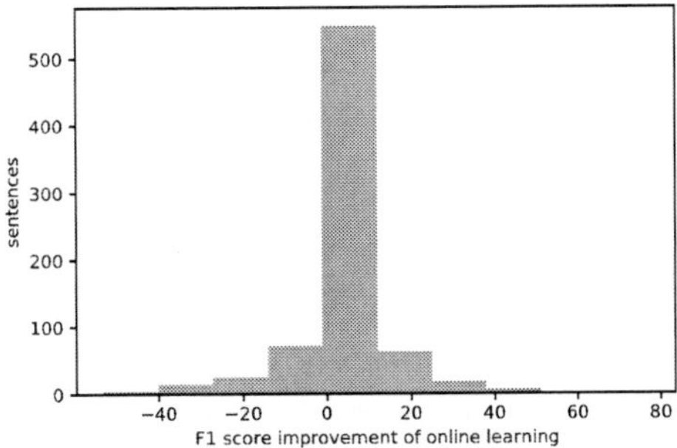

Figure 2: Histogram showing the difference in F1-score with and without online learning in a simulation of annotating the Tiger treebank (higher is better). The improvement is significant with $p < 0.01$.

productive units to analyze new sentences. The parser employs a Tree-Substitution Grammar (TSG) consisting of a set of elementary trees with associated frequencies. The elementary trees are automatically induced from training data in the form of tree fragments attested in two or more trees. Such recurring tree fragments can be efficiently extracted from sets of trees using a tree-kernel approach (Sangati et al., 2010; van Cranenburgh, 2014) which compares pairs of trees in search of common subgraphs. Through the use of indexes of the treebank, this step can be done exactly and exhaustively, instead of needing to resort to approximate methods. Data-driven parsing with discontinuous constituents is done using the grammar formalism of Linear Context-Free Rewriting Systems (LCFRS; Kallmeyer and Maier, 2013), extended to a tree-substitution grammar (van Cranenburgh et al., 2016). Figure 1 shows an example of a derivation with the grammar. Note how discontinuities in elementary trees are marked, specifying where the spans of other elementary trees go as they are combined into a full parse.

This parser is extended with the capability of adding trees to the grammar: online learning. Conceptually, this simply entails adding more exemplars to the model. Since the weights of the elementary trees are simple relative frequencies, there is no expensive parameter estimation involved (compared to, e.g., expectation maximization for latent variable grammars, stochastic gradient descent for deep learning, etc). The set of elementary trees in the grammar is extended with the fragments extracted from the new tree when it is compared to the existing training data. Apart from bookkeeping work such as re-normalizing the relative frequencies and re-indexing grammar rules, updating the grammar is computationally simple and takes less than 1 second. It is therefore feasible to continuously update the grammar during interactive annotation.

Figure 2 shows an evaluation of online learning using a synthetic experiment simulating the annotation of the Tiger treebank. Starting with an initial grammar based on 5000 sentences, candidate parses for new sentences are suggested, and compared to the gold annotation in the treebank. When online learning is enabled, the gold parse is added to the grammar after each sentence. Since both the initial grammar and the new sentences are from the same domain and treebank, the effect is limited, but still there is a clear improvement when online learning is enabled.

Another feature that was added is to improve the handling of sentences that cannot be parsed completely. When a sentence fails to parse, the longest, most probable partial parses are extracted from it in a greedy fashion, until the whole sentence is covered.

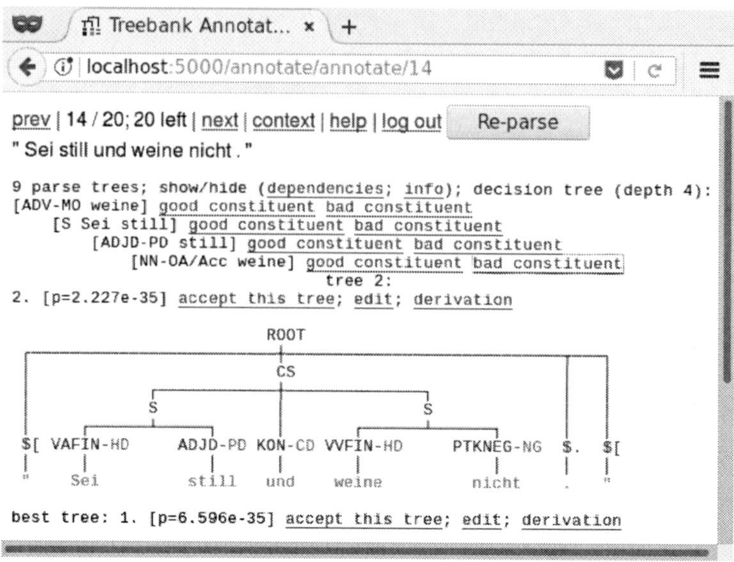

Figure 3: A candidate parse arrived at after following the decision tree of possible parses. The green labels are function tags. Translation: *Be quiet and stop crying.* (from Grimm's fairy tales)

3 User interface

The user interface presents possible candidate parses, which can be selected and edited interactively. Two mechanisms are provided to navigate the potentially long list of similar n-best parses: a decision tree and span constraints.

Upon annotating a new sentence, the user is presented with the most probable analysis. The remaining analyses can be accessed by navigating a decision tree where the nodes ask for the presence of particular constituents that differ between the analyses (Baldridge and Osborne, 2004). We use an entropy-based decision tree method, taking into account the probability distribution of the possible analyses, such that the most probable analyses will require the least number of discriminants. After each discriminant, an example of an analysis confirming to the currently selected discriminants is shown. See Figure 3 for an example.

The decision tree guides the user using the extracted discriminants. Span constraints allow the user to select discriminants. Clicking on a constituent will add a constraint to require or block a particular labeled span, which are then filtered from the list of candidate parses. Additionally, if the desired parse was pruned during parsing, the sentence can be parsed again, potentially producing more trees matching the constraints. See Figure 4 for an example.

In case the correct parse is not among the n-best candidates, the user can select any tree for manual post-editing, in a graphical interface where nodes can be re-attached by drag and drop and labels can be selected from drop down menus. Additionally, a subtree can be selected for re-parsing, after which a replacement can be picked from an n-best list.

4 Active Learning

Active learning is a form of machine learning in which the model takes the initiative of optimizing the selection of new training data to annotate in order to maximize training utility value (for an overview, cf. Settles, 2010). Concretely, this means manipulating the order of sentences to annotate as presented to the user.

A well established technique is uncertainty sampling, which selects sentences of which the model is most uncertain. Uncertainty is measured as the entropy of the probability distribution of possible analyses for a sentence. Using this heuristic, the most difficult sentences will be annotated first. While

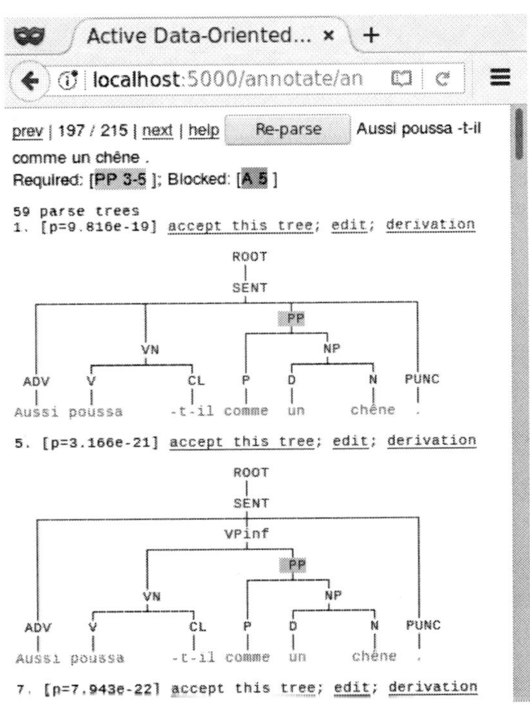

Figure 4: Filtering the list of candidates using span constraints. Here the PP is required, while *chêne* is blocked from being an adjective. Translation: *He also grew like an oak tree* (from Madame Bovary).

this reliably results in steep learning curves, it also means the annotation cost is high and the selected sentences may contain outliers that are difficult but not as useful with respect to the rest of the corpus.

Several works have explored active learning for statistical parsing. Tang et al. (2002) experiments with uncertainty sampling and representativeness ranking, evaluated on a simple treebank of airline reservations. Hwa (2004) presents results on uncertainty sampling with the Penn treebank. Reichart and Rappoport (2009) also adds a clustering method and applies more cognitively grounded cost metrics. Reductions of up to 30 % fewer annotated constituents necessary for a given level of accuracy are shown to be possible in simulations of annotating the Penn treebank. However, whether such reductions also obtain with human annotators has to our knowledge never been confirmed.

In future work we want to explore whether the information in tree fragment distributions and TSG derivations may enable the development of better active learning methods, and run an annotation experiment in which all user interactions are carefully measured.

Acknowledgements

The author is grateful to Laura Kallmeyer and three reviewers for comments. This work was supported by a grant from the German Research Foundation (DFG).

References

Anne Abeillé, Lionel Clément, and François Toussenel. 2003. Building a Treebank for French. In *Treebanks: Building and using parsed corpora*, pages 165–188. Springer.

Jason Baldridge and Miles Osborne. 2004. Active learning and the total cost of annotation. In *Proceedings of EMNLP*, pages 9–16.

Rens Bod. 1992. A computational model of language performance: Data-oriented parsing. In *Proceedings COLING*, pages 855–859.

Sabine Brants, Stefanie Dipper, Silvia Hansen, Wolfgang Lezius, and George Smith. 2002. The Tiger treebank. In *Proceedings of the workshop on treebanks and linguistic theories*, pages 24–41.

Andreas van Cranenburgh. 2014. Extraction of phrase-structure fragments with a linear average time tree kernel. *Computational Linguistics in the Netherlands Journal*, 4:3–16.

Andreas van Cranenburgh, Remko Scha, and Rens Bod. 2016. Data-oriented parsing with discontinuous constituents and function tags. *Journal of Language Modelling*, 4(1):57–111.

Rebecca Hwa. 2004. Sample selection for statistical parsing. *Computational linguistics*, 30(3):253–276.

Laura Kallmeyer and Wolfgang Maier. 2013. Data-driven parsing using probabilistic linear context-free rewriting systems. *Computational Linguistics*, 39(1):87–119.

Mitchell P. Marcus, Mary Ann Marcinkiewicz, and Beatrice Santorini. 1993. Building a large annotated corpus of English: The Penn treebank. *Computational linguistics*, 19(2):313–330.

Roi Reichart and Ari Rappoport. 2009. Sample selection for statistical parsers: cognitively driven algorithms and evaluation measures. In *Proceedings of CoNLL*, pages 3–11.

Federico Sangati, Willem Zuidema, and Rens Bod. 2010. Efficiently extract recurring tree fragments from large treebanks. In *Proceedings of LREC*, pages 219–226.

Remko Scha. 1990. Language theory and language technology; competence and performance. In Q.A.M. de Kort and G.L.J. Leerdam, editors, *Computertoepassingen in de Neerlandistiek*, pages 7–22. LVVN, Almere, the Netherlands. Original title: Taaltheorie en taaltechnologie; competence en performance. English translation: `http://remkoscha.nl/LeerdamE.html`.

Burr Settles. 2010. Active learning literature survey. Tech report, `http://burrsettles.com/pub/settles.activelearning.pdf`.

Min Tang, Xiaoqiang Luo, and Salim Roukos. 2002. Active learning for statistical natural language parsing. In *Proceedings of ACL*, pages 120–127.

CRST: A Claim Retrieval System in Twitter

[1]**Wenjia Ma**, [1]**Wenhan Chao**, [2]**Zhunchen Luo**[†], [1]**Xin Jiang**
[1]School of Computer Science and Engineering, Beihang University
[2]Information Research Center of Military Science
PLA Academy of Military Science
[1,2]Beijing, China
[1]{mawenjia, chaowenhan, xinjiang}@buaa.edu.cn
[2]zhunchenluo@gmail.com

Abstract

For controversial topics, collecting argumentation-containing tweets which tend to be more convincing will help researchers analyze public opinions. Meanwhile, claim is the heart of argumentation. Hence, we present the first real-time claim retrieval system CRST that retrieves tweets containing claims for a given topic from Twitter. We propose a claim-oriented ranking module which can be divided into the offline topic-independent learning to rank model and the online topic-dependent lexicon model. Our system outperforms previous claim retrieval system and argument mining system. Moreover, the claim-oriented ranking module can be easily adapted to new topics without any manual process or external information, guaranteeing the practicability of our system.

1 Introduction

When users search controversial topics in Twitter, they often tend to find some persuasive tweets. Argumentation is known as the most convincing structure, which usually consists of claim and evidence (Toulmin, 1958; Palau and Moens, 2009). However, only when the claim confirmed, can the evidence make sense. To help users swiftly obtain many pre-eminent claims about the query topic from Twitter, we propose CRST, a system that can automatically retrieve claim-oriented tweets.

Given a topic, our task aims to retrieve a list of claim-oriented tweets. We assume a claim-oriented tweet should meet three criteria: (1) the tweet should be topic-related; (2) the tweet clearly supports or opposes the topic; (3) the tweet provides an arguable reason for its stance. For example, "@*mnfa Abortion is not a choice, abortion is the killing of an innocent life.@owillis*" is a tweet related to the topic of "*abortion*". Moreover, it strongly opposes abortion and contains an arguable reason, "`abortion is the killing of an innocent life`". Therefore, it is a claim-oriented tweet.

To the best of our knowledge, this is the first attempt of claim retrieval in Twitter. Most existing works on argument mining in Twitter concentrate on detecting the evidence types (Dusmanu et al., 2017). And the claim retrieval task on documents was first introduced by Roitman et al. (2016). However, due to the short tweet content and specific conventions in Twitter as well as the ambiguous claims made by tweeters, our task is harder than claim retrieval in documents.

CRST integrates search and re-ranking modules to (i) find topic-related tweets, and (ii) rank by the degrees of containing claim. The core NLP part of our system is the claim-oriented ranking module (see Section 2.2 for detail). It can be divided into the offline topic-independent learning to rank model and the online topic-dependent lexicon model. Considering (1) some conventions in Twitter structure tweets and this structuring can be a valuable hint for searching claim-oriented tweets; (2) some claims may be expressed in a general pattern; we use a learning-to-rank framework to integrate Twitter structure information and some general claim pattern features to build an offline topic-independent ranking model. In addition, claims can not exist without topic, so we introduce the topic information to our claim-oriented ranking module. To be more specific, we generate a topic-dependent claim-oriented lexicon online to

---

[†] Corresponding author.

Proceedings of the 27th International Conference on Computational Linguistics: System Demonstrations, pages 43–47
Santa Fe, New Mexico, USA, August 20-26, 2018.

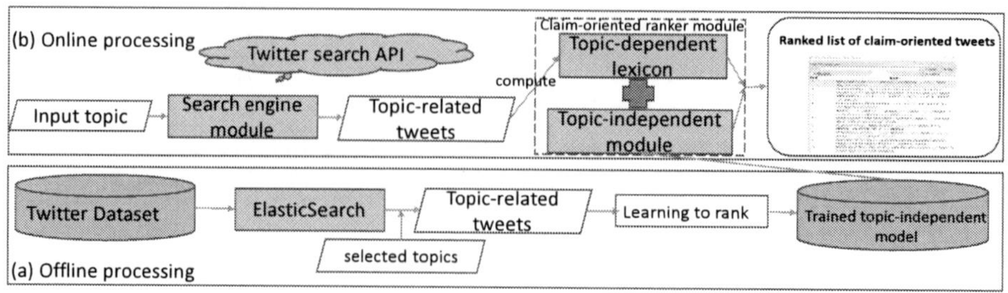

Figure 1: Overview of our system for retrieving claim-oriented tweets.

further elevate the retrieval performance. Experimental results show that our system outperforms other systems on similar tasks.

2 Claim Retrieval System

2.1 System Overview

An overview of our system is shown in Figure 1. We first perform offline steps to process data and to train the topic-independent model (Subfigure a). The online system is illustrated in Subfigure b. In the remainder of this section, we briefly discuss these steps.

Offline Processing In order to build the system, we crawl and index about 60 million English tweets using the Twitter API in 2016. Using these tweets we implement a search engine based on ElasticSearch. Given a query topic, the search engine would present a list of relevant tweets ranked based on the BM25 score. We construct a annotated dataset by searching some selected topics on the search engine (see Section 4.1 for detail). Then, we train a learning-to-rank framework which integrates different kinds of topic-independent features as a topic-independent model.

Online Processing When a user gives a new query topic q, the system performs the following three steps on the fly: (i) *Retrieving related tweets with a real time Twitter search API*, where Tweepy[1] is invoked to retrieve the top-n tweets that are most related to q; (ii) *Ranking the tweets*, where we automatically construct topic-dependent claim-oriented lexicons online and combine it with the offline trained topic-independent module as our ***Claim-oriented Ranking Module*** (elaborate in Section 2.2). (iii) *Visualizing the results*, where the visualization module presents the re-ranked tweets to the user within an interactive graphical interface.

2.2 Claim-oriented Ranking Module

By and large, our retrieval model is a learning-to-rank framework which integrates topic-independent features. Additionally, we use topic-dependent claim-oriented lexicons to further elevate the retrieval performance. Given a query topic q, a list of related tweets T from the Twitter dataset D is calculated as $T = Relevant(D, q)$[2]. The final claim-oriented score function of a tweet t is defined as $FinalScore(t, q) = LTR(T, t) + \lambda ScoreLex(t, Lex_q)$, where $LTR(T, t)$ is a pairwise learning to rank method[3] and $ScoreLex(t, Lex_q)$ is a function[4] using a claim-oriented lexicon Lex_q to construct an claim-oriented score for each tweet t. λ is a hyper parameter obtained through training. And we will elaborate them in the following part.

Topic-independent Module We use learning to rank framework to build our topic-independent model. Learning to rank is a data driven approach that effectively incorporates a bag of features into the retrieval

---

[1] http://www.tweepy.org/

[2] We used Okapi BM25 as a the *Relevant* function.

[3] We use rankSVM (http://www.cs.cornell.edu/people/tj/svm_light/svm_rank.html) to train our ranking model.

[4] We estimate the claim-oriented score of each tweet by calculating the average claim-oriented score over certain terms.

process. We use a linear kernel rankSVM for training and report results for the best setting of parameters. There are three kinds of topic-independent features that we used. (i) *Twitter structural features* refer to conventions that are only used in Twitter, such as "**#**", "**@**", "**RT @**", **URL** and combinations of these conventions. Meanwhile, we also consider whether a tweet is a ***reply*** as a feature. (ii) *Author social features* contain **followers**, **friends** and **status** information, which also play an important role in social media mining work (Luo et al., 2012; Luo et al., 2015). (iii) $GenLex$ is a topic-independent claim-oriented lexicon. We compute the information gain score of each word in tweets which contained in a labeled dataset. Then we choose the top-N scored words to construct $GenLex$. These words, such as "because", "but", "will", are topic-independent words and can reveal general patterns of claim-oriented tweets.

Topic-dependent Claim-oriented Lexicon Since it is impossible to train a supervised model for every topic, we adopt the $ScoreLex(t, Lex_q)$ (mentioned above) by considering it as a topic-dependent problem. The topic-dependent claim-oriented lexicon Lex_q is constructed by $MakeLex(GenLex, T)$, where we measure topic-dependent claim-oriented score of each word w in T, by calculating the co-occurrence frequency of w with words in $GenLex$. Finally, the high scored words will be used to construct a claim-oriented lexicon that refers to query topic q. For example, about topic "abortion", the words in Lex_q are "kill", "murder", "dangerous", etc.

2.3 System Usage

Our system is shown in Figure 2. The interface of our system is implemented using PyQt5. After inputting the query topic q, users can choose to use a claim-oriented score order or time sort. In the former model, our system automatically highlights the words in $GenLex$ to blue, and the words in Lex_q to yellow. This can be seen as a basis for tweets to be considered as containing claims. Additionally, our system allow users viewing details by clicking the tweet.

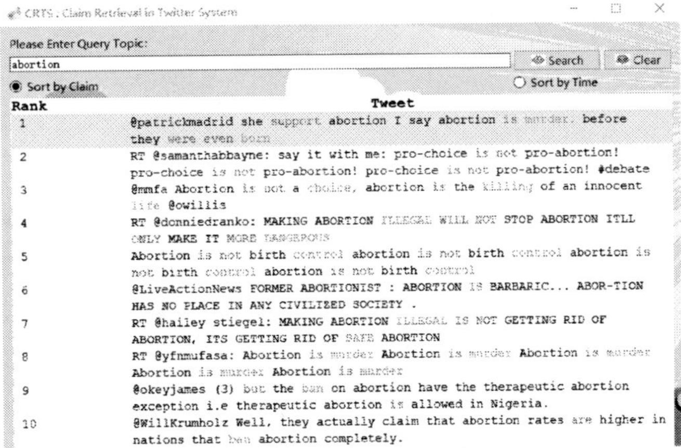

Figure 2: Homepage screenshot of our system.

3 Experimental Result and Case Study

3.1 Evaluation

To evaluate our claim retrieval model, we construct a English Twitter dataset which consists of 2520 tweets from 30 controversial topics[5]. And 586 tweets are identified as containing claims. We use 10-fold cross validation for evaluation, and use MAP as metric.

We use $WikiClaim$ and $TwitArgument$ as baselines. We adopt the features which are used for retrieving claims in wikipedia documents in Roitman et al. (2016), and name it $WikiClaim$.

---

[5]We choose topics from https://www.procon.org/

Rank	Tweet	Reply
1	@patrickmadrid she support abortion I say abortion is murder. before they were even born	1
2	RT @samanthabbayne: say it with me: pro-choice is not pro-abortion! pro-choice is not pro-abortion! pro-choice is not pro-abortion! #debate	0
3	@mmfa Abortion is not a choice, abortion is the killing of an innocent life.@owillis	1
4	RT @donniedranko: MAKING ABORTION ILLEGAL WILL NOT STOP ABORTION ITLL ONLY MAKE IT MORE DANGEROUS	0
5	Abortion is not birth control abortion is not birth control abortion is not birth control abortion is not birth control	0
6	@LiveActionNews FORMER ABORTIONIST : ABORTION IS BARBARIC... ABORTION HAS NO PLACE IN ANY CIVILIZED SOCIETY .	1
7	RT @hailey_stiegel: MAKING ABORTION ILLEGAL IS NOT GETTING RID OF ABORTION, ITS GETTING RID OF SAFE ABORTION	0
8	RT @yfnmufasa: Abortion is murder Abortion is murder Abortion is murder Abortion is murder Abortion is murder	0
9	@okeyjames (3) but the ban on abortion have the therapeutic abortion exception i.e therapeutic abortion is allowed in Nigeria.	1
10	@WillKrumholz Well, they actually claim that abortion rates are higher in nations that ban abortion completely.	1

Table 2: Examples of our system for the querying "abortion".

We also adopt the features which are used for argument identification tasks in Twitter in Theodosis Goudas and Karkaletsis (2015), and name it *TwitArgument*. Considering topic related factor, we combine BM25 with them. As shown in Table 1, our best model (*Best*) which use both learning to rank framework to integrate topic-independent features and topic-dependent claim-oriented lexicon outperforms the baselines significantly.

Methods	MAP
$WikiClaim + BM25$	0.291
$TwitArgument + BM25$	0.328
Best	**0.585**

Table 1: Results of Baselines and our best model. *Best* significantly better than baselines (for $p < 0.01$).

3.2 Case Study

In this section, we demonstrate a scenario of retrieving a query to prove the effectiveness of our system. Table 2 shows the top 10 retrieval results returned by our system when searching for "abortion".

As shown in Table 2, we can figure out that the tweets containing claims are in the top rank such as 1, 2, 3, 4, 5, 6, 7, 8, 10. From these tweet, we can find that many claim-oriented tweets contains a re-tweet feature "*RT @*", it is very possible because of the high forward frequency of valuable claim. As for the "*reply*" features appear many times, it may be because the argumentation always occurs during the discuss or quarrel. At the same time, some structural features like **URL** which is often contained in news or an advertisement rarely appear. In addition, these claim-oriented tweets contain words, like "kill", "life", "murder", which show our model can capture the topic-dependent claim-oriented information.

4   Conclusion

We present the first system that supports users to retrieve claim-containing tweets about controversial topics in Twitter. We train a rankSVM for our learning-to-rank framework and the topic-dependent lexicon is constructed using unlabeled topic-related tweets. Hence, our model can be easily adapted to new emerging topics in Twitter. In addition, our system let the user intuitively obtain the claims, which is certainly helpful in the development of public opinion research. The experimental results show that our system outperforms the previous state-of-art document claim retrieval system and Twitter argument mining system.

Acknowledgements

We appreciate the comments from anonymous reviewers. This work is supported by National Key Research and Development Program of China (Grant No. 2017YFB1402400) and National Natural Science Foundation of China (No. 61602490).

References

Mihai Dusmanu, Elena Cabrio, and Serena Villata. 2017. Argument mining on twitter: Arguments, facts and sources. In *Proceedings of the 2017 Conference on Empirical Methods in Natural Language Processing, EMNLP 2017, Copenhagen, Denmark, September 9-11, 2017*, pages 2317–2322.

Zhunchen Luo, Miles Osborne, and Ting Wang. 2012. Opinion retrieval in twitter. In *Proceedings of the Sixth International Conference on Weblogs and Social Media, Dublin, Ireland, June 4-7, 2012*.

Zhunchen Luo, Miles Osborne, and Ting Wang. 2015. An effective approach to tweets opinion retrieval. *World Wide Web*, 18(3):545–566.

Raquel Mochales Palau and Marie Francine Moens. 2009. Argumentation mining: the detection, classification and structure of arguments in text. In *International Conference on Artificial Intelligence and Law*, pages 98–107.

Haggai Roitman, Shay Hummel, Ella Rabinovich, Benjamin Sznajder, Noam Slonim, and Ehud Aharoni. 2016. On the retrieval of wikipedia articles containing claims on controversial topics. In *International Conference Companion on World Wide Web*, pages 991–996.

Georgios Petasis Theodosis Goudas, Christos Louizos and Vangelis Karkaletsis. 2015. Argument extraction from news, blogs, and social media. In *International Journal on Artificial Intelligence Tools*, pages 287–299.

Stephen Toulmin. 1958. The uses of argument. *Ethics*, 10(1):251–252.

Utilizing Graph Measure to Deduce Omitted Entities in Paragraphs

Eun-kyung Kim, Kijong Han, Jiho Kim, Key-Sun Choi
Semantic Web Research Center
Korea Advanced Institute of Science and Technology (KAIST)
Republic of Korea
{kekeeo,han0ah,hogajiho,kschoi}@kaist.ac.kr

Abstract

This demo deals with the problem of capturing omitted arguments in relation extraction given a proper knowledge base for entities of interest. We introduce the concept of a salient entity and use this information to deduce omitted entities in the paragraph which allows improving the relation extraction quality. The main idea to compute salient entities is to construct a graph on the given information (by identifying the entities but without parsing it), rank it with standard graph measures and embed it in the context of the sentences.

1 Introduction

As the need for structured knowledge for a variety of applications such as knowledge base (KB) completion (Socher et al., 2013), search (Marco and Navigli, 2013), and question-answering (Yahya et al., 2012) has increased, there has been considerable interest in extracting relationships for a large number of documents written in natural language. Relation extraction aims to identify and recognize the semantic relationships between pairs of entities (persons, locations, organizations, etc.) from sentences written in free text and to create them in a structured form.

Most studies in relationship extraction are distantly supervised and only take into account intra-sentence relationships that contain pairs of entities (Mintz et al., 2009; Fan et al., 2014; Zeng et al., 2015). For example, suppose that the following paragraph is given with entities marked by parentheses:"[Cristiano Ronaldo] was born in Madeira. He plays for the Spanish club [Real Madrid C.F.] and the position is a [Forward]." Although the entity mentions do not occur in the same sentence, these sentences convey the team to which "Cristiano Ronaldo" belongs and his position, but this cannot be inferred from each individual sentence. In particular, it is very common for an entity to be omitted from a sentence in Wikipedia–a popular corpus for relation extraction–because Wikipedia pages each focus on only one entity in most cases. This is also a very common phenomenon in text that is written in a language that can omit a subject or object even if it is not a Wikipedia article.

There have been studies into tackling these constraints on relation extraction in two or more sentences (Peng et al., 2017; Quirk and Poon, 2017); these are basically done in a way that increases the number of possible paths between the entities present in other sentences by integrating dependency graphs generated in a single sentence. The dependency graph–the key element of these studies–is known to be effective in relation extraction. However, it is difficult to acquire a highly efficient parser for all languages; thus, the practical application cannot extract relationships in various language environments. As another solution, we can apply a pipelined model to first perform a co-reference resolution (Clark and Manning, 2015) or zero-anaphora resolution (Mitkov, 1999) and then perform relation extraction, but error propagation between processes has been pointed to as a common problem in many natural language processing (NLP) tasks (Quirk and Corston-Oliver, 2006; Yang and Cardie, 2013; Han et al., 2013; Zeng et al., 2015).

This demo aims to overcome these issues by means of a projection in the context of the paragraph into the relationship between tuples in the KB. A paragraph is a series of sentences that fleshes out a coherent theme and maintains a consistent flow, so if an omitted entity exists, it is clear that the reader can

Proceedings of the 27th International Conference on Computational Linguistics: System Demonstrations, pages 48–52
Santa Fe, New Mexico, USA, August 20-26, 2018.

recognize it as an aspect of the subject that will continue being discussed in the paragraph. Therefore, our assumption here is that we can create a coherent graph composed of nodes (i.e. KB entities) and edges (i.e. relationships between entities) in the paragraph. However, in the conventional distant supervision paradigm, entities from the imperfect sentences in a contiguous context will be unreachable. The key to our approach is to first find the most "salient entity" through KB-based graph interpretation without syntactic parsing or other NLP tools and to maximally associate this with unreachable entities in the paragraph.

2 Salient Entity Detection

Normally, a paragraph that consists of a group of sentences deals with a coherent topic, so any reference can be omitted as long as the context provides the subject to which it is referring. In particular, subjects or objects are often omitted when they are obvious from the context. This paper attempts to deal with the null-subject problem to process relation extraction beyond the sentence level; since the subjectivity of an entity can be determined by how it is presented in a paragraph, the "**salience**" of an entity can be computed effectively from what is available in the paragraph itself.

We observed certain cues when identifying salience. Unsurprisingly, salient entities tend to be mentioned in the title or first sentence and are mentioned frequently throughout. However, being included in the title (or first sentence) is neither necessary nor a sufficient condition for salience. Based on these observations, we believe that a KB-based projection of a paragraph that already contains a variety of evidence for an entity is better than developing simple heuristics. This paper defines salient entities as those that have a major impact on the cohesion that occurs in a graph. This assumption is not arbitrary; some of these regularities have been recognized in Centering Theory (Walker et al., 1998). With this goal in mind, we propose a mathematical model and an algorithm to maximize the total connectivity in this situation.

2.1 Task Definition

Let $\mathbf{P}$ and $\mathbf{E}$ be the sets of all paragraphs in a given corpus and the set of all entities in the given KB respectively. Let $\mathbf{E}_p \subset \mathbf{E}$ be the set of entities mentioned in $p \in \mathbf{P}$. We formally define the salient task as learning the function:

$$\sigma : \mathbf{P} \times \mathbf{E} \to \mathbf{R}, \tag{1}$$

where $\sigma(p,e)$ reflects the salience of e in p. We denote the ranking of $\mathbf{E}_p$ according to σ as:

$$\mathbf{x}_p = \left(e_1,...,e_{|\mathbf{E}_p|} | e_i \in \mathbf{E}_p, \sigma(p,e_i) \geq \sigma(p,e_{i+1}) \right), \tag{2}$$

where pairs of entities with tied scores are arbitrarily ordered.

Our ranking function maximizes coherence in the paragraph-driven-graph by adding outgoing edges from the salient entity to other entities. Maximizing cohesion means creating a maximally connected graph that has the minimum number of entities whose deletion from $G = (\mathbf{E}_p, \mathbf{A})$ results in a disconnected or trivial graph, where $\mathbf{A}$ is a set of ordered pairs of entities (e_i, e_j). There are two conditions that constitute $\mathbf{A}$: First, e_i and e_j are in a single sentence; second, e_i is a salient entity and $e_j \in \mathbf{E}_p$. Our objective function is expressed as follows:

$$\kappa(G) = \kappa((\mathbf{E}_p, \mathbf{A})) = \sum_{i=1}^{|\mathbf{E}_p|} \sum_{j=1}^{|\mathbf{E}_p|} y_{ij}, \quad y_{ij} = \begin{cases} w_{ij}, & \text{if}(i,j) \in \mathbf{A} \\ 0, & \text{otherwise} \end{cases}, \tag{3}$$

where w_{ij} represents the number of relations (i.e. weight) associated with (i,j).

3 Evaluation

3.1 Experimental Setup

Our experiments aimed to answer whether the artificially restored sentences create noise in the existing distant supervision model, and whether the deduced entities accurately determine more relationships

(b) Extracted triples (conventional DS paradigm)

(c) Extracted triples by deducing omitted entities

(a) Sentence Augmentation

Figure 1: (a) shows the output after restoring the omitted entity from the input sentences. The restored sentence includes the '***' symbol at the front of each sentence. (b) and (c) show the result of the relation extraction, and the result of using the restored sentence in the step (a), respectively.

from the concealed paragraphs. We conducted experiments on the relation extraction between DBpedia entities in a null-subject language Wikipedia (i.e. Korean). We conducted an experiment performing training and testing using the Korean versions of Wikipedia (dumps on July 2017)[1] as the textual corpus source. We chose the dump of Korean DBpedia KB[2] as the background resource. In this experiment's first stage, we transform Wikipedia's links into entity annotations, and the original sentences of the given corpus can thus be automatically annotated with DBpedia entities. We converted each sentence into a word-level matrix in which each row was a sentence vector extracted from our model. Sentence vectors were learned from the Distributed Memory version of the Paragraph Vector algorithm using training data to automatically learn and predict corresponding relationships by the multi-class logistic regression classifier into one of the 50 relation types in our evaluation dataset.

In the real dataset, the whole labeled sentences have an imbalance in the number of labeled relation types. We found that approximately 85% of relations (of total of 215 relations) have fewer than 1,000 instances, and the amount of data in the top 50 relationships is greater than the rest of the data. Hence, we conducted a relation classification for the top 50 relationships except for those that have very little labeled data. There is no gold annotated dataset under distant supervision, so evaluation typically uses the held-out strategy. A held-out evaluation has the advantage of being automatic, but it can produce biased results because a pair of entities known to have no relationship may actually have a relationship. We solved this problem by creating a gold standard that eliminates false negatives by evaluating people. For this, ten college students judged true or false for the noisy gold test-data generated by the distant supervision assumption[3]. We obtained the precision, recall, and F1-scores for each of the 50 relation types in the experiment then the sum of the weighted averages for each performance measure from each class.

We developed the system to verify the approach to salient entity identification in the experiment as shown in Figure 1. The experimental results show that the effectiveness result of creating large volumes of additional training data to learn the KB relation by obtaining missing entities in relation extraction.

3.2 Result Analysis: Salient Entity Detection Techniques

Table 1 shows the experimental result for our model ($\mathscr{A}$(**Centrality**)) with various competitors to measure the saliency of the entity for the gold test data. For example, other plausible ways to detect saliency are (1) the entity corresponding to the Wikipedia page ($\mathscr{A}$(**Title**)), (2) the most frequent entity in the

---

[1] https://dumps.wikimedia.org/kowiki/
[2] http://downloads.dbpedia.org/2016-10/core-i18n/ko/mappingbased_objects_ko.ttl.bz2
[3] All data used in this experiment are provided in: https://github.com/kekeeo/SASE

Table 1: The results of experiments with various baselines for saliency.

	Precision	Recall	F1-Score
$\mathscr{A}$(Centrality)	**0.58**	**0.54**	**0.52**
$\mathscr{A}$(Title)	0.47	0.42	0.38
$\mathscr{A}$(Max)	0.52	0.48	0.45
$\mathscr{A}$(First)	0.51	0.46	0.43
Standard	0.44	0.40	0.38

paragraph ($\mathscr{A}$(**Max**)), (3) the first entity in the paragraph ($\mathscr{A}$(**First**)). The conventional distant supervised relation extraction corresponds to a single sentence that contains two entities (**Standard**), but we augmented this to tasks for two entities in a paragraph as described in above.

As shown in Table 1, since the method of sentence augmentation by adding the omitted entity to the sentences is higher than the conventional paradigm (i.e. **Standard**), we can see that the proposed sentence augmentation method has increased the positive learning instances for relation extraction. Although the method using centrality obtains superior performance than other heuristic methods, it can be seen that incorrect augmented sentences do not positively affect relation extraction, as shown in the comparative performance between $\mathscr{A}$(**Title**) and **Standard**.

4 Conclusion

This paper demonstrates a method of learning useful context features necessary to classify relations efficiently in a language environment that features frequent subject omissions and a high density of sentences with imperfect sentence components. Our approach provides a simple yet effective method to incorporate paragraph-level information through capturing missing relation argument model. This is the first distant supervision approach that resolves the problem of data sparseness by alleviating distant supervision assumptions for the relation classification of incomplete sentences to the best of our knowledge. This method has promising potential applications in languages that lack advanced NLP tools.

Acknowledgments

This work was supported by Institute for Information & communications Technology Promotion(IITP) grant funded by the Korea government (MSIT) (2013-0-00109, WiseKB: Big data based self-evolving knowledge base and reasoning platform).

References

Kevin Clark and Christopher D. Manning. 2015. Entity-centric coreference resolution with model stacking. In *ACL (1)*, pages 1405–1415. The Association for Computer Linguistics.

Miao Fan, Deli Zhao, Qiang Zhou, Zhiyuan Liu, Thomas Fang Zheng, and Edward Y. Chang. 2014. Distant supervision for relation extraction with matrix completion. In *Proceedings of the 52nd Annual Meeting of the Association for Computational Linguistics (Volume 1: Long Papers)*, pages 839–849, Baltimore, Maryland, June. Association for Computational Linguistics.

Dan Han, Pascual Martínez-Gómez, Yusuke Miyao, Katsuhito Sudoh, and Masaaki Nagata. 2013. Effects of parsing errors on pre-reordering performance for chinese-to-japanese smt. In *PACLIC*. National Chengchi University, Taiwan.

Antonio Di Marco and Roberto Navigli. 2013. Clustering and diversifying web search results with graph-based word sense induction. *Computational Linguistics*, 39(3):709–754.

Mike Mintz, Steven Bills, Rion Snow, and Dan Jurafsky. 2009. Distant supervision for relation extraction without labeled data. In *Proceedings of the Joint Conference of the 47th Annual Meeting of the ACL and the 4th International Joint Conference on Natural Language Processing of the AFNLP: Volume 2 - Volume 2*, ACL '09, pages 1003–1011, Stroudsburg, PA, USA. Association for Computational Linguistics.

Ruslan Mitkov. 1999. Anaphora resolution: The state of the art. Technical report.

Nanyun Peng, Hoifung Poon, Chris Quirk, Kristina Toutanova, and Wen-tau Yih. 2017. Cross-sentence n-ary relation extraction with graph lstms. *Transactions of the Association for Computational Linguistics*, 5:101–115.

Chris Quirk and Simon Corston-Oliver. 2006. The impact of parse quality on syntactically-informed statistical machine translation. In Dan Jurafsky and Éric Gaussier, editors, *EMNLP*, pages 62–69. ACL.

Chris Quirk and Hoifung Poon. 2017. Distant supervision for relation extraction beyond the sentence boundary. In Mirella Lapata, Phil Blunsom, and Alexander Koller, editors, *EACL (1)*, pages 1171–1182. Association for Computational Linguistics.

Richard Socher, Danqi Chen, Christopher D. Manning, and Andrew Y. Ng. 2013. Reasoning with neural tensor networks for knowledge base completion. In Christopher J. C. Burges, Léon Bottou, Zoubin Ghahramani, and Kilian Q. Weinberger, editors, *NIPS*, pages 926–934.

Marilyn Walker, Aravind K. Joshi, and Ellen F. Prince, editors. 1998. *Centering Theory in Discourse*. Clarendon Press, Oxford.

Mohamed Yahya, Klaus Berberich, Shady Elbassuoni, Maya Ramanath, Volker Tresp, and Gerhard Weikum. 2012. Natural language questions for the web of data. In *Proceedings of the 2012 Joint Conference on Empirical Methods in Natural Language Processing and Computational Natural Language Learning*, EMNLP-CoNLL '12, pages 379–390, Stroudsburg, PA, USA. Association for Computational Linguistics.

Bishan Yang and Claire Cardie. 2013. Joint inference for fine-grained opinion extraction. In *ACL (1)*, pages 1640–1649. The Association for Computer Linguistics.

Daojian Zeng, Kang Liu, Yubo Chen, and Jun Zhao. 2015. Distant supervision for relation extraction via piecewise convolutional neural networks. In Lluís Màrquez, Chris Callison-Burch, Jian Su, Daniele Pighin, and Yuval Marton, editors, *Proceedings of the 2014 Conference on Empirical Methods in Natural Language Processing, EMNLP 2015*, pages 1753–1762. The Association for Computational Linguistics.

Transparent, Efficient, and Robust
Word Embedding Access with WOMBAT

Mark-Christoph Müller and **Michael Strube**
Heidelberg Institute for Theoretical Studies gGmbH
Schloss-Wolfsbrunnenweg 35
69118 Heidelberg, Germany
{mark-christoph.mueller|michael.strube}@h-its.org

Abstract

We present WOMBAT, a Python tool which supports NLP practitioners in accessing word embeddings from code. WOMBAT addresses common research problems, including unified access, scaling, and robust and reproducible preprocessing. Code that uses WOMBAT for accessing word embeddings is not only cleaner, more readable, and easier to reuse, but also much more efficient than code using standard in-memory methods: a Python script using WOMBAT for evaluating seven large word embedding collections (8.7M embedding vectors in total) on a simple SemEval sentence similarity task involving 250 raw sentence pairs completes in under ten seconds end-to-end on a standard notebook computer.

1 Motivation

Word embeddings are ubiquitous resources in current NLP which normally come as plain-text files containing collections of <string, real-valued vector> tuples. Each word embedding collection (WEC) is uniquely identified by its combination of 1) training *algorithm*, 2) training *parameters*, and 3) training *data*. The latter, in turn, is characterized by the *textual raw data* and the *preprocessing* that was applied to it.

Word embeddings are often used early on in the system pipeline: in a typical setup, a word embedding file is loaded up-front (*eager loading*), and vectors are looked up in memory and used as replacements for input words. This *native* approach to word embedding access has a couple of limitations with respect to transparency, efficiency, and robustness.

1. Writing code in which WECs are **easily and unambiguously identified** is difficult when each WEC is treated as a monolith in the file system.This way of identifying WECs completely disregards – and, in the worst case, obscures – the fact that these resources might *share* some of their meta data, resulting in different degrees of similarity between WECs: two or more WECs might be identical except for their training window sizes, or except for the fact that some additional postprocessing was applied to one of them. For intrinsic and extrinsic evaluation (Schnabel et al., 2015; Nayak et al., 2016) of the effect of different training parameters on WECs, these parameters need to be accessible explicitly, and not just on the level of file names.

2. Experiments with **large numbers of WECs** do not scale and are inefficient if entire files need to be loaded every time. Experiments involving large numbers of WECs are not uncommon: Baroni et al. (2014) employed 48 different WECs, while Levy et al. (2015) used as many as 672. More recently, Wendlandt et al. (2018) explored the (in)stability of word embeddings by evaluating WECs trained for all combinations of three algorithms (two of them involving a random component), five vector sizes (dimensions), and seven data sets. In order to include the effect of randomness, five sets of WECs with different initializations were trained for the two algorithms, resulting in 385 WECs altogether. Antoniak and Mimno (2018) focused on training *corpora*, in particular on the effect of three different sampling methods. They trained WECs for all combinations of these three methods, four algorithms, six data sets, and two segmentation sizes. To tackle the effect of randomness, they trained repeatedly for 50

Proceedings of the 27th International Conference on Computational Linguistics: System Demonstrations, pages 53–57
Santa Fe, New Mexico, USA, August 20-26, 2018.

times, producing a total of 7.200 WECs. None of these papers provides technical details on how WECs are handled, but the code that is available indicates that the native, eager loading approach seems to be prevalent. More sophisticated, selective access to stored WECs is required to speed up experimentation and also support more ad-hoc, explorative approaches.

3. Finally, **converting unrestricted raw data into units for WEC vector lookup** often amounts to guesswork because the original preprocessing code is not shared together with the WEC resource. Preprocessing – which can involve everything from lowercasing, tokenization, stemming or lemmatization, to stop word and special character removal, right up to detecting and joining multiword expressions – is often underestimated in NLP, and word embedding research is not an exception: For the well-known and widely used GloVe embeddings, the documentation simply states to first use "something like the Stanford Tokenizer"[1]. The 100B word data set used to train the GoogleNews embeddings[2] contains a considerable number of automatically detected multiword expressions. As a result, as many as 2.070.978 of the 3M vocabulary items are phrases joined with one or more "_" characters. Standard preprocessing without access to the same phrase extraction code cannot detect these items and will thus be blind to almost 70% of the GoogleNews WEC vocabulary. Any preprocessing code used in the creation of a WEC resource has to be considered an integral part of that resource. This is the only way to ensure that the resource is fully (re)usable, which in turn is a prerequisite for the reproducibility of experiments utilizing that resource. The topic of *reproducibility* has been around in e.g. computational biology for some time (Sandve et al., 2013), and is also gaining attention in NLP (see e.g. the 4REAL workshops in 2016 and 2018). Already in 2013, Fokkens et al. identified preprocessing, in particular tokenisation, as one of the major sources of errors in their attempts to reproduce NER results.[3]
While some word embedding APIs and toolkits do exist,[4] they mostly focus on providing interfaces for in-memory vector lookup or for higher-level similarity tasks. None of them adresses scalability or preprocessing issues.

2   WOMBAT in a Nut Shell

WOMBAT, the **WO**rd e**MB**edding d**AT**abase, is a light-weight Python tool for more transparent, efficient, and robust access to potentially large numbers of WECs. It supports NLP researchers and practitioners in developing compact, efficient, and reusable code. Key features of WOMBAT are 1. **transparent** identification of WECs by means of a clean syntax and human-readable features, 2. **efficient** *lazy*, on-demand retrieval of word vectors, and 3. increased **robustness** by systematic integration of executable preprocessing code. WOMBAT implements some *Best Practices* for research reproducibility (Sandve et al., 2013; Stodden and Miguez, 2014), and complements existing approaches towards WEC standardization and sharing.[5] The WOMBAT source code including sample WEC data is available at `https://github.com/nlpAThits/WOMBAT`.

WOMBAT provides a single point of access to *existing* WECs. Each plain text WEC file has to be imported into WOMBAT *once*, receiving in the process a set of ATT : VAL identifiers consisting of five system attributes (`algo, dims, dataset, unit, fold`) plus arbitrarily many user-defined ones.

```
from wombat import connector as wb_conn
wbc = wb_conn(path="/home/user/WOMBAT-data/", create_if_missing=True)
wbc.import_from_file("GoogleNews-vectors-negative300.txt",
                     "algo:w2v;dataset:googlenews;dims:300;fold:0;unit:token")
```

Importing the GoogleNews embeddings into WOMBAT.

The above code is sufficient to import the GoogleNews embeddings. The combination of identifiers, provided as a semicolon-separated string, must be unique, but the supplied order is irrelevant. In this

---

[1] `https://github.com/stanfordnlp/GloVe/blob/master/src/README.md`

[2] `https://drive.google.com/file/d/0B7XkCwpI5KDYNlNUTTlSS21pQmM/edit?usp=sharing`

[3] Fokkens et al. (2013) do not address preprocessing for word embeddings, but their conclusions apply just the same.

[4] E.g. `https://radimrehurek.com/gensim/models/word2vec.html`, `https://github.com/3Top/word2vec-api`, `https://github.com/stephantul/reach`, `https://github.com/vecto-ai/vecto`

[5] E.g. `http://vectors.nlpl.eu/repository`, `http://wordvectors.org`, `https://github.com/JaredFern/VecShare`, `http://bit.ly/embeddings`

example, no additional user-defined attributes were assigned, as the publicly available GoogleNews WEC is sufficiently identifiable. For self-trained WECs, user-defined attributes for hyper-parameters including minimum frequency, window size, and training iterations are usually employed.

In WOMBAT, each WEC is stored in a single one-table relational database[6] with a *word* column and a *vector* column as a `float32` NumPy array, which significantly reduces the disk size, e.g. from 12.7 GB to 4.1 GB for GoogleNews. In order to maintain data integrity, the *word* column employs a `unique` database index to prevent multiple entries for the same word.

The most basic WOMBAT operation is the retrieval of embedding vectors from one or more WECs, which are specified by their identifiers. For this, WOMBAT provides a `get_vectors(...)` method supporting a grid search-friendly `ATT:{VAL1,VAL2,...,VALn}` identifier format, which is expanded into `n` atomic identifiers in the supplied order. In addition, several WEC identifiers can be concatenated with `&`. If input words are already preprocessed, they can directly be supplied as a nested Python `list`.

The following code retrieves vectors for the words `theory` and `computation` from all six GloVe WECs and from the GoogleNews WEC, in under two seconds on a standard notebook computer. The special identifier format is used here to specify all four GloVe 6B data sets, which share all properties except for `dims` (vector dimensionality). Other typical uses supported by this format include the evaluation of WECs trained with different hyper-parameters like e.g. `window`.

```
from wombat import connector as wb_conn
wbc = wb_conn(path="/home/user/WOMBAT-data/")
wecs = "algo:glove;dataset:6b;dims:{50,100,200,300};fold:1;unit:token&\
        algo:glove;dataset:42b;dims:300;fold:1;unit:token&\
        algo:glove;dataset:840b;dims:300;fold:0;unit:token&\
        algo:w2v;dataset:googlenews;dims:300;fold:0;unit:token"
v = wbc.get_vectors(wecs, {}, for_input=[["theory", "computation"]], raw=False, as_tuple=True)
```

Retrieving embedding vectors from several WECs.

More often, however, input text is *raw* and needs to be preprocessed into smaller units before word vectors can be retrieved. WOMBAT acknowledges the importance of preprocessing by providing a two-level mechanism for directly integrating user-defined preprocessing code. The first, obligatory level handles the actual preprocessing by piping each raw input line through a `process(...)` method. User-defined Python code implementing this method is directly inserted into the WOMBAT database. When vectors for raw input text are to be retrieved (`raw=True`), the correct preprocessing for each WEC is automatically applied in the background. While each WEC in WOMBAT could have its own preprocessing, the expected input format for many WECs (e.g. GloVe) is almost identical. Only `glove.840B.300d.txt`, e.g., is case-sensitive, while the others are not. This difference, encoded in the WOMBAT meta data as `fold:0` and `fold:1`, is accounted for automatically during preprocessing. Similarly, some WECs might exist in both an unstemmed and a stemmed variant, which can be distinguished by the values `token` and `stem` in the `unit` attribute. These values are also evaluated during preprocessing. The second, optional processing level analyses the token sequence produced by the first level and joins into phrases those adjacent tokens for which vocabulary items exist in the WEC. Currently this is done by a `gensim.models.phrases.Phraser` object, which initially needs to be trained on the tokenized textual raw data *before* WEC training, and which then needs to be applied to this data in order to enrich it with phrase information.

WOMBATs `get_vectors(...)` method returns data as a generic, nested Python data structure. Basically, it is a list containing one two-item tuple for every WEC, where the first item is the WEC identifier, and the second item is a nested structure containing the actual result, including the raw and preprocessed input and a list of <word, vector> tuples. By default, the ordering of this tuple list is undefined, but input ordering can optionally be maintained (`in_order=True`). For most tasks, however, ordering is irrelevant, which is why the more efficient `in_order=False` is the default.

---

[6]We currently use SQLite (`https://sqlite.org`).

```
[                                             # top-level result container
   [                                          # start of result for first WEC
     (
       'algo:glove;dataset:6b;dims:50;fold:1;unit:token', # normalized WEC identifier
       [
         (
           [],                                # raw input as supplied to for_input (empty here since raw=False)
           ['theory','computation'],          # tokens produced by preprocessing (if raw=True)
           [
             (                                # result tuple for 'theory'
               'theory',                      # token exactly as used in lookup
               [0.28217, 0.65819001, ... -0.39082, -0.1266]  # vector as NumPy array
             ),
             (                                # result tuple for 'computation'
               'computation',                 # token exactly as used in lookup
               [-0.25176001, -0.028599, ... 0.31508, 0.25172] # vector as NumPy array
             )
           ]
         )
       ]                                      # end of result for first (and only) input list
     )
   ],                                         # end of result for first (and only) WEC
   ...                                        # potential result for second WEC
]
```

Schematic WOMBAT result format.

3 Sample Use Cases

At this point, the `wombat.analyse` library contains only a few methods (cf. below). Our focus has been on developing a stable, generic, and efficient code base, on top of which more complex and useful functionality (incl. further visualizations, nearest neighbors, etc.) can be implemented.

3.1 Global Sentence Similarity

In order to demonstrate WOMBAT in an actual end-to-end use case, we applied it to a sentence pair similarity ranking task, using the data set from task 1, track 5 of SemEval-2017 (Cer et al., 2017). The data set consists of 250 tab-separated, raw sentence pairs. Since we focus on preprocessing and vector retrieval, we implement a simple baseline approach only, in which sentences are represented as the average vector of their respective word vectors (excluding stop words) and the pairwise distances are computed as cosine distance. The result is a list containing, for each WEC, an ordered list of tuples of the form `<distance, sentence1, sentence2>`. The following code implements the whole process. The distance metric in the `pairwise_distances(...)` method is provided as a parameter, and can be set to any method for computing vector distances (or similarities, in which case the output ordering can be reversed with `reverse=True`).

```
import numpy, scipy.spatial.distance
from wombat import connector as wb_conn
from wombat.analyse import pairwise_distances
wbc = wb_conn(path="/home/user/WOMBAT-data/")
wecs = "algo:glove;dataset:6b;dims:{50,100,200,300};folded:1;unit:token&algo:glove;dataset:42b;dims:300;folded:1;unit:token&\
        algo:glove;dataset:840b;dims:300;folded:0;unit:token&algo:w2v;dataset:googlenews;dims:300;folded:0;unit:token"
infile = "STS.input.track5.en-en.txt"
pp_cache = ()
vecs_1 = wb.get_vectors(wecs, pp_cache, for_input=[numpy.loadtxt(infile, dtype=str, delimiter='\t', usecols=0)], raw=True)
vecs_2 = wb.get_vectors(wecs, pp_cache, for_input=[numpy.loadtxt(infile, dtype=str, delimiter='\t', usecols=1)], raw=True)
pd = pairwise_distances(vecs_1, vecs_2, metric=scipy.spatial.distance.cosine, reverse=False)
```

Global sentence similarity computation with WOMBAT.

The execution time for reading the input file (column 0 and column 1 separately), preprocessing, vector retrieval from seven WECs, vector averaging per sentence, pairwise distance computation, and sorting is under ten seconds on a standard notebook computer.

3.2 Word-Level Sentence Similarity

WOMBAT was originally developed in a research project dealing with scientific publication title similarity, which involved light-weight semantic matching based on WEC-based similarities. Figure 1 shows two sample outputs of WOMBATs `plot_heatmap(...)` method, which accepts as input the generic output vectors produced by `get_vectors(...)`. The two plots show the contribution of phrase-aware preprocessing in the comparison of two publication title strings: the left plot was fed with `<string, vector>` tuples which were created with phrases temporarily disabled, and shows a spurious maximal similarity for the term *net* in the two titles. The right plot, in contrast, was fed with tuples which were created with phrases enabled, including a separate vector for *Petri net*. The plot shows a more differentiated, still high, but not maximal similarity between *Petri net* and *net*, resulting in a more accurate general representation of the to titles' similarities. Heat maps, of course, are standard visualization, but WOMBAT provides methods for their efficient, large-scale creation.

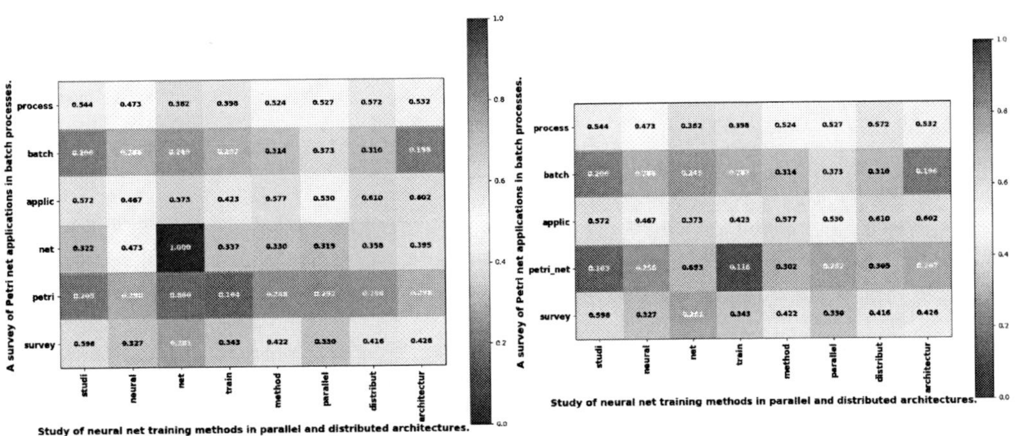

Figure 1: Word-level sentence similarity without (left) and with (right) phrase-aware preprocessing.

Acknowledgements The research described in this paper was conducted in the project *SCAD – Scalable Author Name Disambiguation*, funded in part by the Leibniz Association (grant SAW-2015-LZI-2), and in part by the Klaus Tschira Foundation. We thank the anonymous COLING reviewers for their useful suggestions.

References

Maria Antoniak and David Mimno. 2018. Evaluating the stability of embedding-based word similarities. *TACL*, 6:107–119.

Marco Baroni, Georgiana Dinu, and Germán Kruszewski. 2014. Don't count, predict! A systematic comparison of context-counting vs. context-predicting semantic vectors. In *Proceedings of ACL 2014*, pages 238–247.

Daniel M. Cer, Mona T. Diab, Eneko Agirre, Iñigo Lopez-Gazpio, and Lucia Specia. 2017. Semeval-2017 task 1: Semantic textual similarity - multilingual and cross-lingual focused evaluation. *CoRR*, abs/1708.00055.

Antske Fokkens, Marieke van Erp, Marten Postma, Ted Pedersen, Piek Vossen, and Nuno Freire. 2013. Offspring from reproduction problems: What replication failure teaches us. In *Proceedings of ACL 2013*, pages 1691–1701.

Omer Levy, Yoav Goldberg, and Ido Dagan. 2015. Improving distributional similarity with lessons learned from word embeddings. *TACL*, 3:211–225.

Neha Nayak, Gabor Angeli, and Christopher D. Manning. 2016. Evaluating word embeddings using a representative suite of practical tasks. In *Proceedings of the 1st Workshop on Evaluating Vector-Space Representations for NLP*, pages 19–23.

Geir Kjetil Sandve, Anton Nekrutenko, James Taylor, and Eivind Hovig. 2013. Ten simple rules for reproducible computational research. *PLoS Computational Biology*, 9(10).

Tobias Schnabel, Igor Labutov, David M. Mimno, and Thorsten Joachims. 2015. Evaluation methods for unsupervised word embeddings. In *Proceedings of EMNLP 2015*, pages 298–307.

Victoria Stodden and Sheila Miguez. 2014. Best practices for computational science: Software infrastructure and environments for reproducible and extensible research. *Journal of Open Research Software*, 2(1):1–6.

Laura Wendlandt, Jonathan K. Kummerfeld, and Rada Mihalcea. 2018. Factors influencing the surprising instability of word embeddings. In *Proceedings NAACL-HLT 2018*, pages 2092–2102.

Term Set Expansion based on Multi-Context Term Embeddings: an End-to-end Workflow

Jonathan Mamou,[1] Oren Pereg,[1] Moshe Wasserblat,[1] Ido Dagan,[2] Yoav Goldberg,[2] Alon Eirew,[1] Yael Green,[1] Shira Guskin,[1] Peter Izsak,[1] Daniel Korat[1]

[1]Intel AI Lab, Israel
[2]Department of Computer Science, Bar-Ilan University, Ramat Gan, Israel
[1]`firstname.lastname@intel.com`
[2]`{dagan,yogo}@cs.biu.ac.il`

Abstract

We present SetExpander, a corpus-based system for expanding a seed set of terms into a more complete set of terms that belong to the same semantic class. SetExpander implements an iterative end-to end workflow for term set expansion. It enables users to easily select a seed set of terms, expand it, view the expanded set, validate it, re-expand the validated set and store it, thus simplifying the extraction of domain-specific fine-grained semantic classes. SetExpander has been used for solving real-life use cases including integration in an automated recruitment system and an issues and defects resolution system.[1]

1 Introduction

Term set expansion is the task of expanding a given partial set of terms into a more complete set of terms that belong to the same semantic class. For example, given the partial set of personal assistant application terms like 'Siri' and 'Cortana' as seed, the expanded set is expected to include additional personal assistant application terms such as 'Amazon Echo' and 'Google Now'. Many NLP-based information extraction applications, such as relation extraction or document matching, require the extraction of terms belonging to fine-grained semantic classes as a basic building block. A practical approach to extracting such terms is to apply a term set expansion system. The input seed set for such systems may contain as few as two to ten terms which is practical to obtain.

SetExpander uses a corpus-based approach based on the *distributional similarity hypothesis* (Harris, 1954), stating that semantically similar words appear in similar contexts. Linear bag-of-words context is widely used to compute semantic similarity. However, it typically captures more *topical* and less *functional* similarity, while for the purpose of set expansion, we need to capture more functional and less topical similarity.[2] For example, given a seed term like the programming language 'Python', we would like the expanded set to include other programming languages with similar characteristics, but we would not like it to include terms like 'bytecode' or 'high-level programming language' despite these terms being semantically related to 'Python' in linear bag-of-words contexts.

Moreover, for the purpose of set expansion, a seed set contains more than one term and the terms of the expanded set are expected to be as functionally similar to *all* the terms of the seed set as possible. For example, 'orange' is functionally similar to 'red' (color) and to 'apple' (fruit), but if the seed set contains both 'orange' and 'yellow' then only 'red' should be part of the expanded set. However, we do not want to capture only the term sense; we also wish to capture the granularity within a category. For example, 'orange' is functionally similar to both 'apple' and 'lemon'; however, if the seed set contains 'orange' and 'banana' (fruits), the expanded set is expected to contain both 'apple' and 'lemon'; but if the seed set is 'orange' and 'grapefruit' (citrus fruits), then the expanded set is expected to contain 'lemon' but not 'apple'.

---

[1]A video demo of SetExpander is available at `https://drive.google.com/open?id=1e545bB87Autsch36DjnJHmq3HWfSd1Rv` (some images were blurred for privacy reasons).

[2]We use the terminology introduced by (Turney, 2012): the *topic* of a term is characterized by the nouns that occur in its neighborhood while the *function* of a term is characterized by the syntactic context that relates it to the verbs that occur in its neighborhood.

Proceedings of the 27th International Conference on Computational Linguistics: System Demonstrations, pages 58–62
Santa Fe, New Mexico, USA, August 20-26, 2018.

While term set expansion has received attention from both industry and academia, there are only a handful of available implementations. Google Sets was one of the earliest applications for term set expansion. It used methods like latent semantic indexing to pre-compute lists of similar words (now discontinued). Word Grab Bag[3] builds lists dynamically using word2vec embeddings based on bag-of-word contexts, but its algorithm is not publicly described. State-of-the-art research techniques are based on computing semantic similarity between seed terms and candidate terms in a given corpus and then constructing the expanded set from the most similar terms (Sarmento et al., 2007; Shen et al., 2017).

Relative to prior work, the contribution of this paper is twofold. First, it describes an iterative end-to-end workflow that enables users to select an input corpus, train multiple embedding models and combine them; after which the user can easily select a seed set of terms, expand it, view the expanded set, validate it, iteratively re-expand the validated set and store it. Second, it describes the SetExpander system which is based on a novel corpus-based set expansion algorithm developed in-house; this algorithm combines multi-context term embeddings to capture different aspects of semantic similarity and to make the system more robust across different domains. The SetExpander algorithm is briefly described in Section 2. Our system has been used for solving several real-life use cases. One of them is an automated recruitment system that matches job descriptions with job-applicant resumes. Another use case involves enhancing a software development process by detecting and reducing the amount of duplicated defects in a validation system. Section 4 includes a detailed description of both use cases. The system is distributed as open source software under the Apache license as part of NLP Architect by Intel AI Lab [4]

2   Term Set Expansion Algorithm Overview

Our approach is based on representing any term of a training corpus using word embeddings in order to estimate the similarity between the seed terms and any candidate term.

Noun phrases provide good approximation for candidate terms and are extracted in our system using a noun phrase chunker.[5] Term variations, such as aliases, acronyms and synonyms, which refer to the same entity, are grouped together. We use a heuristic algorithm that is based on text normalization, abbreviation web resources, edit distance and word2vec similarity. For example, *New York, New-York, NY, New York City* and *NYC* are grouped together forming a single term group. Then, we use term groups as input units for embedding training; it enables obtaining more contextual information compared to using individual terms, thus enhancing the robustness of the embedding model.

Our basic algorithm version follows the standard unsupervised set expansion scheme. Terms are represented by their linear bag-of-words window context embeddings using the word2vec toolkit.[6] At expansion time, given a seed of terms, the most similar terms are returned where similarity is estimated by the cosine similarity between the centroid of the seed terms and each candidate term. While word2vec typically uses a linear bag-of-words window context around the focus word, the literature describes other possible context types (Table 1). We found that indeed in different domains, better similarities are found using different context types. The different contexts thus complement each other by capturing different types of semantic relations. Typically, explicit list contexts work well for the automated recruitment system use case, while unary patterns contexts work well for the issues and defects resolution use case (Section 4). To make the system more robust, we extended the basic algorithm to combine multi-context embeddings. Terms are represented with arbitrary context embeddings trained using the generic word2vecf toolkit.[7] Taking the similarity scores between the seed terms and the candidate terms according to each of the different contexts as features, a Multilayer Perceptron (MLP) binary classifier predicts whether a candidate term should be part of the expanded set, where training and development term lists are used for the MLP training. The MLP classifier is implemented on top of Neon,[8] the Intel Nervana Deep Learning Framework. The performance of the algorithm was first evaluated by MAP@n

[3]www.wordgrabbag.com
[4]http://nlp_architect.nervanasys.com/term_set_expansion.html
[5]http://nlp_architect.nervanasys.com/chunker.html
[6]http://code.google.com/archive/p/word2vec
[7]http://bitbucket.org/yoavgo/word2vecf
[8]http://github.com/NervanaSystems/neon

(Mean Average Precision at n). MAP@10, MAP@20 and MAP@50 on an English Wikipedia dataset [9] are respectively 0.83, 0.74 and 0.63.

Context Type	Example sentence	Focus term	Context units
Linear bag-of-words (Mikolov et al., 2013)	*Siri uses voice queries and a natural language user interface.*	*Siri*	*uses, voice queries, natural language user interface*
Explicit lists (Sarmento et al., 2007)	*Experience in Image processing, Signal processing, Computer Vision*	*Image processing*	*Signal processing, Computer Vision*
Syntactic dependency (Levy and Goldberg, 2014)	*Turing studied as an undergraduate ... at King's College, Cambridge.*	*studied*	*(Turing/nsubj), (undergraduate/prep_as), (King's College/prep_at)*
Symmetric patterns (Schwartz et al., 2015)	*Apple and Orange juice drink*	*Apple*	*Orange*
Unary patterns (Rong et al., 2016)	*In the U.S. state of Alaska ...*	*Alaska*	*U.S. state of __*

Table 1: Examples of extracted contexts per context type.

3 System Workflow and Application

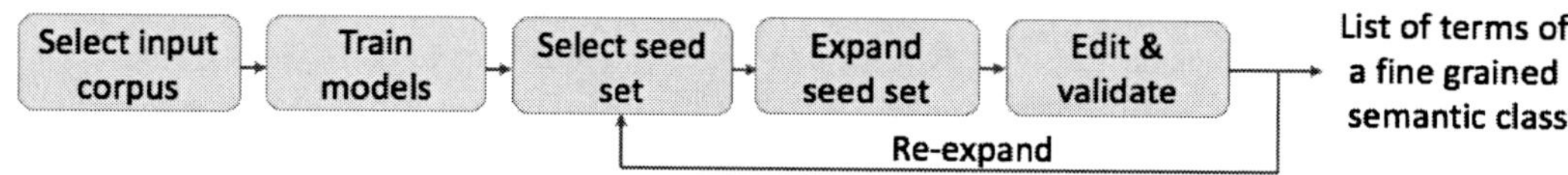

Figure 1: SetExpander end-to-end workflow.

This section describes the iterative end-to-end workflow of SetExpander as depicted in Figure 1. Each step of the flow is performed by the user using the system's user interface (Figures 2 and 3). The first two steps of the flow are to **select an input corpus** and to **train models**. The "train models" step extracts term groups from the corpus and trains the combined term groups embedding models (Section 2). Next, the user is able to **select a seed set** for expansion. Figure 2 shows the seed set selection and expansion user interface. Each row in the displayed table corresponds to a different term group. The term group names are displayed under the 'Expression' column. The 'Filter' text box is used for searching for specific term groups. Upon selecting (clicking) a term group, the context view on the right hand side displays text snippets from the input corpus that include terms that are part of the selected term group (highlighted in green in Figure 2). The user can create a seed set assembled from specific term groups by checking their 'Expand' checkbox (see the red circle in Figure 2). The user can select or set a name for the semantic category of the seed set (see drop down list in Figure 2). Once the seed set is assembled, the user can **expand the seed set** by selecting the Expand option in the tools menu (not shown).

Figure 3 shows the output of the expansion process. The expanded term groups are highlighted in green. The Certainty score represents the relatedness of each expanded term group to the seed set. This score is determined by the MLP classifier (Section 2). The Certainty scores of term groups that were manually selected as part of the seed set, are set to 1. The user can perform **re-expansion** by creating a new seed set based on the expanded terms and the original seed set terms. The user is also able to validate

---

[9]Dataset is described at `http://nlp_architect.nervanasys.com/term_set_expansion.html`.

each expanded item by checking the "Completed" checkbox. The validated list can then be **saved** and later used as a fine-grained taxonomy input to external information-extraction systems.

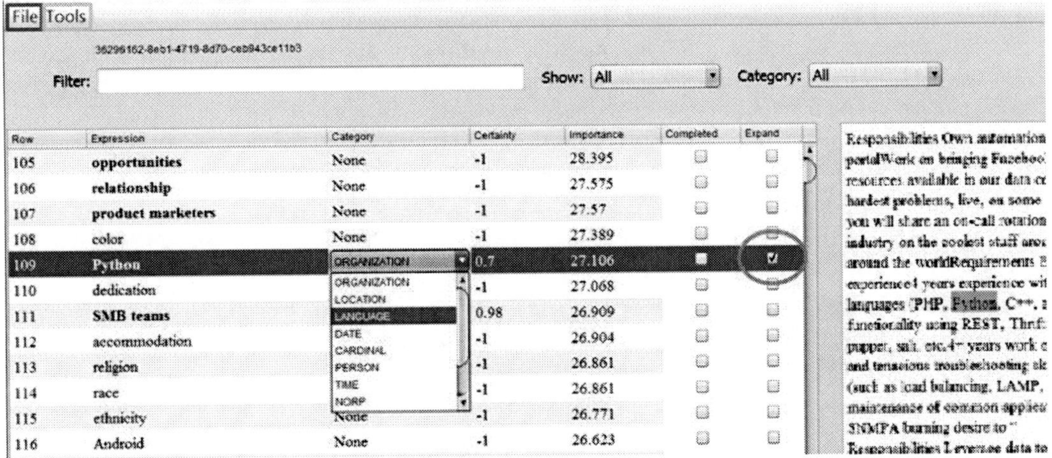

Figure 2: SetExpander user interface for seed selection and expansion.

Row	Expression	Category	Certainty
0	java	LANGUAGE	1
1	Python	LANGUAGE	1
2	JavaScript	LANGUAGE	0.92
3	SQL	LANGUAGE	0.88
4	perl	LANGUAGE	0.84
5	PHP	LANGUAGE	0.82
6	C++	LANGUAGE	0.82
7	TCL	LANGUAGE	0.81
8	ruby	LANGUAGE	0.79
9	visual basic	LANGUAGE	0.77

Figure 3: SetExpander user interface for expansion results output. Seed terms are 'java' and 'python'.

4 Field Use Cases

This section describes two use cases in which SetExpander has been successfully used.

4.1 Automated Recruitment System

Human matching of applicant resumes to open positions in organizations is time-consuming and costly. Automated recruitment systems enable recruiters to speed up and refine this process. The recruiter provides an open position description and then the system scans the organizations resume repository searching for the best matches. One of the main features that affect the matching is the skills list, for example, a good match between an applicant and an open position regarding specific programming skills or experience using specific tools is significant for the overall matching. However, manual generation and maintenance of comprehensive and updated skills lists is tedious and difficult to scale. SetExpander was integrated into such a recruitment system. Recruiters used the system's user interface (Figures 2 & 3) to generate fine-grained skills lists based on small seed sets for eighteen engineering job position categories. We evaluated the recruitment system use case for different skill classes. The system achieved a precision of 94.5%, 98.0% and 70.5% at the top 100 applicants, for the job position categories of Software Machine Learning Engineer, Firmware Engineer and ADAS Senior Software Engineer, respectively.

4.2 Issues and Defects Resolution

Quick identification of duplicate defects is critical for efficient software development. The aim of automated issues and defects resolution systems is to find duplicates in large repositories of millions of software defects used by dozens of development teams. This task is challenging because the same defect may have different title names and different textual descriptions. The legacy solution relied on manually constructed lists of tens of thousands of terms, which were built over several weeks. Our term set expansion application was integrated into such a system and was used for generating domain specific semantic categories such as product names, process names, technical terms, etc. The integrated system enhanced the duplicate defects detection precision by more than 10% and sped-up the term list generation process from several weeks to hours.

5 Conclusion

We presented SetExpander, a corpus-based system for set expansion which enables users to select a seed set of terms, expand it, validate it, re-expand the validated set and store it. The expanded sets can then be used as a domain specific semantic classes for downstream applications. Our system was used in several real-world use cases, among them, an automated recruitment system and an issues and defects resolution system.

Acknowledgements

This work was supported in part by an Intel ICRI-CI grant. The authors are grateful to Sapir Tsabari from Intel AI Lab for her help in the dataset preparation.

References

Zellig S Harris. 1954. Distributional structure. *Word*, 10(2-3):146–162.

Omer Levy and Yoav Goldberg. 2014. Dependency-based word embeddings. In *Proceedings of the 52nd Annual Meeting of the Association for Computational Linguistics (Volume 2: Short Papers)*, volume 2, pages 302–308.

Tomas Mikolov, Ilya Sutskever, Kai Chen, Greg S Corrado, and Jeff Dean. 2013. Distributed representations of words and phrases and their compositionality. In *Advances in neural information processing systems*, pages 3111–3119.

Xin Rong, Zhe Chen, Qiaozhu Mei, and Eytan Adar. 2016. Egoset: Exploiting word ego-networks and user-generated ontology for multifaceted set expansion. In *Proceedings of the Ninth ACM International Conference on Web Search and Data Mining*, pages 645–654. ACM.

Luis Sarmento, Valentin Jijkuon, Maarten de Rijke, and Eugenio Oliveira. 2007. More like these: growing entity classes from seeds. In *Proceedings of the sixteenth ACM conference on Conference on information and knowledge management*, pages 959–962. ACM.

Roy Schwartz, Roi Reichart, and Ari Rappoport. 2015. Symmetric pattern based word embeddings for improved word similarity prediction. In *Proceedings of the Nineteenth Conference on Computational Natural Language Learning*, pages 258–267.

Jiaming Shen, Zeqiu Wu, Dongming Lei, Jingbo Shang, Xiang Ren, and Jiawei Han. 2017. Setexpan: Corpus-based set expansion via context feature selection and rank ensemble. In *Joint European Conference on Machine Learning and Knowledge Discovery in Databases*, pages 288–304. Springer.

Peter D Turney. 2012. Domain and function: A dual-space model of semantic relations and compositions. *Journal of Artificial Intelligence Research*, 44:533–585.

Detecting Heavy Rain Disaster from Social and Physical Sensors

Tomoya Iwakura[*], Seiji Okajima[*], Nobuyuki Igata[*]
Kuhihiro Takeda[†], Yuzuru Yamakage[†], Naoshi Morita[†]
FUJITSU LABORATORIES LTD.[*]
{tomoya.iwakura, okajima.seiji, igata}@jp.fujitsu.com
FUJITSU LIMITED[†]
{takeda.kunihiro, yamakage.yuzuru, morita.naoshi}@jp.fujitsu.com

Abstract

We present our system that assists to detect heavy rain disaster, which is being used in real world in Japan. Our system selects tweets about heavy rain disaster with a document classifier. Then, the locations mentioned in the selected tweets are estimated by a location estimator. Finally, combined the selected tweets with amount of rainfall given by physical sensors and a statistical analysis, our system provides users with visualized results for detecting heavy rain disaster.

1 Introduction

Every year, Japan suffers natural disasters due to torrential rains that cause river overflows, inundation, and landslides. Information on disasters has conventionally been obtained by using physical sensors such as water/rain gauges, weather radars, and meteorological satellites. However, install of physical sensors requires time and cost, and installing a sufficient number of them is not always possible.

Meanwhile, information about natural disasters began being circulated on social media by users nationwide. Among social media, Twitter[1] has received more attention. A characteristic of Twitter is its real-time nature. For example, Twitter has been used as sensors to detect earthquake (Sakaki et al., 2010), flu epidemic (Aramaki et al., 2011), the amount of pollen (Takahashi et al., 2011), and so on. Due to the nature, Twitter is called as a social sensor.

We present our system that identifies heavy rain disaster with social and physical sensors. Our system selects tweets about heavy rain disaster with natural language processing technologies. By combining selected tweets with data obtained from physical sensors and a statistical analysis, our system provides users with visualized results for detecting heavy rain disaster.

This paper is organized as follows. Section 2 describes an overview of our system. In section 3, NLP analyzers used in our system are described. We compare our system with previous systems in Section 4.

2 An Overview of Our System

This section describes our system that can identify heavy rain disaster in the real world from Twitter. Our basic idea is that by selecting tweets that mentioned in tweets and combining the selected tweets with additional information, we can know heavy rain disaster in the real world.

Figure 1 shows an overview of our system. First our system collects tweets with keywords related to heavy rain disaster such as flood, landslide, and so on. Then the searched tweets are selected with NLP analyzers. Our system consists of two main NLP analyzers described in Section 3; a heavy rain information filter and a location estimator. A filter is used to select tweets mentioning heavy rain information and a location estimator annotates the filtered tweets with locations. Then, the filtered tweets are displayed on a map. In addition, combined the

[1]https://twitter.com/

Proceedings of the 27th International Conference on Computational Linguistics: System Demonstrations, pages 63–67
Santa Fe, New Mexico, USA, August 20-26, 2018.

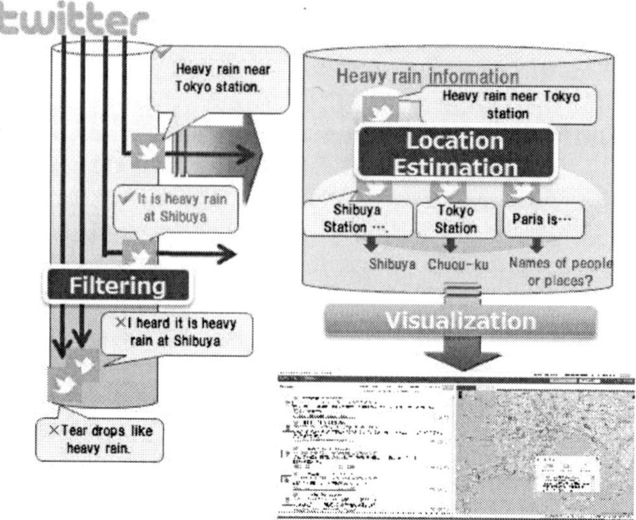

Figure 1: An overview of our system.

selected tweets with amount of rainfall obtained from physical sensors, our system provides users with visualized results for analyzing rain disaster.

Figure 2 shows a snapshot of the display that shows tweets with rainfall data obtained from physical sensors. The display can be used on a Web browser. The screen is divided into the following two displays.

- Time-line display: The left pane of the display shows the time-line. Selected Tweets annotated with location information are displayed in chronological order to facilitate an easy understanding of the latest postings.

- Map display: The map display shows the selected tweets with GPS information, tweets with estimated locations, results of disaster estimation, and the data from physical sensors. The tabs at the top are used to switch the display to a list of images (in thumbnails) that are tagged to the selected tweets. The images are helpful for understanding disaster situations. When a disaster is detected with an anomaly detection described in Section 3, the disaster alert is turned on. The regions estimated as disaster are displayed with a different color on the map like a heatmap.

3 Basic Technologies

This section describes two NLP, filtering and location estimation, and an anomaly detection.

3.1 Filtering

A filter selects heavy rain information from tweets. Even if tweets include words that indicate heavy rain, all the such tweets are not useful for detecting heavy rain disaster. Therefore, we select tweets about reports of sighting of heavy rains; in other words, we exclude information of heavy rains included in news, TV programs, hearsay, and so on.

For example, "Heavy rain made me wet at Shibuya." is a report of sighting of heavy rains. However, "I watched a news about heavy rain on TV." is not. We distinguish such news because such tweets other than sighting of heavy rains do not contribute to know information about heavy rains and become noises.

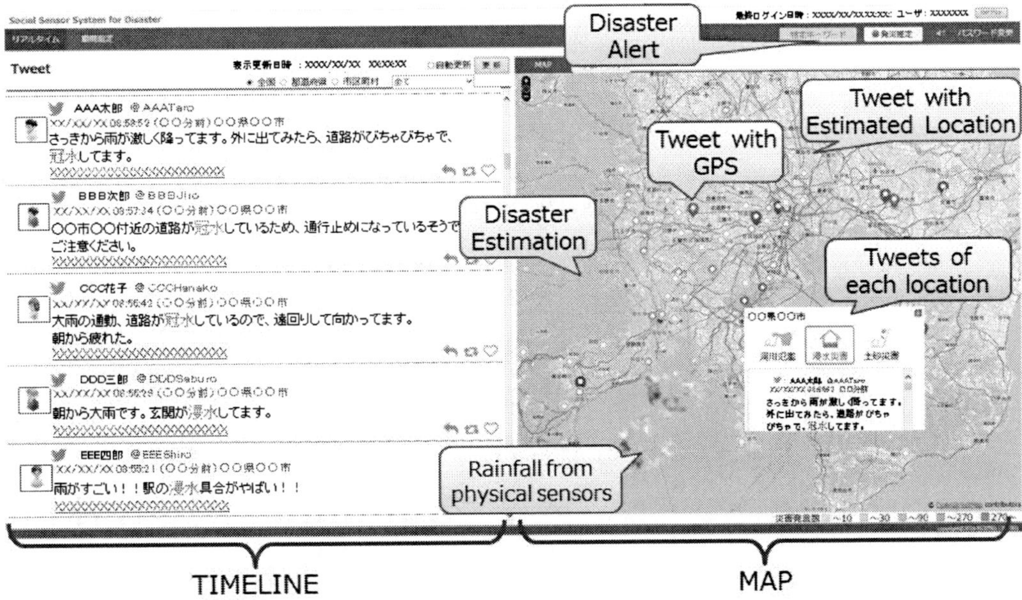

Figure 2: Our interface for displaying a map with selected tweets and rainfalls.

We used a document classifier based on an extended version of (Iwakura, 2017) as a filter. The filter accepts directed graph-based texts, represented as lattices of words with their part-of-speech (POS) tags as an input. A set of n-grams that consist of words and POS tags are learned as rules by the machine learning algorithm.

3.2 Location Estimation

Our location estimator annotates tweets with the latitude and longitude of each location that each tweet mentions. To estimate a location or locations mentioned in a tweet, we use a location estimator that uses dictionary and a machine-learning (Okajima and Iwakura, 2018).

First, our method recognizes candidate locations with a dictionary. Then, in order to filter out irrelevant location given by the dictionary, we use Japanese prefectures referred by a given text. For example, while there are Minato wards in Tokyo, Nagoya, and Osaka, the system can identify which city a mentioned Minato ward is in based on context. We can efficiently filter out irrelevant locations of tweets given by the dictionary with Japanese prefectures referred by tweets because there are almost no cities that have the same name in the same prefectures in Japan.

Prefectures referred by tweets is estimated by a classifier created from automatically generated training data. Considering words included in tweets, we estimated Japanese prefectures referred by tweets.

3.3 Anomaly Detection

We use a heavy rain detection-based on an anomaly detection. As described above, tweets about heavy rains from news, TV programs and hearsay become noises. Therefore, our method identifies heavy rains of each prefecture from tweets selected with the filter and the location estimator. As described in Figure 1, our filter selects tweets mentioned to heavy rains first. Then the location estimator identifies locations mentioned by the selected tweets. Finally, a heavy rain detector estimates whether each Japanese prefecture has heavy rain disaster or not. The heavy rain detector assumes a Poisson distribution and a probability given to a number of

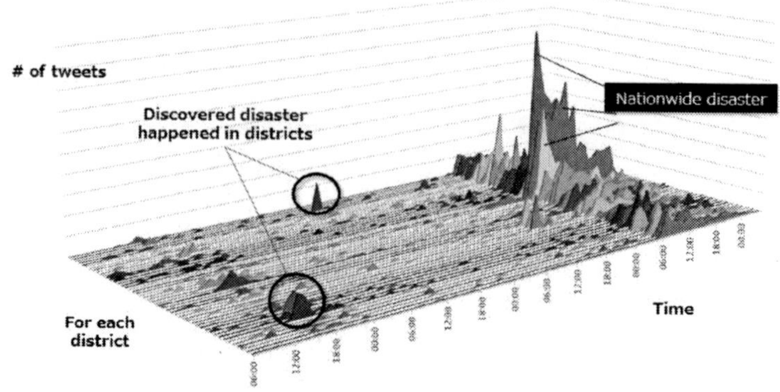

Figure 3: An image of heavy rain detection of each Japanese prefecture with an anomaly detection

tweets of each prefecture on the distribution is used for detecting heavy rains.

Figure 3 shows an image of the heavy rain detector. With estimated locations of tweets, we can identify heavy rain of each prefecture.

4   Related Work

One of the differences from the previous systems is the machine-learning method for filtering. Previous systems (Sakaki et al., 2010; Takahashi et al., 2011) use machine learning algorithms such as SVMs (Platt, 1999) and a boosting-based learner (Iwakura and Okamoto, 2008) that learn models for classifying texts represented by bag-of-words.

In contrast, our system uses a machine-learning-algorithm handles semi-structured texts. By handling semi-structured text, we can consider important substructures of semi-structured texts (Iwakura, 2017).

Another difference is the location estimation. Previous systems also used location information. However, they used locations extracted from user profiles such as GPS information of tweets and user profile (Sakaki et al., 2010), or prefecture level locations identified from user profiles (Takahashi et al., 2011). In contrast, when identifying heavy rain events, we have to identify detailed location information that the events happened. To identify detailed location information, we used a dictionary and context-information (Okajima and Iwakura, 2018).

DISANNA (Mizuno et al., 2016) also analyzes tweets in real time, discovers disaster-related information, and presents it in organized formats based on given queries.

Compared with DISANNA, our system can be used without specifying queries because our system focuses on heavy rain detection and tweets are selected by a filter for the heavy rain detection. In addition, our system also incorporates additional information such as rainfall amounts obtained from real sensors and alerting information.

5   Conclusion

This paper has presented our system that identifies heavy rains by analyzing social media with Natural Language Processing technologies combined with rainfall amounts obtained from physical sensors.

References

Eiji Aramaki, Sachiko Maskawa, and Mizuki Morita. 2011. Twitter catches the flu: Detecting influenza epidemics using twitter. In *EMNLP*, pages 1568–1576.

Tomoya Iwakura and Seishi Okamoto. 2008. A fast boosting-based learner for feature-rich tagging and chunking. In *Proc. of CoNLL'08*, pages 17–24.

Tomoya Iwakura. 2017. Efficient training of adaptive regularization of weight vectors for semi-structured text. In *Proc. of PAKDD'17*, pages 261–272.

Junta Mizuno, Masahiro Tanaka, Kiyonori Ohtake, Jong-Hoon Oh, Julien Kloetzer, Chikara Hashimoto, and Kentaro Torisawa. 2016. WISDOM x, DISAANA and D-SUMM: large-scale NLP systems for analyzing textual big data. In *Proc. of COLING'16 (demo)*, pages 263–267.

Seiji Okajima and Tomoya Iwakura. 2018. Japanese place name disambiguation based on automatically generated training data (to appear). In *Proc. of CICLING'18*.

John C. Platt. 1999. Fast training of support vector machines using sequential minimal optimization. In Bernhard Schölkopf, Christopher J.C. Burges, and Alexander J. Smola, editors, *Advances in Kernel Methods: Support Vector Learning*, pages 185–208. MIT Press.

Takeshi Sakaki, Makoto Okazaki, and Yutaka Matsuo. 2010. Earthquake shakes twitter users: real-time event detection by social sensors. In *WWW*, pages 851–860.

Tetsuro Takahashi, Shuya Abe, and Nobuyuki Igata. 2011. Can twitter be an alternative of real-world sensors? In *HCI (3)*, pages 240–249.

Simulating Language Evolution: A Tool for Historical Linguistics

Alina Maria Ciobanu, Liviu P. Dinu
Faculty of Mathematics and Computer Science, University of Bucharest
Human Language Technologies Research Center, University of Bucharest
`alina.ciobanu@my.fmi.unibuc.ro, ldinu@fmi.unibuc.ro`

Abstract

Language change across space and time is one of the main concerns in historical linguistics. In this paper, we develop a language evolution simulator: a web-based tool for word form production to assist in historical linguistics, in studying the evolution of the languages. Given a word in a source language, the system automatically predicts how the word evolves in a target language. The method that we propose is language-agnostic and does not use any external knowledge, except for the training word pairs.

1 Introduction

Natural languages are living eco-systems, they are constantly in contact and, by consequence, they change continuously. Two of the fundamental questions in historical linguistics are the following (Rama and Borin, 2014): i) *How are languages related?* and ii) *How do languages change across space and time?*. In this paper, we focus on the second question. More specifically, we investigate how words enter a target language from a source language.

Traditionally, both problems were investigated with comparative linguistics instruments (Campbell, 1998) and required a manual process. Most of the previous approaches to word form production relied on phonetic transcriptions. They built on the idea that, given the phonological context, sound changes follow certain regularities across the entire vocabulary of a language. The proposed methods (Eastlack, 1977; Hartman, 1981) required a list of known sound correspondences as input, collected from dictionaries or published studies.

Modern approaches impose the use and development of quantitative and computational methods in this field (McMahon et al., 2005; Heggarty, 2012; Atkinson, 2013), or even cross-disciplinary methods (such as those borrowed from biology). Nowadays, given the development of the machine learning techniques, computers are able to learn sound or character correspondences automatically from pairs of known related words. Beinborn et al. (2013) proposed such a method for cognate production, using the orthographic form of the words, and applying a machine translation method based on characters instead of words. The orthographic approach relies on the idea that sound changes leave traces in the orthography and alphabetic character correspondences represent, to a fairly large extent, sound correspondences (Delmestri and Cristianini, 2010). Aligning the related words to extract orthographic changes from one language to another has proven very effective, when applied to both the orthographic (Gomes and Lopes, 2011) and the phonetic (Kondrak, 2000) form of the words . For the task of cognate production based on the orthography of the words, besides the character-based machine translation approach mentioned above, another contribution belongs to Mulloni (2007), who introduced an algorithm for cognate production based on edit distance alignment and the identification of orthographic cues when words enter a new language. Another probabilistic approach to word form production is based on building generative models from the phylogenetic tree of languages, modeling the evolution of the languages and capturing various aspects of language change (Bouchard-Côté et al., 2009; Hall and Klein, 2010).

Proceedings of the 27th International Conference on Computational Linguistics: System Demonstrations, pages 68–72
Santa Fe, New Mexico, USA, August 20-26, 2018.

2 Simulating Language Evolution

We propose a method for word form production based on the orthography of the words, building on the idea that orthographic changes represent sound correspondences to a fairly large extent (Delmestri and Cristianini, 2010). Given the form of a word u in a source language L_1, our system predicts the form v of the word u in a target language L_2, in the hypothesis that the word v will be derived in L_2 from the word u.

From the alignment of the related words in the training set we learn orthographic cues and patterns for the changes in spelling. We use the alignment as input for a sequence labeling system (assigning a sequence of labels to a sequence of tokens), based on an approach that has been proven useful for cognate production (Ciobanu, 2016; Dinu and Ciobanu, 2017), proto-word reconstruction (Ciobanu and Dinu, 2018) and for generating transliterations (Ammar et al., 2012).

We conduct our experiments on Romanian as a target language, and experiment with 10 source languages from which words entered in Romanian.

2.1 Word Alignment

To align pairs of words we employ the Needleman-Wunsch global alignment algorithm (Needleman and Wunsch, 1970), with the orthographic form of the words as input sequences and a very simple substitution matrix, which gives equal scores to all substitutions, disregarding diacritics (e.g., we ensure that e and $é$ are matched). For example, for the Romanian word *descifrabil* (meaning *decipherable*), borrowed from the French word *déchiffrable*, the alignment is as follows:

```
d  é  -  c  h  i  f  f  r  a  b  -  l  e
d  e  s  c  -  i  f̌  -  r  a  b  i  l  -
```

2.2 Sequence Labeling

The words in the source language are the sequences, and the characters are the tokens. Our purpose is to obtain, for each input word, a sequence of characters that compose its related word in the target language. To this end, we use first- and second-order conditional random fields (CRFs) (Lafferty et al., 2001). For each character in the source word (after the alignment), the corresponding label is the character which occurs on the same position in the target word. In case of insertions, the characters are added to the previous label. We account for affixes separately: we add two extra characters B and E, marking the beginning and the end of an input word. In order to reduce the number of labels, for input tokens that are identical to their labels we replace the label with $*$. For the previous example, the labels are as follows:

```
B  d  é  c  h  i  f  f  r  a  b  l  e  E
↓  ↓  ↓  ↓  ↓  ↓  ↓  ↓  ↓  ↓  ↓  ↓  ↓  ↓
*  *  es *  -  *  *  -  *  *  bi *  -  *
```

As features for the sequence labeling system, we use character n-grams in a window of size w around the current token.

2.3 Experiments

We run experiments on a dataset of word-etymon pairs (Ciobanu and Dinu, 2014), from which we extract Romanian words having etymons in 10 languages. The dataset was built from an aggregation of machine-readable dictionaries[1] that contains information about the etymology of the words.The dataset is structured as a list of word pairs having the form: $w_1(L_1) \rightarrow w_2(L_2)$, where word w_2 entered L_2 from the L_1 word w_1. Example: *victoria (Latin) $\rightarrow$ victorie (Romanian)*. We use subsets of 800 word pairs for each language, to have an equal size that allows a comparison between source languages. The results are reported in Table 1. In Table 2 we show examples of our system's output.

We split the datasets in subsets for training, development and testing with a ratio of 3:1:1. We use the CRF implementation provided by the Mallet toolkit for machine learning (McCallum, 2002). We perform

---

[1] `https://dexonline.ro`

Source language	Baseline		Our system	
	EDIT (un-normalized)	**EDIT** (normalized)	**EDIT** (un-normalized)	**EDIT** (normalized)
English	2.04	0.23	1.33	0.15
French	2.16	0.24	1.42	0.15
Italian	2.60	0.32	1.62	0.23
Latin	2.75	0.34	1.76	0.22
Neo-Greek	2.39	0.29	1.82	0.24
Old Slavic	2.34	0.33	1.84	0.27
German	2.36	0.32	2.00	0.29
Turkish	1.88	0.27	2.01	0.29
Portuguese	2.95	0.52	2.50	0.43
Spanish	3.22	0.53	3.06	0.50

Table 1: Word form production for Romanian words.

a grid search for the number of iterations in $\{1, 5, 10, 25, 50, 100\}$ and for the size of the window w in $\{1, 2, 3\}$. We use a "majority class" type of baseline that does not take context into account, as described by Ciobanu (2016).

We use the edit distance (Levenshtein, 1965) between the produced words and the gold standard to evaluate the performance of our method. We use both an un-normalized and a normalized version of the edit distance. To obtain the normalization, we divide the edit distance by the length of the longer string.

We use lemmas (dictionary word forms) as input. We further experiment with some additional pre-processing steps on the input data (diacritics removal and stemming). The results are slightly improved when diacritics are not taken into account. Stemming does not improve performance, which shows that Romanian is a complex language, and foreign influences, in the case of new words entering the language, occur in the root of the words as well. Our system obtains the best results for English and French as source languages. The languages ranked higher are those with which Romanian had the most intense cultural collaboration, either more recently (English, for example), or in the past (Italian and French). The word production performance is lower even for related languages (as Portuguese and Spanish); these languages are more remote from Romania, from a geographical point of view, and this might have made the contact between languages more difficult.

Source language	Word	5-best productions
English	immunopathology	**imunopatologie**, immunopatologie, imunopafologie, imunopatologi, imunopathologie
French	opaliser	opalizare, **opaliza**, opalizară, opalizat, opalizăre
Italian	nivellazione	nivellaţie, nivellaţieu, **nivelaţie**, nivellaţiea, nivellaţiune
Latin	desideratum	desiderat, **deziderat**, desiderati, desideratu, deziderati
Neo-Greek	atherina	atherină, **aterină**, atherina, aterina, atherinire
Old Slavic	stihija	**stihie**, stihii, stihi, stihij, stihij
German	schabotte	şabottă, şabot, şabott, **şabotă**, şabotte
Turkish	peškeš	peşkeş, pešcheş, **peşcheş**, peşkşš, peşkeš
Portuguese	terneça	**tinereţe**, tinereçă, tinereţă, tinereçe, tereţe
Spanish	sainete	sainet, **sainetă**, sainete, săinet, saine

Table 2: Examples of word form production for Romanian words. We highlight the correct productions in bold.

3   A Tool for Historical Linguistics

We built a web application[2] to expose our system for word production. Its purpose is to assist linguists studying language evolution and language change, by providing n-best lists of possible word productions, when words enter a target language from a given source language. Its main impact is that it will narrow down the possibilities worth investigating when reconstructing a language, or when investigating language evolution.

The users of the application enter the source word, select the source language (from the possible 10 languages) and the system simulates the evolution of the word in Romanian. The web interface is rendered in Figure 1, along with an example produced by our system: given the source French word *documentaire*, the system produces a 10-best list of word forms in Romanian, having the correct word (*documentar*) on the first position.

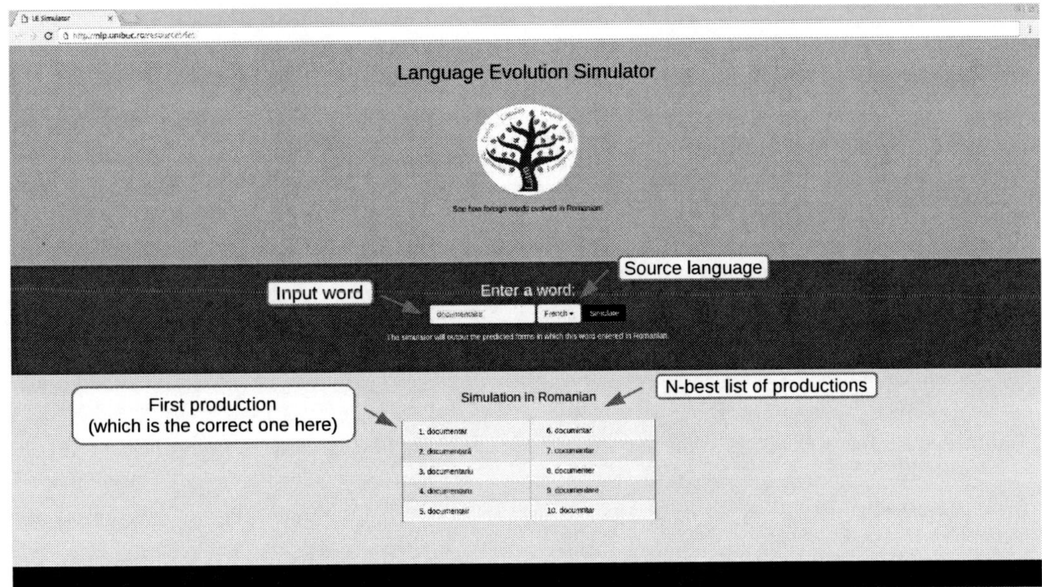

Figure 1: Language evolution simulator tool.

4   Conclusions

In this paper, we presented an automatic method for word form production, based on the orthography of the words. We experimented with Romanian as a target language and multiple source languages. We developed a language evolution simulator: a tool to be used in historical linguistics, to help in the investigation of language evolution. Given words in a source language, the system automatically predicts how they evolve in a target language.

As future work, we intend to enhance the system with more target languages, as we gain access to more data, to extend the user interface to handle blocks of text, not only single words as input, and to incorporate more types of relationships between words (cognate production and proto-word production) into the application.

Acknowledgments

We thank the anonymous reviewers for their helpful and constructive comments. The contribution of the authors to this paper is equal. Research supported by UEFISCDI, project number 53BG/2016.

---

[2]`http://nlp.unibuc.ro/resources/les`

References

Waleed Ammar, Chris Dyer, and Noah A Smith. 2012. Transliteration by sequence labeling with lattice encodings and reranking. In *Proceedings of the 4th Named Entity Workshop*, pages 66–70.

Quentin D Atkinson. 2013. The Descent of Words. *Proceedings of the National Academy of Sciences*, 110(11):4159–4160.

Lisa Beinborn, Torsten Zesch, and Iryna Gurevych. 2013. Cognate Production using Character-based Machine Translation. In *Proceedings of IJCNLP 2013*, pages 883–891.

Alexandre Bouchard-Côté, Thomas L. Griffiths, and Dan Klein. 2009. Improved Reconstruction of Protolanguage Word Forms. In *Proceedings of NAACL 2009*, pages 65–73.

Lyle Campbell. 1998. *Historical Linguistics. An Introduction.* MIT Press.

Alina Maria Ciobanu and Liviu P. Dinu. 2014. An Etymological Approach to Cross-Language Orthographic Similarity. Application on Romanian. In *Proceedings of EMNLP 2014*, pages 1047–1058.

Alina Maria Ciobanu and Liviu P. Dinu. 2018. Ab Initio: Latin Proto-word Reconstruction. In *Proceedings of COLING 2018*.

Alina Maria Ciobanu. 2016. Sequence Labeling for Cognate Production. In *Proceedings of KES 2016*, pages 1391–1399.

Antonella Delmestri and Nello Cristianini. 2010. String Similarity Measures and PAM-like Matrices for Cognate Identification. *Bucharest Working Papers in Linguistics*, 12(2):71–82.

Liviu P. Dinu and Alina Maria Ciobanu. 2017. Romanian Word Production: an Orthographic Approach Based on Sequence Labeling. In *Proceedings of CICLing 2017*.

Charles L. Eastlack. 1977. Iberochange: A Program to Simulate Systematic Sound Change in Ibero-Romance. *Computers and the Humanities*, 11:81–88.

Luís Gomes and José Gabriel Pereira Lopes. 2011. Measuring Spelling Similarity for Cognate Identification. In *Proceedings of EPIA 2011*, pages 624–633.

David Hall and Dan Klein. 2010. Finding Cognate Groups Using Phylogenies. In *Proceedings of ACL 2010*, pages 1030–1039.

Steven Lee Hartman. 1981. A Universal Alphabet for Experiments in Comparative Phonology. *Computers and the Humanities*, 15:75–82.

Paul Heggarty. 2012. Beyond Lexicostatistics: How to Get More out of "Word List" Comparisons. In *Quantitative Approaches to Linguistic Diversity: Commemorating the Centenary of the Birth of Morris Swadesh*, pages 113–137. Benjamins.

Grzegorz Kondrak. 2000. A New Algorithm for the Alignment of Phonetic Sequences. In *Proceedings of NAACL 2000*, pages 288–295.

John D. Lafferty, Andrew McCallum, and Fernando C. N. Pereira. 2001. Conditional Random Fields: Probabilistic Models for Segmenting and Labeling Sequence Data. In *Proceedings of ICML 2001*, pages 282–289.

Vladimir I. Levenshtein. 1965. Binary Codes Capable of Correcting Deletions, Insertions, and Reversals. *Soviet Physics Doklady*, 10:707–710.

Andrew Kachites McCallum. 2002. MALLET: A Machine Learning for Language Toolkit. http://mallet.cs.umass.edu.

April McMahon, Paul Heggarty, Robert McMahon, and Natalia Slaska. 2005. Swadesh Sublists and the Benefits of Borrowing: an Andean Case Study. *Transactions of the Philological Society*, 103(2):147–170.

Andrea Mulloni. 2007. Automatic Prediction of Cognate Orthography Using Support Vector Machines. In *Proceedings of the ACL Student Research Workshop*, pages 25–30.

Saul B. Needleman and Christian D. Wunsch. 1970. A General Method Applicable to the Search for Similarities in the Amino Acid Sequence of Two Proteins. *Journal of Molecular Biology*, 48(3):443–453.

Taraka Rama and Lars Borin. 2014. Comparative Evaluation of String Similarity Measures for Automatic Language Classification. In George K. Mikros and Jn Macutek, editors, *Sequences in Language and Text*. De Gruyter Mouton.

A Unified RvNN Framework for End-to-End Chinese Discourse Parsing

Chuan-An Lin[1], Hen-Hsen Huang[1], Zi-Yuan Chen[1], and Hsin-Hsi Chen[1,2]

[1]Department of Computer Science and Information Engineering
National Taiwan University, Taipei, Taiwan
[2]MOST Joint Research Center for AI Technology and All Vista Healthcare, Taipei, Taiwan
{calin, hhhuang}@nlg.csie.ntu.edu.tw
{b02902017, hhchen}@ntu.edu.tw

Abstract

This paper demonstrates an end-to-end Chinese discourse parser. We propose a unified framework based on recursive neural network (RvNN) to jointly model the subtasks including elementary discourse unit (EDU) segmentation, tree structure construction, center labeling, and sense labeling. Experimental results show our parser achieves the state-of-the-art performance in the Chinese Discourse Treebank (CDTB) dataset. We release the source code with a pre-trained model for the NLP community. To the best of our knowledge, this is the first open source toolkit for Chinese discourse parsing. The standalone toolkit can be integrated into subsequent applications without the need of external resources such as syntactic parser.

Title and Abstract in Chinese

適用於點對點中文語篇剖析的遞迴類神經網路統一架構

中文語篇剖析有四項子任務，包含初級語篇單元分割、剖析樹建立、主次關係識別、語篇關係辨識等。本文展示一個點對點中文語篇剖析器，並提出一套統一架構，可以對輸入之中文篇章直接產生完整的中文語篇剖析結果。我們的剖析器以遞迴類神經網路為基礎，同時對四項子任務進行學習，在中文語篇樹庫（CDTB）資料集上，達到最先進的效能。我們釋出了這個剖析器的原始碼與預先訓練完成的模型，立即可用。據我們所知，這是第一個開放原始碼的中文剖析工具集，而且這套獨立的工具集不須依賴外部資源（如句法剖析器），便於下游應用的整合。

1 Introduction

Discourse parsing is aimed at identifying how the discourse units are related with each other, forming the hierarchical structure of an article. As pointed out by Mann and Thompson (1988), no part in an article is completely isolated. The discourse structure provides critical information to understand an article. NLP tasks such as summarization (Louis et al., 2010), information retrieval (Lioma et al., 2012), and text categorization (Ji and Smith, 2017) have been shown benefited from the information extracted by discourse parsing.

Prior work of Chinese discourse parsing focuses on intra-sentential parsing (Huang and Chen, 2012). The CoNLL 2016 Shared Task deals with shallow parsing (Xue et al., 2016). So far, there is quite less work on complete hierarchical Chinese discourse parsing at paragraph or article level (Kang et al., 2016). The subtasks in Chinese discourse parsing depend on each other. In a pipelined system, there may be a severe issue of error propagation among elementary discourse unit (EDU) segmentation, connective recognition, parse tree construction, and relation labeling (Kang et al., 2016). The other problem is that prior Chinese discourse parser relies on linguistic features extracted by external third party packages. This is an important issue especially for a pipeline system. Extracting feature from free text is also an issue, while most systems rely on external syntactic parser for providing informations to do the above tasks. For a toolkit targeting real-world applications, a standalone system is more robust and easy to

Proceedings of the 27th International Conference on Computational Linguistics: System Demonstrations, pages 73–77
Santa Fe, New Mexico, USA, August 20-26, 2018.

deploy. Inspired by Li et al. (2014a), in this work we propose an end-to-end Chinese discourse parser
that performs EDU segmentation, discourse tree construction, and discourse relation labeling in a unified
framework based on recursive neural network (RvNN) proposed by Goller and Kuchler (1996). The
RvNN model learns to construct the structured output through merging children nodes to parent nodes
in the bottom-up fashion. Within the RvNN paradigm, recurrent neural network (RNN) is employed to
model the representations from word segments, discourse units, to the whole paragraph. RNN like long
short-term memory (LSTM) neural network (Hochreiter and Schmidhuber, 1997) is reportedly successful
in learning the text representation. In the prediction stage, we use the CKY algorithm to deal with both
local and global information during the construction of discourse parse tree, eliminating the gap between
the bottom-up approach and top-down annotation schemes.

The contribution of this work is three-fold: (1) We release a ready-to-use toolkit for end-to-end Chinese discourse parsing. To the best of our knowledge, this is the first publicly available toolkit for Chinese
discourse parsing.[1] (2) We propose a novel unified RvNN framework for end-to-end discourse parsing.
Experimental results show our model achieves the state-of-the-art performance. (3) Without the need for
external resources like syntactic parser, our standalone end-to-end parser can be easily integrated into
subsequent applications. The open source package can be even adapted to other languages.

The rest of this paper is organized as follows. We present our unified RvNN framework in Section
2. In Section 3, the performance of our system is evaluated and compared with that of previous work.
Section 4 concludes the remarks.

2 System Description

The architecture of our united framework for end-to-end Chinese discourse parsing is shown in Figure 1.
For a given text, we first segment the text into m text segments $\mathbf{w}^1, \mathbf{w}^2, \mathbf{w}^3, ..., \mathbf{w}^m$ by using punctuation
marks as delimiter, where $\mathbf{w}^i = (w_1^i, \ldots, w_{n_j}^i)$ forms the sequence of words in the ith text segment. The
words are fed into an embedding layer, and $\mathbf{w}^i$ is then represented as $\mathbf{e}^i = (e_1^i, \ldots, e_{n_j}^i)$. Then, an LSTM
encoder is trained to convert $\mathbf{e}^i$ into the segment representation $\mathbf{s}^i$, and $\mathbf{s}^1, \mathbf{s}^2, \mathbf{s}^3, ..., \mathbf{s}^m$ serve as the input
for the RvNN. Through the RvNN, segments are hierarchically joined to discourse units (DUs) in the
bottom-up fashion. Finally, a single discourse parse tree is constructed, and the sense and the centering
relations of each join are labeled.

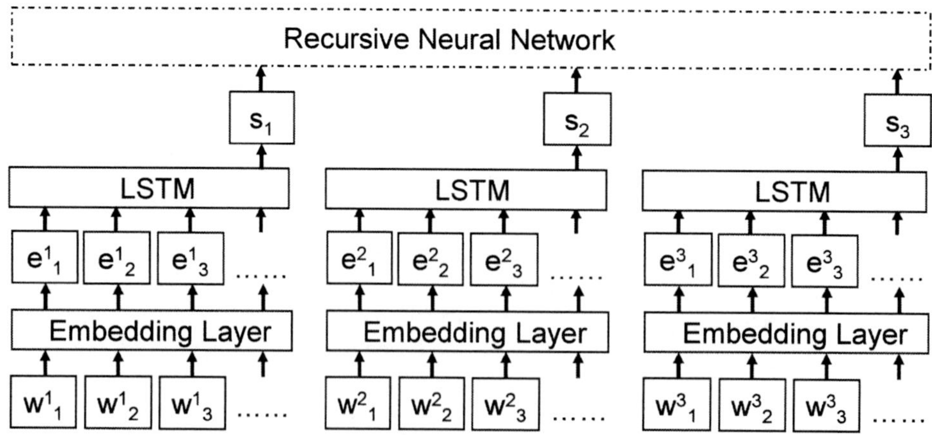

Figure 1: Architecture of our unified RvNN discourse parser.

---

[1] http://nlg.csie.ntu.edu.tw/nlpresource/cdp/

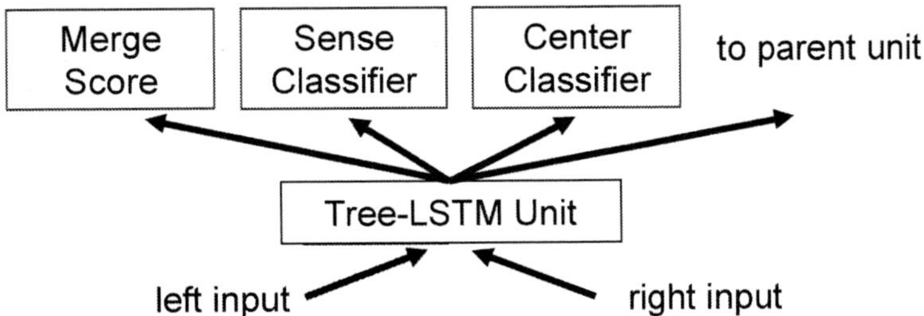

Figure 2: Tree-LSTM unit used in the recursive neural network.

2.1 Recursive Neural Network

Figure 2 illustrates the unit in our RvNN based on the Tree-LSTM unit (Tai et al., 2015). Given the left and the right inputs (i.e. two text segments or two DUs), the Tree-LSTM composition function produces a representation for the new tree node. The Tree-LSTM unit generalizes the LSTM unit to the tree-based input. Similar to LSTM, Tree-LSTM makes use of intermediate states as a pair of an active state representation $\vec{h}$ and a memory representation $\vec{c}$. We use the version similar to (Bowman et al., 2016) as the formula:

$$
(1) \quad \begin{bmatrix} \vec{i} \\ \vec{f_l} \\ \vec{f_r} \\ \vec{o} \\ \vec{g} \end{bmatrix} = \begin{bmatrix} \sigma \\ \sigma \\ \sigma \\ \sigma \\ \tanh \end{bmatrix} \left(W_{\text{comp}} \begin{bmatrix} \vec{h}_s^1 \\ \vec{h}_s^2 \end{bmatrix} + \vec{b}_{\text{comp}} \right)
$$

$$
(2) \quad \vec{c} = \vec{f_l} \odot \vec{c}_s^2 + \vec{f_r} \odot \vec{c}_s^1 + \vec{i} \odot \vec{g}
$$

$$
(3) \quad \vec{h} = \vec{o} \odot \tanh(\vec{c})
$$

where σ is the sigmoid activation function, $\odot$ is the element-wise product, and the pairs $\langle \vec{h}_s^1, \vec{c}_s^1 \rangle$ and $\langle \vec{h}_s^2, \vec{c}_s^2 \rangle$ are input from its two children tree nodes. The output of Tree-LSTM is the pair $\langle \vec{h}, \vec{c} \rangle$. Note that the Tree-LSTM unit is designed for binary tree. We handle the multinuclear with the same scheme as Kang et al. (2016).

The representations $\vec{h}$ and $\vec{c}$ produced by Tree-LSTM are taken for the following four usages: merge scoring, sense labeling, center labeling, and the input for the upper Tree-LSTM unit. In the prediction stage, the representation will be first sent into the merge scorer to measure the probability of the join of its two children tree nodes:

$$
(4) \quad \vec{p_m} = \text{softmax}(W_m \begin{bmatrix} \vec{h} \\ \vec{c} \end{bmatrix} + \vec{b}_m)
$$

The output $\vec{p_m}$ is a 2-dimensional vector, representing the probabilities of to-merge and not-to-merge.

Similarly, the sense classifier and the center classifier compute the probability distributions $\vec{p_s}$ and $\vec{p_c}$, respectively, as follows:

$$
(5) \quad \vec{p_s} = \text{softmax}(W_s \begin{bmatrix} \vec{h} \\ \vec{c} \end{bmatrix} + \vec{b}_s)
$$

$$
(6) \quad \vec{p_c} = \text{softmax}(W_c \begin{bmatrix} \vec{h} \\ \vec{c} \end{bmatrix} + \vec{b}_c)
$$

For sense labeling, $\vec{p_s}$ consists of 6 values constituting the probabilities of the following six senses: causality, coordination, transition, explanation, subEDU, and EDU. Our end-to-end parser constructs the discourse parse tree from the text segments, EDUs, and to non-leaf DUs in a united framework. The first four of the six senses are used to label the discourse relation between DUs, while the last two senses are used for EDU segmentation. For center labeling, $\vec{p_c}$ consists of 3 values constituting the probabilities of the three center categories including front, latter, and equal. Center labeling is only performed on DUs.

2.2 Parser Training

To train the RvNN, the positive instances are the tree nodes extracted from the discourse parse trees in Chinese Discourse Treebank (CDTB) dataset developed by Li et al. (2014b). On the other hand, the negative instances are derived from the ill-joined discourse trees. We select arbitrary two neighboring subtrees and merge them into a new tree. The new tree is regarded as a negative instance if it is inconsistent with the ground-truth. The losses of the merging scorer, the sense classifier, and the center classifier, denoted as $\mathcal{L}_m$, $\mathcal{L}_s$, and $\mathcal{L}_c$, respectively, are measured with cross-entropy. The loss function is defined as:

$$(7) \quad \mathcal{L} = \begin{cases} \mathcal{L}_m, & \text{if the instance is negative} \\ \mathcal{L}_m + \mathcal{L}_s + \mathcal{L}_c, & \text{otherwise} \end{cases}$$

We use stochastic gradient decent (SGD) with the learning rate of 0.1 for parameter optimization.

2.3 Parse Tree Construction

In the prediction stage, we construct the discourse parse tree based on the predictions made by Tree-LSTM. The Cocke–Younger–Kasami (CKY) algorithm (Younger, 1967) is employed to maximize the probability of the whole parse tree. The dynamic programing algorithm simulates the recursive parsing procedure, considering local and global information jointly.

3 Experiments

We compare our model LSTM-RvNN with the baseline model proposed by Kang et al. (2016). To the best of our knowledge, it is the only existing Chinese discourse parser at the paragraph level. We also evaluate our model given the golden EDUs. The standard evaluation tool PARSEVAL (Carlson et al., 2001) is performed to measure the F-score of the tree structure prediction.

Table 1 shows the experimental results. The F-scores of EDU segmentation, parse tree construction (Structure), parse tree construction with sense labeling (+Sense), parse tree construction with center labeling (+Center), and parse tree construction with both sense and center labeling (Overall) are reported. In general, our model outperforms the baseline model in every aspect except EDU segmentation. Even so, the final discourse parse trees constructed and labeled by our model are more accurate.

Model	EDU	Structure	+Sense	+Center	Overall
Baseline with golden EDU		52.3%	33.8%	23.9%	23.2%
LSTM-RvNN with golden EDU		**64.6%**	**42.7%**	**38.5%**	**35.0%**
Baseline	**93.8%**	46.4%	28.8%	23.1%	20.0%
LSTM-RvNN	87.2%	**49.5%**	**32.6%**	**28.8%**	**26.8%**

Table 1: System performances in F-score.

4 Conclusion

This paper demonstrates an end-to-end Chinese discourse parser that performs the CDT-style parsing without the need of external resources such as syntactic parser. We propose a unified framework based on RvNN to model the subtasks jointly. Experimental results show our parser achieves the state-of-the-art performance in the CDTB dataset. We release the source code of our parser with a ready-to-use pre-trained model for the NLP community. To the best of our knowledge, this is the first toolkit for Chinese discourse parsing.

Acknowledgements

This research was partially supported by Ministry of Science and Technology, Taiwan, under grants MOST-106-2923-E-002-012-MY3 and MOST-107-2634-F-002-011-.

References

Samuel R. Bowman, Jon Gauthier, Abhinav Rastogi, Raghav Gupta, Christopher D. Manning, and Christopher Potts. 2016. A fast unified model for parsing and sentence understanding. In *Proceedings of the 54th Annual Meeting of the Association for Computational Linguistics (ACL'16)*, pages 1466–1477, August.

Lynn Carlson, Daniel Marcu, and Mary Ellen Okurowski. 2001. Building a discourse-tagged corpus in the framework of rhetorical structure theory. In *Proceedings of the Second SIGdial Workshop on Discourse and Dialogue (SIGDIAL'01)*, pages 1–10.

C. Goller and A. Kuchler. 1996. Learning task-dependent distributed representations by backpropagation through structure. In *Proceedings of the 1996 IEEE International Conference on Neural Networks*, volume 1, pages 347–352 vol.1, Jun.

Sepp Hochreiter and Jürgen Schmidhuber. 1997. Long short-term memory. *Neural Comput.*, 9(9):1735–1780, November.

Hen-Hsen Huang and Hsin-Hsi Chen. 2012. Contingency and comparison relation labeling and structure prediction in chinese sentences. In *Proceedings of the 13th Annual Meeting of the Special Interest Group on Discourse and Dialogue (SIGDIAL'12)*, pages 261–269.

Yangfeng Ji and Noah A. Smith. 2017. Neural discourse structure for text categorization. In *Proceedings of the 55th Annual Meeting of the Association for Computational Linguistics (ACL'17)*, pages 996–1005, July.

Xiaomian Kang, Haoran Li, Long Zhou, Jiajun Zhang, and Chengqing Zong. 2016. An end-to-end chinese discourse parser with adaptation to explicit and non-explicit relation recognition. In *Proceedings of the CoNLL-16 shared task*, pages 27–32, August.

Jiwei Li, Rumeng Li, and Eduard Hovy. 2014a. Recursive deep models for discourse parsing. In *Proceedings of the 2014 Conference on Empirical Methods in Natural Language Processing (EMNLP'14)*, pages 2061–2069, October.

Yancui Li, Wenhe Feng, Jing Sun, Fang Kong, and Guodong Zhou. 2014b. Building chinese discourse corpus with connective-driven dependency tree structure. In *Proceedings of the 2014 Conference on Empirical Methods in Natural Language Processing (EMNLP'14)*, pages 2105–2114, Doha, Qatar, October. Association for Computational Linguistics.

Christina Lioma, Birger Larsen, and Wei Lu. 2012. Rhetorical relations for information retrieval. In *Proceedings of the 35th International ACM SIGIR Conference on Research and Development in Information Retrieval (SIGIR'12)*, pages 931–940.

Annie Louis, Aravind Joshi, and Ani Nenkova. 2010. Discourse indicators for content selection in summarization. In *Proceedings of the SIGDIAL 2010 Conference*, pages 147–156, Tokyo, Japan, September. Association for Computational Linguistics.

William C Mann and Sandra A Thompson. 1988. Rhetorical structure theory: Toward a functional theory of text organization. *Text-Interdisciplinary Journal for the Study of Discourse*, 8(3):243–281.

Kai Sheng Tai, Richard Socher, and Christopher D. Manning. 2015. Improved semantic representations from tree-structured long short-term memory networks. *Association for Computational Linguistics*.

Nianwen Xue, Hwee Tou Ng, Sameer Pradhan, Attapol Rutherford, Bonnie Webber, Chuan Wang, and Hongmin Wang. 2016. Conll 2016 shared task on multilingual shallow discourse parsing. In *Proceedings of the CoNLL-16 shared task*, pages 1–19, TOBEFILLED-Ann Arbor, Michigan, August. Association for Computational Linguistics.

Daniel H Younger. 1967. Recognition and parsing of context-free languages in time n3. *Information and control*, 10(2):189–208.

A Web-based Framework for Collecting and Assessing Highlighted Sentences in a Document

Sasha Spala[1], Franck Dernoncourt[2], Walter Chang[2], Carl Dockhorn[1]
[1]Adobe Systems, [2]Adobe Research
{sspala,dernonco,wachang,cdockhor}@adobe.com

Abstract

Automatically highlighting a text aims at identifying key portions that are the most important to a reader. In this paper, we present a web-based framework[1] designed to efficiently and scalably crowdsource two independent but related tasks: collecting highlight annotations, and comparing the performance of automated highlighting systems. The first task is necessary to understand human preferences and train supervised automated highlighting systems. The second task yields a more accurate and fine-grained evaluation than existing automated performance metrics.

1   Introduction

As people have access to an increasingly larger amount of information, technologies may enable them to consume that information more efficiently. Existing technologies have focused on automated summarization techniques. However, summarization techniques are not fully mature: emphasis mistakes are frequent and may cause the reader to miss crucial points in the summarized document. To address this issue, as an alternative to summarization, key portions of a document can instead be highlighted (or made more visible by bold, italic, etc)Highlights appear within their context (unlike a summary), and the impact of 'bad" highlights is of much lower consequence than 'bad" summaries.

We believe highlights to be motivated by reading intentions. Thus, we must determine if a difference exists between extractive summary sentences and human highlights. The framework presented in this paper allows users to efficiently and scalably crowdsource two related tasks: collecting highlight annotations, and comparing the performance of automated highlighting systems.

2   Related Work

Highlighting is one of the most common methods of annotation (Baron, 2009), making it a popular content annotation method for increasing comprehension in many reading domains. Passive highlighting, or highlights that already appear in text, has been shown in several studies to be a useful tool for information retention and comprehension (Fowler and Barker, 1974; Lorch Jr., 1989; Lorch Jr et al., 1995).

Rath (1961) asked human annotators to retrieve the "most representative" sentences in a document and failed to find significant human agreement for both human-retrieved and machine-retrieved sentences; Daumé (2004) showed that when instructed to choose the "most important" sentences from a passage, humans still fell short of significant agreement. Though Daumé (2004) had low expectations for human agreement for summarization, we believe that the effect of *inline* content, such as highlights, could significantly increase the efficacy of this task.

We explored several annotation frameworks, but none of them are designed for collecting and assessing highlights. For example, MAE (Stubbs, 2011) allows annotators to select entire spans of text and assign categories and labels to those spans, but did not allow researchers to normalize user input; one must rely on annotators to select the correct length of input and, in our case, define sentence boundaries. Similarly, BRAT (Stenetorp et al., 2012) makes it difficult to select a sentence with exact boundaries without post-processing annotator input.

---

[1]https://github.com/Franck-Dernoncourt/sentence-highlighting

Proceedings of the 27th International Conference on Computational Linguistics: System Demonstrations, pages 78–81
Santa Fe, New Mexico, USA, August 20-26, 2018.

3 Framework Design

3.1 Overview

We present in the next two sections the interfaces corresponding to the two use cases of our framework: direct highlight annotation, and human evaluation of highlighting systems. For each of these two use cases, the framework collects a wide range of behind-the-scenes data during annotator interactions, including intermediate highlights (versus the final version of highlights an annotator is satisfied with) and the time spent on each section of a document. From the collected data, we can infer a variety of important information , such as how often users adjust their highlights, and whether users scroll across documents to skim the content, or read every word.

Our annotation framework is lightweight, requiring only a Node.js server, which is simple to deploy on Linux, macOS, or Windows.

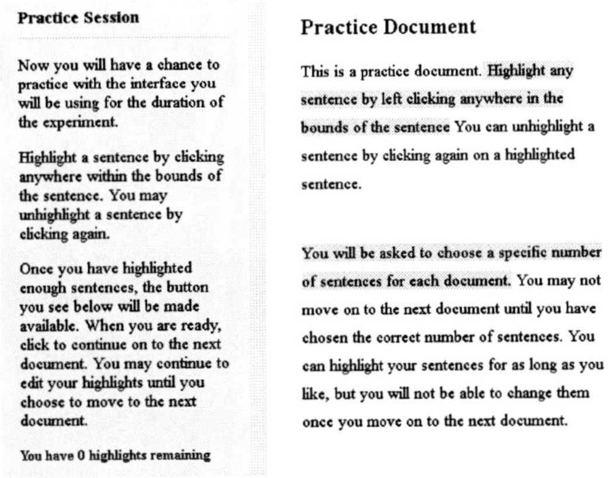

Figure 1: Interface for direct highlight annotation. Annotators may highlight or unhighlight any sentence by clicking on it.

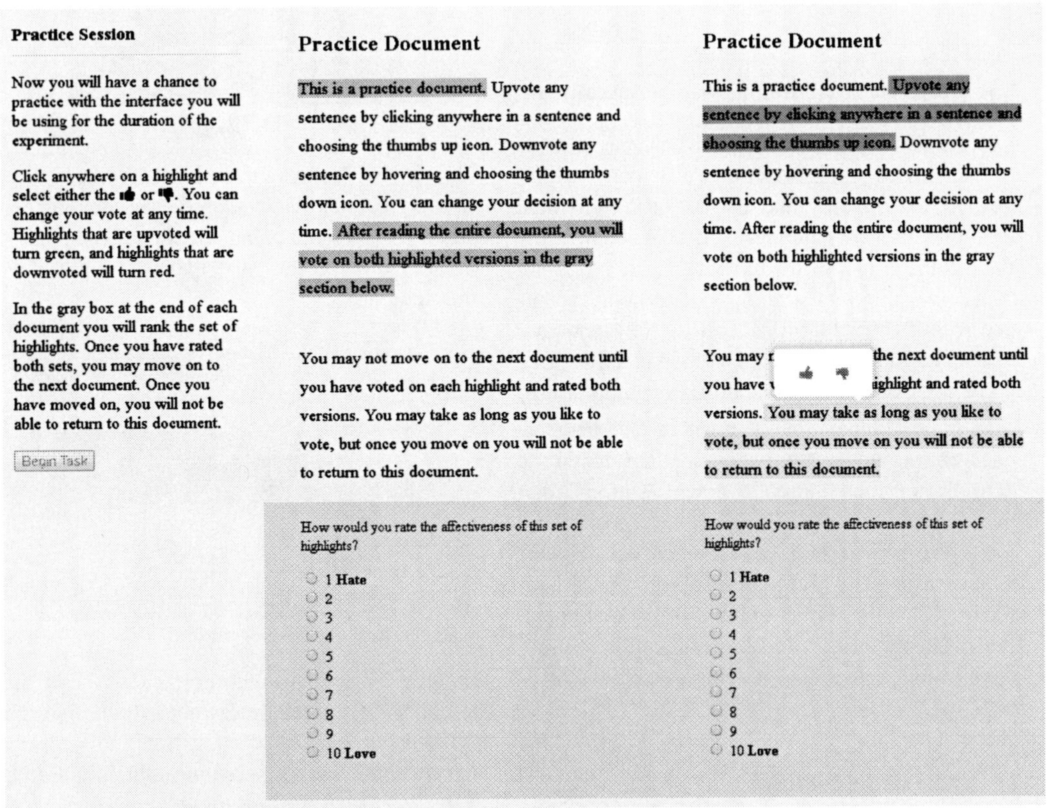

Figure 2: Interface for highlighting system assessment. Participants are presented with two versions of the same text with different highlights. Participants must upvote (green) or downvote (red) each highlight, then give a global grade between 1 and 10 for each of the two versions.

3.2 Use Case 1: Highlight Annotation Collection

Figure 1 presents the interface used to collect provided highlight annotations. Annotators are asked to highlight sentences that would make document comprehension easier and faster for another naive reader. A counter in the left column updates the number of highlights remaining as annotators work through each document.

Clicking anywhere within the boundaries of a sentence highlights the entire sentence in yellow. Annotators are allowed to highlight and unhighlight as many times as desired, but are not able to revisit the same document after moving to the next document. All annotators are required to complete a brief tutorial session before beginning that demonstrates the interface controls.

This highlight collection phase attempts to simplify user interaction; Highlighting and unhighlighting can be done with a single left click. There are no color variations; the text size for the left panel and the document title and content stay consistent throughout the task.

3.3 Use Case 2: Highlight System Assessment

Figure 2 presents the interface where participants evaluate highlighting systems. Participants are instructed to "upvote" and "downvote" individual highlights that they believe will help identify the main point(s) of the document. Participants are shown two different highlighted versions, generated from two highlighting systems. Systems are randomized and anonymized, both in location (e.g., left or right side of the content frame) and pairing.

To handle annotation of positive and negative votes on individual highlights, we introduced the "thumbs up" and "thumbs down" buttons, displayed after left clicking anywhere within the boundaries of a highlighted sentence. Participants must vote on every highlight displayed on the document. Once they reach the end of the document, they must rate the two versions of the highlights on a one-to-ten scale before moving to the next document.

4 Analysis Reporting

To help researchers analyze the results, our framework provides analysis scripts, written in Python 3. In this section, we present some of these analyses.

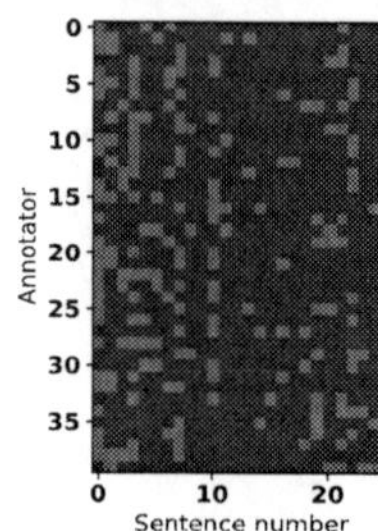

Figure 3: Binary heatmap showing annotator highlights. Red and blue cells correspond to highlighted and non-highlighted sentences, respectively. Each row represents an annotator, each column a sentence in the document.

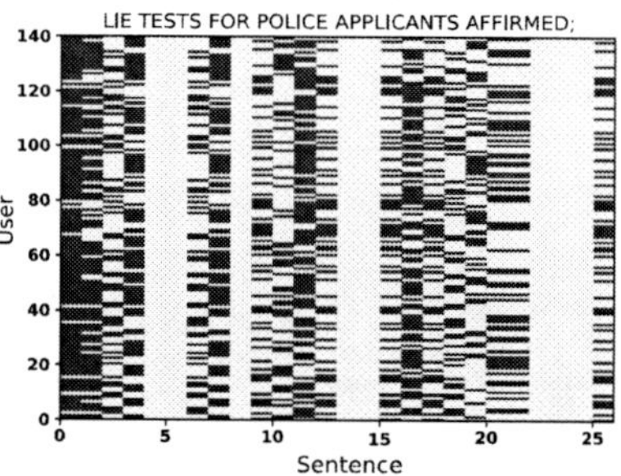

Figure 4: Representation of highlight votes, where green and red cells represent up- and down votes, respectively, and cream reflects that the model shown to the participant did not highlight that sentence.

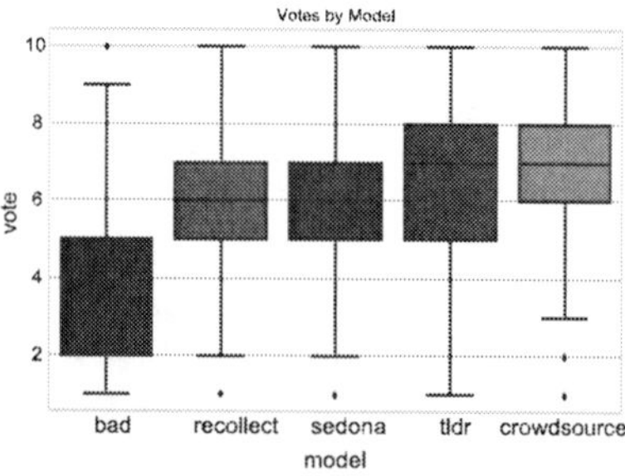

Figure 5: Vote distribution by model. "Bad" is an a model that selects intentionally bad highlights; "crowdsource" displays the highlights most often chosen by annotators during highlight collection; "sedona" (Elhoseiny et al., 2016), "recollect" (Modani et al., 2015; Modani et al., 2016) and "tldr" (smmry.com) are extractive summarization models that are used to select which sentences to highlight.

4.1 Use Case 1: Highlight Annotation Results

After annotators highlight sentences in a document, the annotations may be viewed as a binary heatmap, as shown in Figure 3. The heatmap may be used to identify highlight clusters (e.g., if highlights tend to be located at the beginning of the document) as well as an approximate overview of the inter-annotator agreement. The Krippendorff Alpha score (Krippendorff, 2011) is computed, which indicates the overall agreement across all annotators.

4.2 Use Case 2: Highlight Assessment Results

Figure 4 displays up- and down-votes on all sentences in a document, for all automated highlighting models. It can be used to visually determine the consistency of the annotators. E.g., ideally if a sentence is worth being highlighted, it should be upvoted across all annotators, regardless of the model that highlighted it.

Figure 5 contains one boxplot for each model. Specifically, each boxplot represents the distribution of participants' votes that they cast on a document that was highlighted by the model corresponding to the boxplot.

5 Conclusion

In this paper, we have presented a web-based framework designed to efficiently and scalably crowdsource the collection of highlight annotations as well as the human comparison of the performance of automated highlighting systems. The interface is highly customizable, easy to tune, and, based on our experience the framework with Amazon Mechanical Turk, easily understood by annotators. The framework as well as its source code is freely available. We hope it will help foster research in the field of automated highlighting.

References

[Baron2009] Dennis Baron. 2009. *A better pencil: Readers, writers, and the digital revolution*. Oxford Uni. Press.

[Daumé III and Marcu2004] Hal Daumé III and Daniel Marcu. 2004. Generic sentence fusion is an ill-defined summarization task. In *Text Summarization Branches Out Workshop at ACL*.

[Elhoseiny et al.2016] Mohamed Elhoseiny, Scott Cohen, Walter Chang, Brian Price, and Ahmed Elgammal. 2016. Automatic annotation of structured facts in images. In *5th Workshop on Vision and Language*.

[Fowler and Barker1974] Robert L. Fowler and Anne S. Barker. 1974. Effectiveness of highlighting for retention of text material. *Journal of Applied Psychology*, 59(3):358–364.

[Krippendorff2011] Klaus Krippendorff. 2011. Computing krippendorff's alpha-reliability.

[Lorch Jr et al.1995] R.F. Lorch Jr, E. Pugzles Lorch, and M.A. Klusewitz. 1995. Effects of typographical cues on reading and recall of text. *Contemporary Educational Psychology*, 20(1):51–64.

[Lorch Jr.1989] R. F. Lorch Jr. 1989. Text-signaling devices and their effects on reading and memory processes. *Educational Psychology Review*, 1(3):209–234.

[Modani et al.2015] Natwar Modani, Elham Khabiri, Harini Srinivasan, and James Caverlee. 2015. Creating diverse product review summaries: a graph approach. In *ICWISE*, pages 169–184. Springer.

[Modani et al.2016] Natwar Modani, Balaji Vasan Srinivasan, and Harsh Jhamtani. 2016. Generating multiple diverse summaries. *International Conference on Web Information Systems Engineering*.

[Rath et al.1961] G.J. Rath, A. Resnick, and T.R. Savage. 1961. The formation of abstracts by the selection of sentences. part i. sentence selection by men and machines. *JAIST*, 12(2):139–141.

[Stenetorp et al.2012] Pontus Stenetorp, Sampo Pyysalo, Goran Topić, Tomoko Ohta, Sophia Ananiadou, and Jun'ichi Tsujii. 2012. BRAT: a web-based tool for NLP-assisted text annotation. In *ACL Demonstrations*.

[Stubbs2011] Amber Stubbs. 2011. MAE and MAI: lightweight annotation and adjudication tools. In *Proceedings of the 5th Linguistic Annotation Workshop*, pages 129–133. Association for Computational Linguistics.

Cool English: A Grammatical Error Correction System Based on Large Learner Corpora

Yu-Chun Lo, Jhih-Jie Chen, Ching-Yu Yang, Jason S. Chang
Department of Computer Science
National Tsing Hua University
{howard.lo, jjc, chingyu, jason}@nlplab.cc

Abstract

This paper presents a grammatical error correction (GEC) system that provides corrective feedback for essays. We apply the neural sequence-to-sequence model, which is frequently used in machine translation and text summarization, to this GEC task. The model is trained on EF-Cambridge Open Language Database (EFCAMDAT), a large learner corpus annotated with grammatical errors and corrections. Evaluation shows that our system achieves competitive performance on a number of publicly available testsets.

1 Introduction

The rise of English as a global language has motivated research and development in computer-assisted language learning systems. However, learning a second or foreign language is not at all easy, especially in the area of writing. Due to the limited vocabulary and inadequate command of grammar, second language learners are prone to misspelled words and write ungrammatical sentences. The demand for grammatical error correction (GEC) has encouraged researchers to develop technology to support the writing process.

Correcting grammatical errors with statistical machine translation (SMT) techniques has gained great success (Brockett et al., 2006). Translating an ungrammatical sentence into a correct one can effectively handle all types of errors simultaneously (Rozovskaya and Roth, 2014). More recently, Rozovskaya and Roth (2016) compares the strength and the weakness of classifier-based and SMT-based approaches, and integrates both of them to build a hybrid GEC system.

Recently, Yuan and Briscoe (2016) presents the very first word-based neural machine translation (NMT) model for GEC and proposes a two-step approach to handle the rare word problem. Xie et al. (2016) proposes a character-based NMT model, achieving open vocabulary machine translation. Sennrich et al. (2016) purposes a subword-based model with Byte-Pair Encoding (BPE) algorithm, which only splits rare words and leaves frequent words unsegmented.

The remainder of this paper is structured as follows. In section 2, we describe our system implementation. Then, we describe the experiment settings in section 3. We report our system performance and discuss the evaluation results in section 4. Finally, we conclude our paper and explore the future direction of GEC research in section 5.

2 The GEC System

In this section, we present *GEC Cool English*, a web-based system where users can write their essays and get corrective feedback (available at https://nlp-ultron.cs.nthu.edu.tw/gec/). The correction process is divided into three steps. First, we use *spaCy*[1] to tokenize input sentences (Honnibal and Johnson, 2015). Second, the tokenized sentences are converted into lowercase and fed into the NMT model for inference. We then re-capitalize the model predictions using *truecaser*[2]. Finally, to give easy-to-read feedback, we convert the result into an informative visual expression instead of the NMT model

[1] https://spacy.io
[2] https://github.com/nreimers/truecaser

Proceedings of the 27th International Conference on Computational Linguistics: System Demonstrations, pages 82–85
Santa Fe, New Mexico, USA, August 20-26, 2018.

output directly. Words to be deleted are marked with *strikethrough* and colored red, while words to be inserted are colored green (as shown in Figure1).

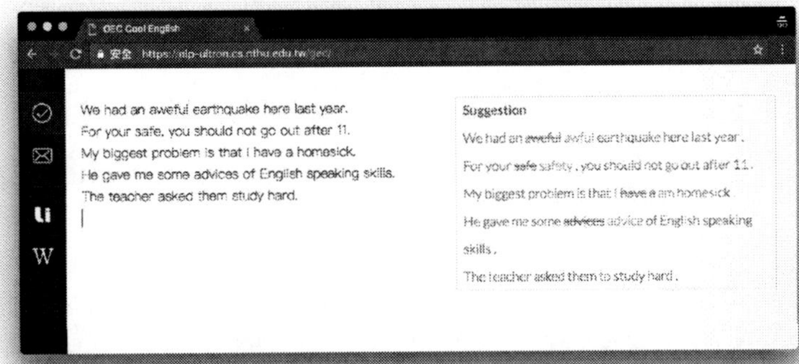

Figure 1: The screenshot of the system *GEC Cool English*

2.1 Model Implementation

We build our NMT model upon the neural sequence-to-sequence (Seq2Seq) framework proposed by Luong et al. (2015), where both encoder and decoder are recurrent neural networks (RNNs). We further extend our NMT model by adding residual connections among the recurrent layers, which has suggested improving the gradient flow during training. To select the best NMT model for our GEC system, we explore word-based model (WORD) and subword-based model (SUBWORD). Our NMT models are implemented with *OpenNMT* (Klein et al., 2017), a comprehensive library for training and deploying NMT models.

3 Experiments

3.1 Dataset

For training data, we use the EF-Cambridge Open Language Database (EFCAMDAT) (Geertzen et al., 2013), which is currently the largest publicly available learner corpus. EFCAMDAT contains about 1.2 million essays with over 83 million words written by approximately 174 thousand learners with a variety of CEFR levels (A1-C2). We extract parallel sentences from those essays, resulting in about 7 million pairs of parallel sentences and 2.4 million of them contain at least one edit. To the best of our knowledge, we are the first group to exploit EFCAMDAT corpus for GEC tasks.

To compare our systems with other works, we also use the following frequently used learner corpora: the Lang-8 Corpus of Learner English (L8) [3], the Cambridge First Certificate English (FCE) exam scripts (Yannakoudakis et al., 2011), which is a subset of *proprietary* Cambridge Learner Corpus (CLC), and the NUS Corpus of Learner English (NUCLE).

For development and test data, we use the JHU FLuency-Extended GUG corpus (JFLEG) (Napoles et al., 2017), which is designed for evaluating fluency and grammaticality. JFLEG corpus consists of 1,501 pairs of erroneous and corrected sentences, in which 754 pairs are development data and 747 pairs test data.

3.2 Preprocessing

First, noisy sentences are excluded: sentences with URLs, E-mail, XML-like tags, etc., sentences less than 3 words or more than 50 tokens, and sentences that start with a non alphabetic character or do not end with a punctuation mark. Next, name entities are recognized with *spaCy* and correct spelling errors on non-name-entity tokens with *Enchant*. [4] We then re-capitalize sentences with *truecaser* and correct wrongly tokenized contractions and remove consecutive punctuation marks and convert tokens

---

[3] http://cl.naist.jp/nldata/lang-8
[4] https://github.com/AbiWord/enchant

System	Training data	Data size	GLEU(dev)	GLEU(test)
Previous systems				
Chollampatt et al. (2016)	L8 + NUCLE	2.7M	46.3	50.1
Yuan and Briscoe (2016)	CLC	1.9M	47.2	52.1
Ji et al. (2017)	L8 + CLC + NUCLE	2.6M	49.0	53.4
Sakaguchi et al. (2017)	L8 + FCE + NUCLE	720K	49.9	54.0
Our system				
WORD	L8 + FCE + NUCLE	720K	46.3	53.8
WORD	EFCAMDAT	2M	44.2	51.6
SUBWORD	L8 + FCE + NUCLE	720K	46.1	53.6
SUBWORD	EFCAMDAT	2M	44.9	52.1

Table 1: Evaluation on JFLEG test set

into lowercase. Finally, we exclude the parallel sentences in which the token edit distance more than 50% of the length of the source sentence. Through our text cleaning pipeline, 2 million parallel sentences from EFCAMDAT and 720K parallel sentences from L8 + FCE + NUCLE are left for training.

3.3 Hyperparameters and Training Details

The vocabulary size are 50K and 35K respectively for the models trained on EFCAMDAT and L8 + FCE + NUCLE. The sequence length is limited to 50 words for both source and target sentences. The diemension of word embedding is set to 300. The encoder is a 2-layer bi-directional Long Short Term Memory networks (LSTM) and the decoder is a 2-layer LSTM. The hidden layer size of both encoder and decoder is set to 512. We perform *UNK* replacement by copying the source token with the highest attention score. We train our models by *scheduled sampling* (Bengio et al., 2015) and follow the *curriculum learning* strategy using linear decay scheduling. The schedule sampling rate is set to 0.5. We optimize our model using ADAM optimizer with learning rate 0.001 without learning rate decay. The maximum gradient norm is set to 1. The batch size is set to 64. We apply dropout on both input tokens and embeddings, and train our models with *variational dropout* (Gal and Ghahramani, 2016). All dropout probabilities are set to 0.3. Finally, beam search is used to optimize hypotheses with beam size set to 5 and maximum sequence length set to 50. Each model is trained for 20 epochs on NVIDIA 1080 Ti GPU within one day.

4 Evaluation and Discussions

Table 1 shows our systems achieves competitive performance comparing to the previous state-of-the-art systems.

It is worth mentioning that our text cleaning pipeline significantly improves the performance of models trained on the EFCAMDAT corpus (WORD: $49.08 \rightarrow 51.63$; SUBWORD: $50.37 \rightarrow 52.05$). Especially spelling error correction and converting tokens into lowercase alleviate the rare word problem and reduce the vocabulary size of NMT for faster training.

The results show that the models trained on the L8 + FCE + NUCLE outperform the ones trained on EFCAMDAT. One possible reason may due to the large vocabulary size and inconsistent annotations in EFCAMDAT. For example, "discuss about N." should be always corrected to "discuss N.", but only 162 out of 849 are corrected. One interesting insight is that subword-based model generally performs better than word-based model, simply because it handles the rare word problem more effectively. But in our experiments, we found that, in EFCAMDAT, the subword-based model performs better than the word-based model, but in L8 + FCE + NUCLE, the word-based model achieves similar performance as the subword-based model does. The reason might be that, the vocabulary size of 35K is sufficient enough for a word-based model to cover all the vocabularies in L8 + FCE + NUCLE, thus less effected by the rare word problem. In contrast, the word-based model with the vocabulary size of 50K is still insufficient to cover the diverse vocabulary of EFCAMDAT, thus perform worse than the subword-based model. We believe that pre-processing and selecting training data through active learning could reduce the vocabulary size and cope with the rare word problem, thus further improving a word-based model.

5 Conclusions

We have presented a GEC system that gives corrective feedback for the erroneous sentence. Our system achieves competitive performance on the JFLEG test set with publicly available learner corpora comparing to the previous state-of-the-art NMT based systems.

Many avenues for future research exists. For example, we could remove or correct inconsistent annotations based on statistical and grammatical analysis. As an effect to reduce vocabulary size, we could perform contextual spelling error correction as a first and separate step before the NMT process.

References

Samy Bengio, Oriol Vinyals, Navdeep Jaitly, and Noam Shazeer. 2015. Scheduled sampling for sequence prediction with recurrent neural networks. In *NIPS*.

Chris Brockett, William B Dolan, and Michael Gamon. 2006. Correcting esl errors using phrasal smt techniques. In *Proceedings of the 2006 ACL*, pages 249–256. Association for Computational Linguistics.

Shamil Chollampatt, Duc Tam Hoang, and Hwee Tou Ng. 2016. Adapting grammatical error correction based on the native language of writers with neural network joint models. In *Proceedings of EMNLP*, pages 1901–1911.

Yarin Gal and Zoubin Ghahramani. 2016. A theoretically grounded application of dropout in recurrent neural networks. In *NIPS*.

Jeroen Geertzen, Theodora Alexopoulou, and Anna Korhonen. 2013. Automatic linguistic annotation of large scale l2 databases: The ef-cambridge open language database. In *Proceedings of SLRF 2012*.

Matthew Honnibal and Mark Johnson. 2015. An improved non-monotonic transition system for dependency parsing. In *Proceedings of the 2015 EMNLP*, pages 1373–1378.

Jianshu Ji, Qinlong Wang, Kristina Toutanova, Yongen Gong, Steven Truong, and Jianfeng Gao. 2017. A nested attention neural hybrid model for grammatical error correction. *arXiv preprint arXiv:1707.02026*.

Guillaume Klein, Yoon Kim, Yuntian Deng, Jean Senellart, and Alexander Rush. 2017. Opennmt: Open-source toolkit for neural machine translation. *Proceedings of ACL 2017, System Demonstrations*, pages 67–72.

Thang Luong, Hieu Pham, and Christopher D. Manning. 2015. Effective approaches to attention-based neural machine translation. In *EMNLP*.

Courtney Napoles, Keisuke Sakaguchi, and Joel Tetreault. 2017. Jfleg: A fluency corpus and benchmark for grammatical error correction. In *Proceedings of the EACL*, volume 2, pages 229–234.

Alla Rozovskaya and Dan Roth. 2014. Building a state-of-the-art grammatical error correction system. *Transactions of the Association of Computational Linguistics*, 2(1):419–434.

Alla Rozovskaya and Dan Roth. 2016. Grammatical error correction: Machine translation and classifiers. In *Proceedings of the 2016 ACL*, volume 1, pages 2205–2215.

Keisuke Sakaguchi, Matt Post, and Benjamin Van Durme. 2017. Grammatical error correction with neural reinforcement learning. In *Proceedings of the 8th IJCNLP*, pages 366–372.

Rico Sennrich, Barry Haddow, and Alexandra Birch. 2016. Neural machine translation of rare words with subword units. *CoRR*, abs/1508.07909.

Ziang Xie, Anand Avati, Naveen Arivazhagan, Dan Jurafsky, and Andrew Y Ng. 2016. Neural language correction with character-based attention. *arXiv preprint arXiv:1603.09727*.

Helen Yannakoudakis, Ted Briscoe, and Ben Medlock. 2011. A new dataset and method for automatically grading esol texts. In *Proceedings of the 49th Annual Meeting of the Association for Computational Linguistics: Human Language Technologies-Volume 1*, pages 180–189. Association for Computational Linguistics.

Zheng Yuan and Ted Briscoe. 2016. Grammatical error correction using neural machine translation. In *Proceedings of the 2016 NAACL-HLT*, pages 380–386.

Appraise Evaluation Framework for Machine Translation

Christian Federmann
Microsoft Translator
One Microsoft Way
Redmond, WA 98052, USA
`chrife@microsoft.com`

Abstract

We present Appraise, an open-source framework for crowd-based annotation tasks, notably for evaluation of machine translation (MT) output. This is the software used to run the yearly evaluation campaigns for shared tasks at the WMT Conference on Machine Translation. It has also been used at IWSLT 2017 and, recently, to measure human parity for machine translation for Chinese to English news text. The demo will present the full end-to-end life cycle of an Appraise evaluation campaign, from task creation to annotation and interpretation of results.

1 Motivation

Human evaluation of machine translation is the ultimate measure of translation quality. However, due to data collection effort and annotation cost, many experiments and publications do not report results from human evaluation and rely on scores computed by automated metrics such as BLEU (Papineni et al., 2002) instead. We believe that machine translation researchers should be able to conduct manual annotation campaigns at scale, without having to re-implement the necessary infrastructure from scratch. Since 2007, development of the Appraise evaluation framework for machine translation has supported the research community, trying to bring more human evaluation into MT research.

2 Introduction

The Appraise framework has become a standard tool for machine translation evaluation. It is used for shared tasks at the yearly Conference on Machine Translation (WMT) (Bojar et al., 2017) and has been adopted at last year's IWSLT 2017 workshop (Cettolo et al., 2017). The Microsoft Translator team utilises the software for its internal quality monitoring. Figure 1 shows the annotation user interface.

Figure 1: Screenshot of user interface for source-based direct assessment as implemented in Appraise.

Proceedings of the 27th International Conference on Computational Linguistics: System Demonstrations, pages 86–88
Santa Fe, New Mexico, USA, August 20-26, 2018.

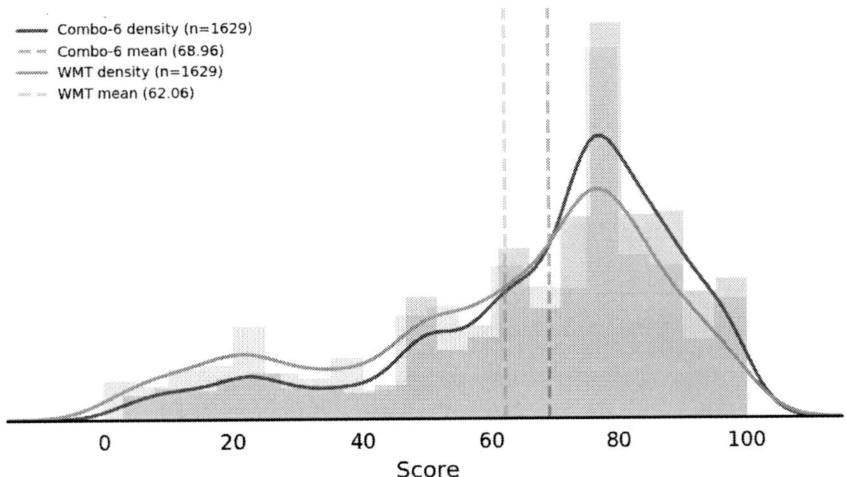

Figure 2: Visualisation of Appraise direct assessment results for Chinese to English news translation.

In 2018, Appraise was used as part of a research project which proved human parity for machine translation of Chinese to English news text (Awadalla et al., 2018), based on a large-scale evaluation campaign run using an Appraise system hosted on Azure. Figure 2 shows a graph visualising results from this work, comparing score distributions for the human parity system (COMBO-6) and the original WMT17 reference translation (WMT).

Our system demonstration provides an end-to-end overview on all aspects of a machine translation evaluation campaign within Appraise. We first describe input data, task creation, and campaign setup, including best practices regarding user and team management. Then, we show the annotation interface and discuss how annotator reliability is measured and monitored, allowing to detect spammers assigning random scores to candidate translations. We describe how statistical significance testing (Wilcoxon, 1945; Mann and Whitney, 1947; Riezler and Maxwell, 2005) can help to solve this problem. Lastly, we explain how final campaign results can be computed, extracted and visualised effectively, so that results are easily interpretable.

We also describe the annotation system's Python-based architecture and highlight implementation details as well as lessons learnt during ten years of human evaluation campaigns based on Appraise.

3 License

Appraise source code is available on GitHub[1] and is shared under a permissive license[2].

4 Conclusion

Our system demonstration explains the full end-to-end life cycle of an Appraise evaluation campaign. It gives an in-depth look into a decade of research on machine translation evaluation, including in-sights from several WMT campaigns as well as the evaluation part of Microsoft's recent human parity research breakthrough. This should lead to interesting discussions.

Acknowledgements

The author thanks the anonymous reviewers for their feedback. Appraise is developed incorporating feedback from the research community, participants of WMT and IWSLT shared tasks, and Microsoft. This support is crucial for the evolution of Appraise and, thus, much appreciated. Thank you!

---

[1]See https://github.com/cfedermann/Appraise/
[2]See https://github.com/cfedermann/Appraise/blob/master/appraise/LICENSE

References

Hany Hassan Awadalla, Anthony Aue, Chang Chen, Vishal Chowdhary, Jonathan Clark, Christian Federmann, Xuedong Huang, Marcin Junczys-Dowmunt, Will Lewis, Mu Li, Shujie Liu, Tie-Yan Liu, Renqian Luo, Arul Menezes, Tao Qin, Frank Seide, Xu Tan, Fei Tian, Lijun Wu, Shuangzhi Wu, Yingce Xia, Dongdong Zhang, Zhirui Zhang, and Ming Zhou. 2018. Achieving human parity on automatic chinese to english news translation. March.

Ondřej Bojar, Rajen Chatterjee, Christian Federmann, Yvette Graham, Barry Haddow, Shujian Huang, Matthias Huck, Philipp Koehn, Qun Liu, Varvara Logacheva, Christof Monz, Matteo Negri, Matt Post, Raphael Rubino, Lucia Specia, and Marco Turchi. 2017. Findings of the 2017 Conference on Machine Translation (WMT17). In *Proceedings of the Second Conference on Machine Translation, Volume 2: Shared Task Papers*, pages 169–214, Copenhagen, Denmark, September. Association for Computational Linguistics.

Mauro Cettolo, Marcello Federico, Luisa Bentivogli, Jan Niehues, Sebastian Stüker, Katsuitho Sudoh, Koichiro Yoshino, and Christian Federmann. 2017. Overview of the IWSLT 2017 Evaluation Campaign. In *Proceedings of the 14th International Workshop on Spoken Language Translation (IWSLT)*, pages 2–12, Tokyo, Japan, December. IWSLT.

Christian Federmann. 2012. Appraise: An Open-Source Toolkit for Manual Evaluation of Machine Translation Output. *The Prague Bulletin of Mathematical Linguistics*, 98:25–35, September.

Christian Federmann. 2017. Appraise on Aure: A cloud-based, multi-purpose evaluation framework. In *Proceedings of the EAMT 2017: User Studies and Project/Product Descriptions*, page 32, Prague, Czech Republic, May. European Association for Machine Translation (EAMT).

Henry B Mann and Donald R Whitney. 1947. On a test of whether one of two random variables is stochastically larger than the other. *The Annals of Mathematical Statistics*, pages 50–60.

Kishore Papineni, Salim Roukos, Todd Ward, and Wei-Jing Zhu. 2002. Bleu: a method for automatic evaluation of machine translation. In *Proceedings of the 40th annual meeting on association for computational linguistics*, pages 311–318. Association for Computational Linguistics.

Stefan Riezler and John T Maxwell. 2005. On Some Pitfalls in Automatic Evaluation and significance Testing for MT. In *Proceedings of the ACL Workshop on Intrinsic and Extrinsic Evaluation Measures for Machine Translation and/or Summarization*, pages 57–64, Stroudsburg, PA, USA, June. Association for Computational Linguistics.

Frank Wilcoxon. 1945. Individual Comparisons by Ranking Methods. *Biometrics Bulletin*, 1(6):80–83.

KIT Lecture Translator:
Multilingual Speech Translation with One-Shot Learning

Florian Dessloch, Thanh-Le Ha, Markus Müller, Jan Niehues, Thai-Son Nguyen, Ngoc-Quan Pham,
Elizabeth Salesky, Matthias Sperber, Sebastian Stüker, Thomas Zenkel, Alexander Waibel
Karlsruhe Institute of Technology, Karlsruhe, Germany; Carnegie Mellon University, Pittsburgh, PA, USA
`firstname.lastname@kit.edu`

Abstract

In today's globalized world we have the ability to communicate with people around the world. However, in many situations the language barrier still presents a major issue. For example, many foreign students studying at KIT are initially unable to follow a lecture in German. Therefore, we offer an automatic simultaneous interpretation service for students.

To fulfill this task, we have developed a low-latency translation system adapted to the lecture domain which covers several language pairs. While the switch from traditional statistical machine translation to neural machine translation (NMT) significantly improved performance, to integrate NMT into the speech translation framework required several adjustments. We have addressed the run-time constraints and different types of input. Furthermore, we utilized one-shot learning to easily add new topic-specific terms to the system. In addition to better performance, NMT also enabled us increase our covered languages through the use of multilingual models. Combining these techniques, we are able to provide an adapted speech translation system for several European languages.

1 Introduction

In today's globalized world we have the opportunity to communicate with people all over the world. But, often the language barrier still poses a challenge and prevents communication. At KIT, there are many international students from around the world. To deal with the language barrier and support foreign students in lectures, KIT offers an automatic lecture translation (LT) service in many lecture halls. When a lecture begins, a recording client is triggered which records the lecturer's speech and presentation screen, and sends them to our simultaneous LT system which returns both the transcription and translation in real-time via a web interface.

Starting from the initial version of lecture translation (Fügen et al., 2006), our system has continuously developed (Kolss et al., 2008; Cho et al., 2013). In 2012, the LT system was first operated in several lecture halls in KIT with limited coverage; German was the primary spoken language, translated into English. We now support both German and English as input languages with three additional target languages: French, Spanish, and Italian. Furthermore, a preliminary multilingual system for 24 languages is also available. In order to provide efficient recognition and translation services to the students, we address the following research areas: 1) **Low-latency**: Transcription and translation needs to be synchronized with the speech of the lecturer as much as possible. How can we provide systems with very low latency? 2) **Multilingualism**: How can we minimize the effort and maintenance needed to train and support many languages? 3) **Adaptation**: Which adaptation techniques are applicable for online and low-latency speech translation?

2 Low-latency Speech Translation Framework

Speech is simultaneously recorded by a recording client and sent to a server. There, the three main components of the system, automatic speech recognition (ASR), segmentation, and machine translation

Proceedings of the 27th International Conference on Computational Linguistics: System Demonstrations, pages 89–93
Santa Fe, New Mexico, USA, August 20-26, 2018.

(MT), transcribe and translate the audio, which is shown to the user in an interface. The segmentation system is a monolingual translation system that adds case and punctuation information to the ASR output, and segments it into appropriate sentences for the translation system. While the main use-case is online translation, where the user can follow the lecture concurrently on his smart phone or laptop, we also offer a web-based archive for viewing previously recorded lectures.

One of the main weaknesses in earlier versions of our speech translation framework was the latency of the system. Since MT systems are usually trained on the sentence-level, the translation would only be displayed if the whole sentence was recognized. In order to overcome this drawback, we extended our framework to handle intermediate outputs (Niehues et al., 2016). This allows us to display a translation for a partly recognized sentence, and later update it with the full sentence translation. The same technique is also applied to display intermediate hypotheses from the speech recognition which is described in Section 3.

3   Automatic Speech Recognition

We utilize the DNN-HMM model to build our ASR component. We trained a deep neural network with several lectures' audio to model many thousands of context-dependent phonemes. We also utilized lecturers' materials such as lecture notes and reading materials to build adapted vocabulary and language models for the scheduled lectures. While using phoneme-based acoustic modeling is stable for many different languages, the automatic adaptation of vocabulary and language model allows us to significantly improve transcription quality based on information from the lectures of the same course and lecturer. A further advantage to the DNN-HMM model for our use case is that it is a very efficient model for building low-latency ASR systems. The latency of our ASR system has to be very low to keep transcription and translation as synchronized with the speech of the lecturer as possible.

Low-latency ASR   By using a dynamic decoding framework for ASR, we can avoid the detection of audio segments, and incrementally perform decoding as soon as a fraction of speech is recorded. This so-called run-on incremental recognition helps us avoid the latency caused by waiting for the end of the current segment. Normally, only at the end of an utterance is the most probable hypothesis determined. However, since waiting until the end of the utterance leads to a high latency, we detect when a part of the hypothesis becomes stable and can be kept.

Lecture Dictionary Adaptation   The web interface allows lecturers to upload lecture materials such as slides and reading materials that will be accessible for download by students. We make additional use of these materials by automatically extracting out-of-vocabulary (OOV) words which are not recognizable by the default ASR system. We generate automatic pronunciations for these word, and map them to a common word to obtain language model probabilities. This is based on the intuition that these words are likely to occur in the lecture and should possess higher probability. Adaptation is performed on a per-lecture basis so that each lecture has its own specialized vocabulary.

4   Neural Machine Translation

The main advancement over previous lecture translation systems is the switch from SMT to NMT, and the necessary adaptations to do so. In order to use NMT in our framework, we had to develop several adaptations. First, we improved the run-time for the monolingual translation system by using a dedicated target encoding. Secondly, we used multi-task learning to improve the performance on translating the partial sentences necessary in low-latency translation. Finally, we developed methods to easily integrate topic-specific terms. But the switch also allowed us to significantly increase our language coverage.

Monolingual MT   Automatic speech recognition (ASR) systems typically do not generate punctuation marks or reliable casing. To create segments and better match typical MT training conditions, we use a monolingual NMT system to add sentence boundaries, insert proper punctuation, and add case where appropriate before translating (Cho et al., 2017). To train, we create parallel data where the source is the lowercased sentence with all punctuation removed, and the target is features indicating case with punctuation attached. The output vocabulary is then quite small; less than 100. Rare source words are replaced with POS tags. The training data is randomly segmented so that segment boundaries and punctuation types are well-distributed throughout the corpus. At test time, we follow the sliding window technique describe in (Cho et al., 2017), and always keep the previous l_w words as context.

Adaption to Speech   Since we are using the low-latency framework described in Section 2, the system does not only need to translate complete sentences, but also partial sentences. In phrase-based MT, this did not pose a problem. But if the NMT system is only trained on complete sentences, it learns to always generate complete sentences. Therefore, it will fantasize an ending for an incomplete sentence. We address this problem by additionally training the system to translate partial sentences. Accordingly, we first generate artificial training data. To improve corrections while maintaining performance, we use multi-task learning and train the model to perform both tasks, the translation of partial sentences and the translation of full sentences (Niehues et al., 2018).

One-Shot Learning   In addition to overall translation quality, we identify the importance of translating rare events which do not appear many times in the training data but are critical to individual lectures They can be difficult to translate using NMT, but it is crucial for the system to translate them consistently. In order to incorporate external translations into the system, we designed a framework that allows the model to dynamically interact with external knowledge bases via both data augmentation and modeling (Pham et al., 2018). During training, we pre-train phrase-tables with the parallel corpora, and use them to annotate possible translations for the rare-words that appear less than 3 times in the training data. We consider word-splitting methods such as BPE crucial efficiently represent words that do not appear in the training data, and therefore allow proper annotation. By using the COPY-NET the model is able to learn a bias towards the annotation, which might otherwise have be assigned very small probabilities by the NMT softmax function. Finally, we use reinforcement learning to guide the search operation to encourage copying the annotation into the generated sequence.

Multilingual MT   In order to build a single neural translation model able to translate into more than twenty European languages, we follow the approach described in (Pham et al., 2017). Our goal is to keep the neural architecture as compact as possible while still maintaining parity with the translation quality of systems trained on individual language pairs on the same data. Fundamentally, we our system shares its main components across languages: the encoder, the decoder and the attention layer, but employs different softmax output layers and word embedding layers for different target languages based on their vocabularies. In this way, the system does not need to calculate over all the words from all target languages.

5   Results

WERs and Latency of the ASR   In Table 1 , we present the performance of our multilingual speech recognition component in term of word error rates (WER) and word latency. The word latency is measured as the difference between the time a word is spoken and the time when its transcription is available at the display component. Since words span a duration we use their end time. Each test set consists of about 20-30 lecture talks. Typically, recognized words will appear in the display client about 1 second after real-time. The archived WERs without adaption are below 20.0% for all languages.

#	Language	WER (%)	Word Latency (s)
1	English	15.2	0.84
2	German	19.4	1.03
3	Spanish	14.1	0.79
4	French	19.3	1.11
5	Italian	17.5	0.94

Table 1: WER and Latency of The ASR

Input	Das binäre *Zahlensystem* ist ...
Baseline:	The binary *payment system* is ...
One-Shot:	The binary *numeral system* is ...

Table 2: An example of one-shot learning

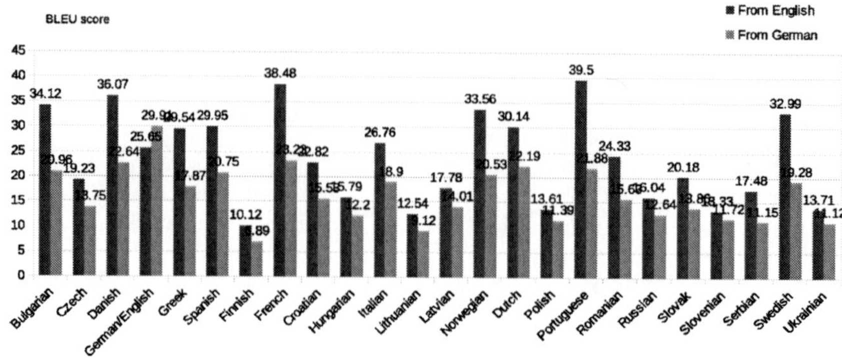

Figure 1: MT Performance when translating from English or German to 24 European languages

Machine Translation   Figure 1 shows the results of the multilingual system, translating from English and German to 24 European languages using a single model trained on the multilingual data. Compared to a standard bilingual system trained on the same data, it achieves better performance: for English↔German, we see 25.65 BLEU as compared to 24.92 translating into German, and 29.91 BLEU as compared to 28.74 translating into English. The results confirm our assumption that multilingual information helps to improve low-resourced translation systems trained individually.

This system achieves its best BLEU scores translating from English to Portuguese and German to English. This is reasonable, as there are adequate amounts of data in those directions and there are related languages which can assist by providing additional context. At the other end of the spectrum, the system obtains its worst results when translating into Finnish as there is not much parallel training data, and Finnish is the most morphologically-rich language in our set, further impoverishing the data condition.

When translating in specific domains, words which are generally rare can be incredibly important to translate correctly. For example, if we consider a lecture about the binary numeral system or *Zahlensystem*, it is necessary to translate this term or the meaning of the lecture is lost. One-shot learning allows us to do so, as shown in Table 2. Without one-shot learning, we have not seen this term before. Using byte-pair encoding, the system is generate a translation for *Zahlensystem*, but it incorrectly generates the translation *payment system* for the similar German word *Zahlsystem*. By adding the phrase {*Zahlensystem # numeral system*} to our memory, we are able to correctly translate this word in context.

6   Conclusion

This paper describes recent advancements for low-latency speech-to-text translation. Using several techniques, we were able to use fully neural methods for the machine translation component of our system. Further, by using multi-task and reinforcement learning, we were able to use NMT in a low-latency framework that can be easily adapted to new topics. These neural methods have allowed us to significantly increase our covered languages. Our multilingual model is able to translate from two source languages to 24 target languages, while fitting in memory on a moderate-size GPU.

References

Eunah Cho, Christian Fügen, Teresa Herrmann, Kevin Kilgour, Mohammed Mediani, Christian Mohr, et al. 2013. A real-world system for simultaneous translation of german lectures. In *INTERSPEECH*.

Eunah Cho, Jan Niehues, and Alex Waibel. 2017. Nmt-based segmentation and punctuation insertion for real-time spoken language translation. *Proc. Interspeech 2017*, pages 2645–2649.

Christian Fügen, Muntsin Kolss, Dietmar Bernreuther, Matthias Paulik, Sebastian Stüker, Stephan Vogel, and Alex Waibel. 2006. Open domain speech recognition & translation: Lectures and speeches. In *ICASSP*.

Muntsin Kolss, Matthias Wölfel, Florian Kraft, Jan Niehues, Matthias Paulik, and Alex Waibel. 2008. Simultaneous german-english lecture translation. In *IWSLT 2008*, pages 174–181.

Jan Niehues, Thai-Son Nguyen, Eunah Cho, Thanh-Le Ha, Kevin Kilgour, Markus Müller, Matthias Sperber, Sebastian Stüker, and Alexander Waibel. 2016. Dynamic transcription for low-latency speech translation.

J. Niehues, N-Q Pham, T-L Ha, M. Sperber, and A. Waibel. 2018. Low-latency neural speech translation. In *Proceedings of the 19th Annual Conference of the International Speech Communication Association (Interspeech 2018)*, Hyderabad, India.

Ngoc-Quan Pham, Matthias Sperber, Elizabeth Salesky, Thanh-Le Ha, Jan Niehues, and Alexander Waibel. 2017. KIT's Multilingual Neural Machine Translation systems for IWSLT 2017. *IWSLT 2017*.

Ngoc-Quan Pham, Jan Niehues, and Alex Waibel. 2018. Towards one-shot learning for rare-word translation with external experts. In *Proceedings of the Second Workshop on Neural Machine Translation*. Association for Computational Linguistics.

Graphene: A Context-Preserving Open Information Extraction System

Matthias Cetto[1], Christina Niklaus[1], André Freitas[2], and **Siegfried Handschuh[1]**

[1] Faculty of Computer Science and Mathematics, University of Passau

`{matthias.cetto, christina.niklaus, siegfried.handschuh}@uni-passau.de`

[2] School of Computer Science, University of Manchester

`andre.freitas@manchester.ac.uk`

Abstract

We introduce Graphene, an Open IE system whose goal is to generate accurate, meaningful and complete propositions that may facilitate a variety of downstream semantic applications. For this purpose, we transform syntactically complex input sentences into clean, compact structures in the form of core facts and accompanying contexts, while identifying the rhetorical relations that hold between them in order to maintain their semantic relationship. In that way, we preserve the context of the relational tuples extracted from a source sentence, generating a novel lightweight semantic representation for Open IE that enhances the expressiveness of the extracted propositions.

1 Introduction

Information Extraction (IE) is the task of turning the unstructured information expressed in natural language (NL) text into a structured representation in the form of relational tuples consisting of a set of arguments and a phrase denoting a semantic relation between them: $\langle arg1; rel; arg2 \rangle$. Unlike traditional IE methods, Open IE is not limited to a small set of target relations known in advance, but rather extracts all types of relations found in a text. In that way, it facilitates the domain-independent discovery of relations extracted from text and scales to large, heterogeneous corpora such as the Web. Since its introduction by Banko et al. (2007), a large body of work on the task of Open IE has been described. By analyzing the output of state-of-the-art systems (e.g., (Mausam et al., 2012; Del Corro and Gemulla, 2013; Angeli et al., 2015)), we observed three common shortcomings.

First, relations often span over long nested structures or are presented in a non-canonical form that cannot be easily captured by a small set of extraction patterns. Therefore, such relations are commonly missed by state-of-the-art approaches. Second, current Open IE systems tend to extract propositions with long argument phrases that can be further decomposed into meaningful propositions, with each of them representing a separate fact. Overly specific constituents that mix multiple - potentially semantically unrelated - propositions are difficult to handle for downstream applications, such as question answering (QA) or textual entailment tasks. Instead, such approaches benefit from extractions that are as compact as possible. Third, state-of-the-art Open IE systems lack the expressiveness needed to properly represent complex assertions, resulting in incomplete, uninformative or incoherent propositions that have no meaningful interpretation or miss critical information asserted in the input sentence.

To overcome these limitations, we developed an Open IE framework called "Graphene" that transforms syntactically complex NL sentences into clean, compact structures that present a canonical form which facilitates the extraction of accurate, meaningful and complete propositions. The contributions of our work are two-fold. First, to remove the complexity of determining intricate predicate-argument structures with variable arity from syntactically complex input sentences, we propose a two-layered transformation process consisting of a clausal and phrasal disembedding layer. It removes clauses and phrases that convey no central information from the input and converts them into independent context sentences, thereby reducing the source sentence to its main information. In that way, the input

Proceedings of the 27th International Conference on Computational Linguistics: System Demonstrations, pages 94–98
Santa Fe, New Mexico, USA, August 20-26, 2018.

is transformed into a **novel hierarchical representation in the form of core facts and accompanying contexts**. Second, we **identify the rhetorical relations by which core sentences and their associated contexts are connected in order to preserve their semantic relationship**. These two innovations enable us to enrich extracted relational tuples of the form $\langle arg1; rel; arg2 \rangle$ with contextual information that further specifies the tuple and to establish semantic links between them, resulting in a novel lightweight semantic representation for Open IE that provides highly informative extractions and thus supports their interpretability in downstream applications. The source code is available at `https://github.com/Lambda-3/Graphene`.

2   The System in a Nutshell

Graphene makes use of a two-layered transformation stage consisting of a clausal and phrasal disembedding layer, which is followed by a final relation extraction (RE) stage. It takes a text document as an input and returns a set of semantically typed and interconnected relational tuples. The workflow of our approach is displayed in Figure 1.

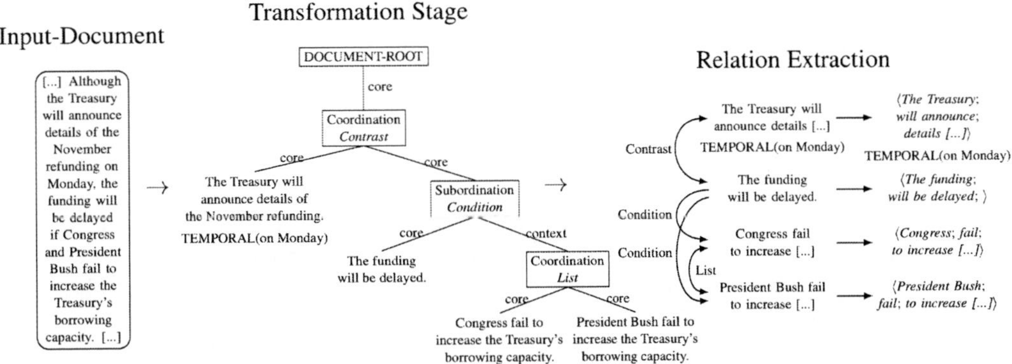

Figure 1: Extraction workflow for an example sentence.

2.1   Transformation Stage

During the transformation process, source sentences that present a complex linguistic structure are converted into a hierarchical representation of core facts and associated contexts that are connected by rhetorical relations capturing their semantic relationship similar to Rhetorical Structure Theory (RST) (Mann and Thompson, 1988). These compact, syntactically sound structures ease the problem of recognizing predicate-argument relations that are contained in the input without losing their semantic dependencies.

Clausal Disembedding.   In the clausal disembedding layer, we split up complex multi-clause sentences that are composed of *coordinated* and *subordinated clauses*, *relative clauses*, or *attributions* into simpler, stand-alone sentences that contain one clause each. This is done in a recursive fashion so that we obtain a hierarchical structure of the transformation process comparable to the diagrams used in RST. As opposed to RST, however, the transformation process is carried out in a top-down fashion, starting with the input document and using a set of hand-crafted syntactic rule patterns that define how to split up, transform and recurse on complex syntactic patterns[1]. Each split will create two or more simplified sentences that are connected with information about (1) their constituency type depicting their semantic relevance (*coordinate* or *subordinate*) and (2) the rhetorical relation that holds between them. The constituency type infers the concept of nuclearity from RST, where coordinate sentences (which we call *core sentences*) represent nucleus spans that embody the central part of information, while subordinate sentences (*context sentences*) represent satellite spans that provide background information on the nucleus. The classification of the rhetorical relations is based on both syntactic and lexical features. While

---

[1]The complete rule set can be found online: `https://github.com/Lambda-3/Graphene/blob/master/wiki/supplementary/syntactic-simplification-patterns.pdf`

former are manifested in the phrasal composition of a sentence's phrasal parse tree, latter rely on a set of manually defined cue phrases. In this way, a hierarchical tree representation of the recursive transformation process for the whole document is constructed which we denote as *discourse tree*. Its leaf nodes represent the simplified sentences that were generated during the clausal disembedding layer.

Phrasal Disembedding. After recursively dividing multi-clause sentences into stand-alone sentences that contain one clause each, they are further simplified on a phrasal level. For this purpose, sentences are processed separately and transformed into simpler structures by extracting the following phrasal components from the input: *prepositional phrases, participial phrases, adjectival/adverbial phrases, appositive phrases, lead noun phrases, coordinations of verb phrases, enumerations of noun phrases* and *purposes*. This task is assisted by the sentence simplification system described in Niklaus et al. (2016).

2.2 Relation Extraction

After the transformation stage, RE is performed by using the simplified sentences as an input. The framework is designed to accept any type of RE implementation which is able to extract relational tuples from single sentences. The identified rhetorical relations from the transformation stage are then mapped to the corresponding relational tuples in the form of simple and linked contextual arguments (see Section 3). As a result, different approaches for RE can be complemented with contextual information that further specifies the extracted relational tuples. In that way, a new layer of semantics is added to the task of RE that can be used in other NLP tasks (see Section 6).

3 Output Format

In order to represent contextual relations between propositions, the default representation of a relational tuple of the form $\langle arg1; rel; arg2 \rangle$ needs to be extended. Therefore, we present a novel lightweight semantic representation for Open IE that is both machine processable and human readable. It extends a binary subject-predicate-object tuple $t \leftarrow (rel, arg_{subj}, arg_{obj})$ with: a unique identifier id; information about the contextual hierarchy, the so-called *context-layer* cl; and two sets of semantically classified contextual arguments C_S (*simple contextual arguments*) and C_L (*linked contextual arguments*), yielding the final representation of (id, cl, t, C_S, C_L) tuples. The *context-layer* cl encodes the contextual hierarchy of core and contextual facts. Propositions with a context-layer of 0 carry the core information of a sentence, whereas propositions with a context-layer of $cl > 0$ provide contextual information about propositions with a context-layer of $cl - 1$. Both types of contextual arguments C_S and C_L provide (semantically classified) contextual information about the statement expressed in t. Whereas a simple contextual argument $c_S \in C_S, c_S \leftarrow (s, r)$ contains a textual expression s that is classified by the semantic relation r, a linked contextual argument $c_L \in C_L, c_L \leftarrow (id(z), r)$ refers to the content expressed in another proposition z.

To facilitate the inspection of the extracted propositions, a human-readable format, called *RDF-NL*, is generated by Graphene (see Figure 2). In this format, propositions are grouped by sentences in which they occur and are represented by tab-separated strings for the identifier id, context-layer cl and the core extraction that is represented by the binary relational tuple $t \leftarrow (rel, arg_{subj}, arg_{obj})$: subject argument arg_{subj}, relation name r and object argument arg_{obj}. Contextual arguments (C_S and C_L) are indicated by an extra indentation level to their parent tuples. The representation of a contextual argument consists of a type string and a tab-separated content. The type string encodes both the context type (S for a simple contextual argument $c_S \in C_S$ and L for a linked contextual argument $c_L \in C_L$) and the classified semantic relation (e.g. *Cause, Purpose*), if present. The content of a simple contextual argument is the textual expression, whereas the content of a linked contextual argument is the identifier of the target proposition.

Besides, the framework can materialize its relations into a graph serialized under the N-Triples[2] specification of the Resource Description Framework (RDF) standard. In that way, the consumption of the extracted relations by downstream applications is facilitated. A detailed description as well as some examples of the machine-readable RDF format are available online[3].

---

[2]https://www.w3.org/TR/n-triples
[3]https://github.com/Lambda-3/Graphene/blob/master/wiki/RDF-Format.md

```
Although the Treasury will announce details of the November refunding on Monday, the funding
will be delayed if Congress and President Bush fail to increase the Treasury's borrowing capacity.

#1    0    the Treasury     will announce     details of the November refunding
   S:TEMPORAL      on Monday
   L:CONTRAST        #2

#2    0    the funding     will be delayed
   L:CONTRAST        #1
   L:CONDITION       #3
   L:CONDITION       #4

#3    1    Congress      fail    to increase the Treasury 's borrowing capacity

#4    1    president Bush    fail    to increase the Treasury 's borrowing capacity
```

Figure 2: Proposed representation format (RDF-NL) - human readable representation.

4 Usage

Graphene can be either used as a Java API, imported as a Maven dependency, or as a service which we provide through a command line interface or a REST-like web service that can be deployed via docker. A demonstration video is available online[4].

5 Benchmarking

We evaluated the performance of our Open IE system Graphene using the benchmark framework proposed in Stanovsky and Dagan (2016), which is based on a QA-Semantic Role Labeling corpus with more than 10,000 extractions over 3,200 sentences from Wikipedia and the Wall Street Journal[5]. This benchmark allowed us to compare our framework with a set of state-of-the-art Open IE approaches in recall and precision (see Figure 3). With a score of 50.1% in average precision, Graphene achieves the best performance of all the systems in extracting accurate tuples. Considering recall, our framework (27.2%) is able to compete with the best-performing baseline approaches (32.5% and 33.0%). The interested reader can refer to Cetto et al. (2018) for more details.

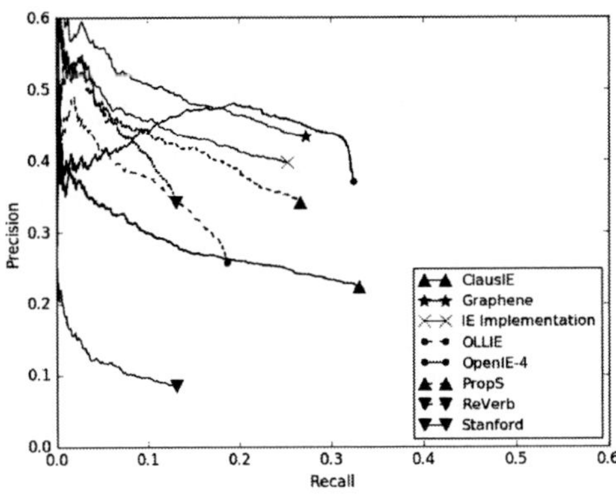

Figure 3: Performance of Graphene.

6 Application Scenarios of the Lightweight Semantic Open IE representation

The resulting lightweight semantic representation of the source text in the form of a two-layered hierarchy of semantically-linked relational tuples can be used to facilitate a variety of artificial intelligence tasks, such as building QA systems, creating text summarization applications or supporting semantic inferences.

For example, QA systems could build upon the semantically typed and interconnected relational tuples produced by our Open IE system Graphene to investigate the dependencies between extracted propositions (such as causalities, attributions and local or temporal contexts) and map specific question types to the corresponding semantic relationships when querying the underlying data. Based on the example given in Figure 2, one can imagine the following user query:

<u>*Under which circumstances*</u> *will the funding be delayed?*

Here, the system could infer from the interrogative expression *"Under which circumstances?"* to search for propositions that are linked to the extraction stating that ⟨*the funding*; *will be delayed*; ∅⟩

---

[4] https://asciinema.org/a/bvhgIP8ZEgDwtmRPFctHyxALu?speed=3
[5] available under https://github.com/gabrielStanovsky/oie-benchmark

by a conditional (CONDITION) relation. Accordingly, in this scenario the system is expected to return propositions #3 and #4 of Figure 2.

7   Conclusion

We presented Graphene, an Open IE system that transforms sentences which present a complex linguistic structure into a novel hierarchical representation in the form of core facts and accompanying contexts which are connected by rhetorical relations capturing their semantic relationship. In that way, the input text is turned into clean, compact structures that show a canonical form, thus facilitating the extraction of accurate, meaningful and complete propositions based on a novel lightweight semantic representation consisting of a set of semantically typed and interconnected relational tuples. In the future, we aim to port this idea to languages other than English.

References

Gabor Angeli, Melvin Jose Johnson Premkumar, and Christopher D. Manning. 2015. Leveraging linguistic structure for open domain information extraction. In *Proceedings of the 53rd Annual Meeting of the Association for Computational Linguistics and the 7th International Joint Conference on Natural Language Processing*, pages 344–354. ACL.

Michele Banko, Michael J. Cafarella, Stephen Soderland, Matt Broadhead, and Oren Etzioni. 2007. Open information extraction from the web. In *Proceedings of the 20th International Joint Conference on Artifical Intelligence*, pages 2670–2676. Morgan Kaufmann Publishers Inc.

Matthias Cetto, Christina Niklaus, André Freitas, and Siegfried Handschuh. 2018. Graphene: Semantically-linked propositions in open information extraction. In *Prooceedings of COLING 2018. To appear.*

Luciano Del Corro and Rainer Gemulla. 2013. Clausie: Clause-based open information extraction. In *Proceedings of the 22Nd International Conference on World Wide Web*, pages 355–366. ACM.

William C Mann and Sandra A Thompson. 1988. Rhetorical structure theory: Toward a functional theory of text organization. *Text-Interdisciplinary Journal for the Study of Discourse*, 8(3):243–281.

Mausam, Michael Schmitz, Stephen Soderland, Robert Bart, and Oren Etzioni. 2012. Open language learning for information extraction. In *Proceedings of the 2012 Joint Conference on Empirical Methods in Natural Language Processing and Computational Natural Language Learning*, pages 523–534. ACL.

Christina Niklaus, Bernhard Bermeitinger, Siegfried Handschuh, and André Freitas. 2016. A sentence simplification system for improving relation extraction. In *Proceedings of COLING 2016: System Demonstrations.*

Gabriel Stanovsky and Ido Dagan. 2016. Creating a large benchmark for open information extraction. In *Proceedings of the 2016 Conference on Empirical Methods in Natural Language Processing (EMNLP)*. ACL.

LanguageNet: Learning to Find Sense Relevant Example Sentences

Shang-Chien Cheng[1]**, Jhih-Jie Chen**[2]**, Ching-Yu Yang**[2]**, Jason S. Chang**[2]
[1]Institute of Information Systems and Applications
National Tsing Hua University
[2]Department of Computer Science
National Tsing Hua University
{ashleycheng, jjc, chingyu, jason}@nlplab.cc

Abstract

In this paper, we present a system, *LanguageNet*, which can help second language learners to search for different meanings and usages of a word. We disambiguate word senses based on the pairs of an English word and its corresponding Chinese translations in a parallel corpus, UM-Corpus. The process involved performing word alignment, learning vector space representations of words and training a classifier to distinguish words into groups of senses. *LanguageNet* directly shows the definition of a sense, bilingual synonyms and sense relevant examples.

1 Introduction

The polysemy of words, namely words with more than one sense, is one of the major challenges for English as a Second or Other Language (ESOL) learners. The issue of disambiguating polysemous words has attracted considerable attention to the NLP community. In order to derive and provide information about word senses, large knowledge based semantic lexicons have been developed, such as WordNet (Miller, 1995) and *BabelNet* (Navigli and Ponzetto, 2012). These resources are useful as a sense inventory for many NLP tasks. However, these knowledge bases contain few or even no example sentences. Thus, it is important to obtain more sense relevant WordNet examples, which can be more useful for language learners, or for training sense-aware NLP systems. Previous work has pointed out that *"two languages are more informative"* and there is typically *"one sense per translation"*, since different word senses typically translate differently into a foreign language. Intuitively, sense relevant examples could be obtained using parallel corpora to distinguish word sense based on counterpart translations.

For example, the word *"plant"* has at least two different meanings in English: one is ORGANISM and the other is BUILDING, with corresponding Chinese translations 植物 and 工廠. Consider the two senses of the word *"plant"*. The good example for the sense ORGANISM not "The *plant* has 300 workers.", which is irrelevant to the sense, but rather "Rice is a model *plant*". The Chinese translation of the first sentence is "該工廠有300餘名工人。", while the translation for the second sentence is "水稻是用於研究的模式植物。". The two Chinese translations of plant for the sense of building and organism is respectively "工廠" and "植物". Intuitively, by learning the characteristic translations of the category (ORGANISM or BUILDING) of a word sense, we can identify the meaning of head word in the given sentence, and thus retrieving sense relevant examples.

We use Chinese translations of a English head word, HW in a parallel corpus to disambiguate and identify the word sense of HW in WordNet, expected to provide example sentences for different senses of a word. Our approach learns how to effectively classify a word into its intended senses by using a collection of word-translation pairs (e.g., e-HowNet) and a class system based on basic level concepts in WordNet.

The rest of the paper is organized as follows. We review the related work in the next section. Next, we present our method for automatically learning to classify Chinese translations to possible set of senses and expected to provide good examples. Then we introduce the system design and interface. Finally, we exploit the great potential of the system and envision the future works.

Proceedings of the 27th International Conference on Computational Linguistics: System Demonstrations, pages 99–102
Santa Fe, New Mexico, USA, August 20-26, 2018.

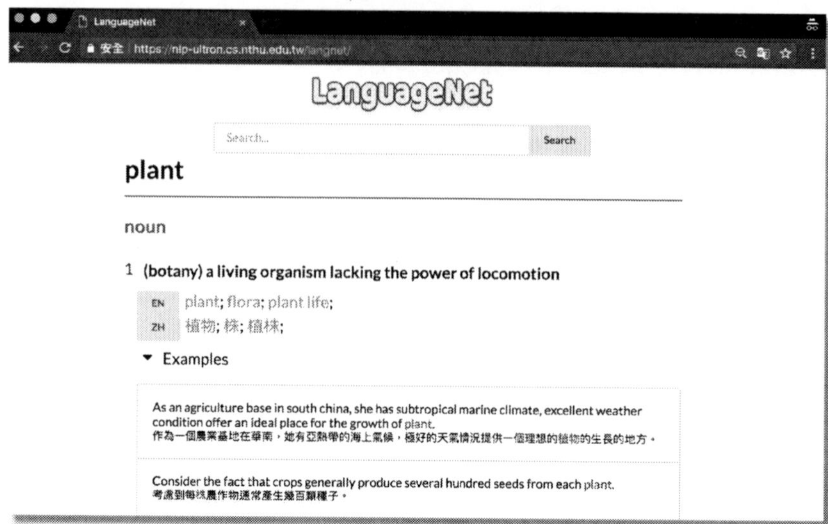

Figure 1: Example using *LanguageNet* typing "plant".

2   Related Work

Word sense disambiguation (WSD) has been an area of active research. WSD involves predicting the intended sense of a word in context based on a predefined set of senses. (Resnik and Yarowsky, 1999) use translate distinctions in the foreign language to identify sense distinctions in the source language for word sense disambiguation.

Recent work (e.g., Guo et al. (2014)), Upadhyay et al. (2017) also use parallel or mutilingual corpora to learn muti-sense vectors and capture different meanings of the same word in word sense disambiguation. In the area of word embedding, Chen et al. (2014) and Iacobacci et al. (2016) propose to use word embeddings instead of surface word as features to improve WSD performance. Yuan et al. (2016) propose to use similarity based on word embedding to identify the intended word sense.

3   Method

Problem Statement: We are given a polysemy W. We want to disambiguating the meaning of a word in sentences from a parallel corpus by providing bilingual examples for different senses of a word. Our goal is to find good examples for a given sense in *WordNet*. For this, we use a word-aligned parallel corpus, and then extract and classify translations for each W in question. Once the translations are classified and sense-tagged, we can then select example sentences for a given word sense.

3.1   Aligning and Extracting Word Translations

We use a large English-Chinese parallel corpus, UM-Corpus to obtain diverse kind of translations of a source-language word (Tian et al., 2014). For this, we use a word aligner, *fast align* (Dyer et al., 2013) to produce word alignments between the source words and translations in a parallel corpus. Then, for every pair of English word and translation, we computes pair similarity based on Dice coefficient and extract and classify translation words which frequently appear together with Dice similarity higher than a threshold. In the final step, we use these pairs of English and Chinese words to select example sentences and generate sense-tagged data.

3.2   Translation Similarity and Sense Labeling

In order to classify a given translation, we need a similarity measure between translations. First, we train a vector space representations of words using *word2vec* (Mikolov et al., 2013) on Chinese Wikipedia. Then, we define sense categories based on WordNet hierarchy (the top-level hypernym), and take a

Table 1: Example of word-translation pairs for training the classifier under two sense categories related to "plant"

Sense Category	Words	Translations
plant	grass, moss, fungus, ginkgo, crop	草類, 苔類, 菌類, 銀杏, 作物
building complex	factory, mill, sander, workshop	廠家, 製造廠, 研磨機, 製造場

Table 2: Result of classification under sense categories and corresponding gloss in WordNet related to the word "plant"

Translations	Sense category	Gloss in WordNet
植物, 植株	Plant	(botany) a living organism lacking the power of locomotion
工廠, 裝置, 廠	Building complex	buildings for carrying on industrial labor

collection of word-translation pairs (W, T) in c (e.g., *E-HowNet*) and assign each translation T to its all possible sense categories of the English word W based on WordNet hierachy and a list of Basic Level Concepts. Since nouns have the explicit hierarchical structure of hypernym relationship in WordNet, we focus on noun senses. Although these (T, CAT) pairs may contain errors, we use them to train a classifier for tagging translations and apply the word embeddings trained with *word2vec* as features. We used 2,442 sense categories of noun based on WordNet concept and take word-translation pairs of 14,991 nouns from the bilingual dictionary for training. Table 1 displays example word-translation pairs for classifying translations related to the two sense categories related to "plant".

3.3 Classifying Chinese Translation to WordNet Senses

To identify the sense of a polysemy and its Chinese translation, we use the support vector machine (SVM) classifier trained on the sense category and translation, as described in the previous subsection. We use only unambiguous words with only one sense category (even when there are more than one WordNet sense). The feature is simply the word embedding of the translation. The output of the model are sense categories with probability and the probable category coinciding with the given English word will be returned as the output. We train a model to predict each sense category based on vector of translation T. If an ambiguous word has two senses, our SVM classifier use the feature vectors generated from training data of these two sense categories to learn a hyperplane which separates these two senses in high dimensional space. Given a translation of the word, the classifier then predict the sense category by its word vector and predict the sense according to the side of the hyperplane the vector lies in. After classification, we convert the category to the relevant sense to the English word belonging to this category. Table 2 displays the result of classification under sense categories and corresponding gloss in WordNet related to the word "plant".

3.4 Selecting example sentences

Finally, the Chinese translations of a English polysemous word which we extracted from corpus are sense-tagged. To help the user quickly and straightforwardly learn the usage for each sense of a word, good examples are really important. Therefore, we adopt the GDEX method (Adam Kilgarriff, 2008) to select representative sentences in candidates with translations of the same sense from the parallel corpus. The GDEX method score sentences by considering sentence length, word frequency, the presence of pronouns, location of the head word, and most importantly collocations.

3.5 *LanguageNet*

Our goal is to disambiguate word sense based on WordNet and provide sense relevant examples for the user using the additional information of Chinese translations of a English polysemy word. The preliminary evaluation shows that the system can predict the relevant sense category with an accuracy rate of over 90% for a set of 12 words used in the WSD evaluation literature. We develop *LanguageNet* as a web application, which can assist second language learners to search for different meanings and usages of a word. We extracted 5,148 nouns in the UM-corpus to disambiguate senses and produce a bilingual word sense dataset for the system. An example *LanguageNet* search for the word "plant" is shown in Figure 1. *LanguageNet* has determined the intended senses of "plant" in sentences by predicting the sense class of the counterpart Chinese translations (e.g., 植物, 工廠, 廠, 植株). *LanguageNet* is accessible at (`http://nlp-ultron.cs.nthu.edu.tw/langnet/`).

4 Conclusion and Future Work

LanguageNet not only shows the definition and synonyms for each sense of a word, but also provides good sense relevant examples for the user. The preliminary assessment shows *LanguageNet* can provide reasonable accurate sense relevant translations and examples to support learning English with learner's native language (e.g., Chinese).

LanguageNet provide the best of the both worlds by combining a dictionary and a concordance to help English learners. Alternatively, the sense-labeled data can also be used by an NLP system to exploit semantic information. As future work, we plan to use the sense-labeled data to improve other WSD tasks and train the sense-specific word embeddings.

References

Katy McAdam Michael Rundell Pavel Rychlý Adam Kilgarriff, Miloš Husák. 2008. Gdex: Automatically finding good dictionary examples in a corpus. In Janet DeCesaris Elisenda Bernal, editor, *Proceedings of the 13th EURALEX International Congress*, pages 425–432, Barcelona, Spain, jul. Institut Universitari de Linguistica Aplicada, Universitat Pompeu Fabra.

Xinxiong Chen, Zhiyuan Liu, and Maosong Sun. 2014. A unified model for word sense representation and disambiguation. In *Proceedings of the 2014 Conference on Empirical Methods in Natural Language Processing (EMNLP)*, pages 1025–1035.

Chris Dyer, Victor Chahuneau, and Noah A Smith. 2013. A simple, fast, and effective reparameterization of ibm model 2. Association for Computational Linguistics.

Jiang Guo, Wanxiang Che, Haifeng Wang, and Ting Liu. 2014. Learning sense-specific word embeddings by exploiting bilingual resources. In *Proceedings of COLING 2014, the 25th International Conference on Computational Linguistics: Technical Papers*, pages 497–507.

Ignacio Iacobacci, Mohammad Taher Pilehvar, and Roberto Navigli. 2016. Embeddings for word sense disambiguation: An evaluation study. In *Proceedings of the 54th Annual Meeting of the Association for Computational Linguistics (Volume 1: Long Papers)*, volume 1, pages 897–907.

Tomas Mikolov, Ilya Sutskever, Kai Chen, Greg S Corrado, and Jeff Dean. 2013. Distributed representations of words and phrases and their compositionality. In *Advances in neural information processing systems*, pages 3111–3119.

George A Miller. 1995. Wordnet: a lexical database for english. *Communications of the ACM*, 38(11):39–41.

Roberto Navigli and Simone Paolo Ponzetto. 2012. Babelnet: The automatic construction, evaluation and application of a wide-coverage multilingual semantic network. *Artificial Intelligence*, 193:217–250.

Philip Resnik and David Yarowsky. 1999. Distinguishing systems and distinguishing senses: New evaluation methods for word sense disambiguation. volume 5, pages 113–133. Cambridge University Press.

Liang Tian, Derek F Wong, Lidia S Chao, Paulo Quaresma, Francisco Oliveira, and Lu Yi. 2014. Um-corpus: A large english-chinese parallel corpus for statistical machine translation. In *LREC*, pages 1837–1842.

Shyam Upadhyay, Kai-Wei Chang, Matt Taddy, Adam Kalai, and James Zou. 2017. Beyond bilingual: Multisense word embeddings using multilingual context. *arXiv preprint arXiv:1706.08160*.

Dayu Yuan, Julian Richardson, Ryan Doherty, Colin Evans, and Eric Altendorf. 2016. Semi-supervised word sense disambiguation with neural models. *arXiv preprint arXiv:1603.07012*.

Automatic Curation and Visualization of Crime Related Information from Incrementally Crawled Multi-source News Reports

Tirthankar Dasgupta, Abir Naskar, Rupsa Saha and **Lipika Dey**

TCS Innovation Lab, India
(dasgupta.tirthankar, abir.naskar, rupsa.s, lipika.dey)@tcs.com

Abstract

In this paper, we demonstrate a system for the automatic extraction and curation of crime-related information from multi-source digitally published News articles collected over a period of five years. We have leveraged the use of deep convolution recurrent neural network model to analyze crime articles to extract different crime related entities and events. The proposed methods are not restricted to detecting known crimes only but contribute actively towards maintaining an updated crime ontology. We have done experiments with a collection of 5000 crime-reporting News articles span over time, and multiple sources. The end-product of our experiments is a crime-register that contains details of crime committed across geographies and time. This register can be further utilized for analytical and reporting purposes.

1 Introduction

News articles from different sources regularly report crime incidents that contain details of crime, information about accused entities, details of the investigation process and finally details of judgment(Westphal, 2008). These details are not all published together, but pour in over time. A curated crime knowledge base with organized information about criminal activities and possible associated criminals is beneficial to a wide variety of end-users(Westphal, 2008; Furtado et al., 2010; Hassani et al., 2016; Arulanandam et al., 2014). While law-enforcers of a region have access to details of crime committed within their own jurisdiction, a shared knowledge-base containing information curated from open sources can be used by them to track criminal activities in other regions(Chau et al., 2002). These knowledge bases are also in demand by financial organizations who want to make use of these profiles to check on the credit-worthiness of a customer. Regulatory agencies also want to use these knowledge bases to verify legal compliance. Crime and corruption, common scourges of modern societies, top the list of problems cited by public entities in emerging and developing nations.

There are many challenges of such automatic information curation. Ensuring verifiability and reliability of information sources is a prime concern for curators. Handling factual variations or contradictions needs intelligent methods for disambiguation. Incremental compiling of facts from sources generated over a period of time also needs efficient entity resolution and linking mechanisms to ensure information continuity. While the present work addresses the later challenges, we do not delve deeper into the issue of information reliability but rather assume that News articles collected from reliable agencies supply authentic information.

The salient features of the demonstration are: a) We have leveraged deep convolution recurrent neural network to extract different crime related entities and events from News documents. This includes, *name of the accused, name of the victim, nature of crime, geographic location, date and time, law enforcement, charges bought, and action taken (if any) against the accused.* b) The model is trained over a dataset of 5000 documents that spans across time, different sources- containing a multiplicity of reporting on particular topics. c) We have done experiments with a collection of 1000 new News articles. The end-product of our experiments is a crime-register that contains details of crime committed across geographies and time. This register can be further utilized for analytical and reporting purposes.

Proceedings of the 27th International Conference on Computational Linguistics: System Demonstrations, pages 103–107
Santa Fe, New Mexico, USA, August 20-26, 2018.

2 System Architecture

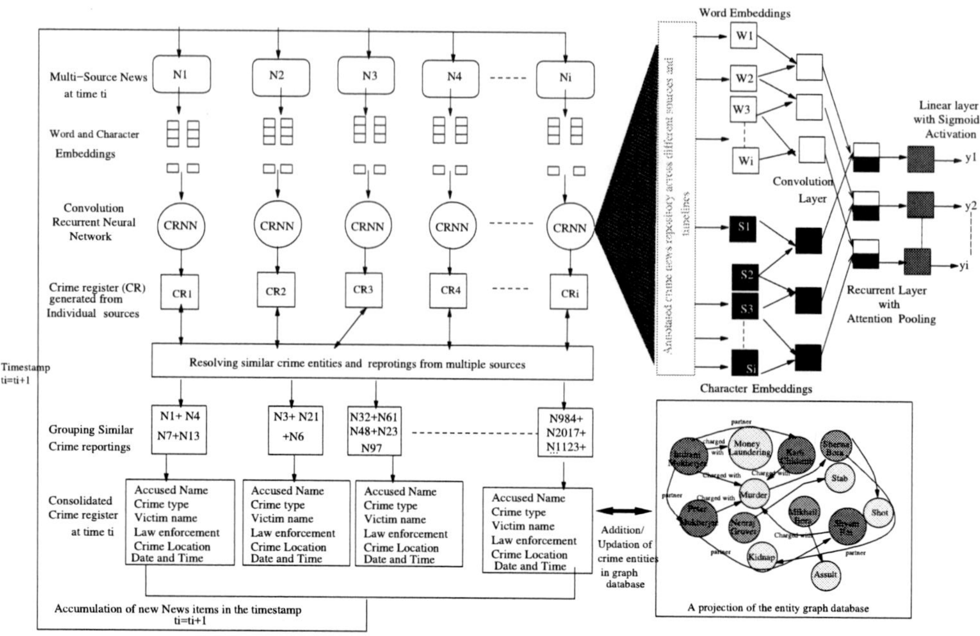

Figure 1: Overview of the crime event and entity extraction architecture.

The overall architecture depicted in Figure 1, consists of seven primary units: a) *Multi-source news accumulation*, b) Crime entity extraction using Convolution Recurrent Neural Network(CRNN) c) Creating *temporary crime registers*, d) *grouping similar crime reporting*, e) Updated *crime register*, and g) Reinforcement mechanism.

Multi-source news accumulation: The proposed system consists of multiple web crawlers that continuously crawls crime news events from 10 different sources in a near runtime manner.

Crime entity extraction using Convolution Recurrent Neural Network(CRNN): Output of the crawlers are passed to the crime entity extraction unit to extract the following crime components: *name of the accused, name of the victim, nature of crime, geographic location, date and time, law enforcement, charges bought, and action taken (if any) against the accused.* The input to the CRNN are a sequence of word and characters embeddings. We use the GloVe word vector representations of dimension 300 (Pennington et al., 2014). Both the word and character embeddings are passed to the convolution layer (CNN). CNNs works best in determining local features from texts. The CNN applies a linear transformation to all K windows in the given sequence of vectors. Given a word representations $X_1, X_2, ...X_l$, the convolution layer first concatenates these vectors to form a vector $\bar{x}$ of length $l.d_{LT}$ and then uses $Conv(\bar{x}) = W.(x) + b$ to calculate the output vector of length d_c. Where, **W** and **b** are the weights that the network learns. The output of the CNN layer is passed to the RNN layer. We have used bidirectional LSTMs (Bi-LSTM) networks that are connected so that both future and past sequence context can be examined. After obtaining the intermediate layers from the Bi-LSTM, we use an attention pooling layer over the sentence representations. The attention pooling helps to acquire the weights of sentence contribution to final quality of the text. This is represented as: $a_i = \tanh(W_a.h_i + b_a)$, $\alpha_i = \frac{e^{w_\alpha.a_i}}{\sum e^{w_\alpha.a_i}}$, $O = \sum(\alpha_i.h_i)$. Where W_a, w_α are weight matrix and vector respectively, b_a is the bias vector, a_i is attention vector for i-th sentence, and α_i is the attention weight of i-th sentence. We apply a sigmoid function to limit the possible scores to the range $[0, 1]$. The mapping of the linear layer after applying the sigmoid activation function is given by $s(x) = sigmoid(w.x + b)$. Where, x is the input vector, w is the weight vector, and b is bias value.

Creating crime register for individual news sources: Once the target components are extracted, we create a temporary crime register of crime entities extracted from each of the individual source news items. Figure 2 and Figure 3 illustrates the basic working of the crime extraction tool. In the left panel of Figure 2, there are series of news headline corresponding to a particular date. Once a headline is selected, the corresponding news details are displayed in the middle panel. Corresponding to the detailed news all the respective crime entities and events were extracted and labeled in different colors. There are number of instances where the same crime event is reported in multiple news sources in different ways. There are also issues related to information richness of one source as compared to other. In particular we have observed that regional news sources cover deeper information rather than nationalized news sources. In addition to this there are severe issues related to entity resolution both within the document as well as outside the document. For example, *"Sailesh Patel"* may be referred as *"Sailesh"* or *"Patel"* in other articles. In order to resolve such entities, we have used the BMI measure as discussed in (Lau et al., 2008; Lau et al., 2009). Also, resolution of such named entities help grouping similar crime reporting together. Thus, it is also important to ensemble information across different news sources together and construct a unified knowledge representation.

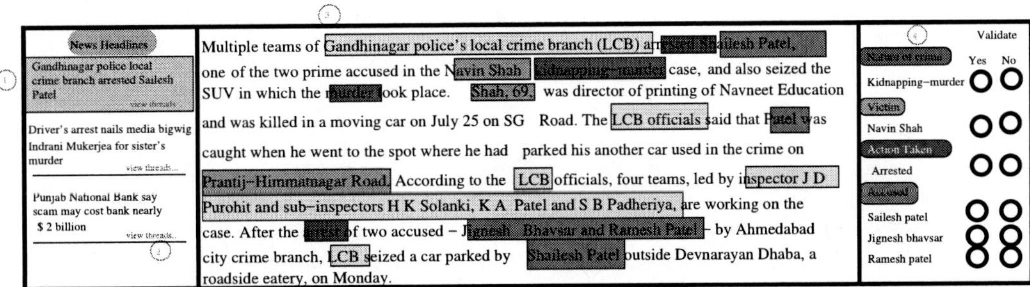

Figure 2: Working of the crime extraction module. The extracted labels are marked in color.

Tracking new progress and outcomes: As discussed earlier, all the details of a crime incident are not published together, but gradually reported over time. This may span between days to months to year. Over the time information regarding the crime incident changes and new outcomes emerges. For example, in Figure 2 our system demonstrates how a particular crime incident about "Sheena Bora murder case" changes over time with new accused names, crime type and victims. Therefore, it becomes extremely difficult for a curator to manually keep track of all the records form the past repositories. With respect to this, the present system plays an important role in automatically identifying, tracking, and maintaining crime incidents that last over years. Once the crime entities of similar crime reports are grouped together, the entities along with their relations are then stored in an crime ontological structure. If a new entity arrives, then the corresponding ontology along with its relations will be updated in the repository.

As discussed earlier, the proposed system in mainly developed to assist analysts and knowledge workers for exploring, reviewing and visualize textual data. With respect to this an important feature of the proposed system is its ability to adapt based on the users feedback. For example, in Figure 2 the system provides option to the user to change the system predicted outputs. Based on the users output, the system has the capability to retrain its classification and extraction model. This in turn help create new and enriched models.

2.1 Experimentation and Evaluation

In order to evaluate, we took another set of 1000 news articles from 3 different sources over the period of five years. Each of the articles were manually annotated by a group of experts. The annotation process involves identifying the major crime components as discussed earlier. The system is evaluated by comparing its output with that of the expert annotations. We quantify the performance score in terms of the precision(P), recall(Re), and F-measure(F). Table 1 reports the comparison of performance of

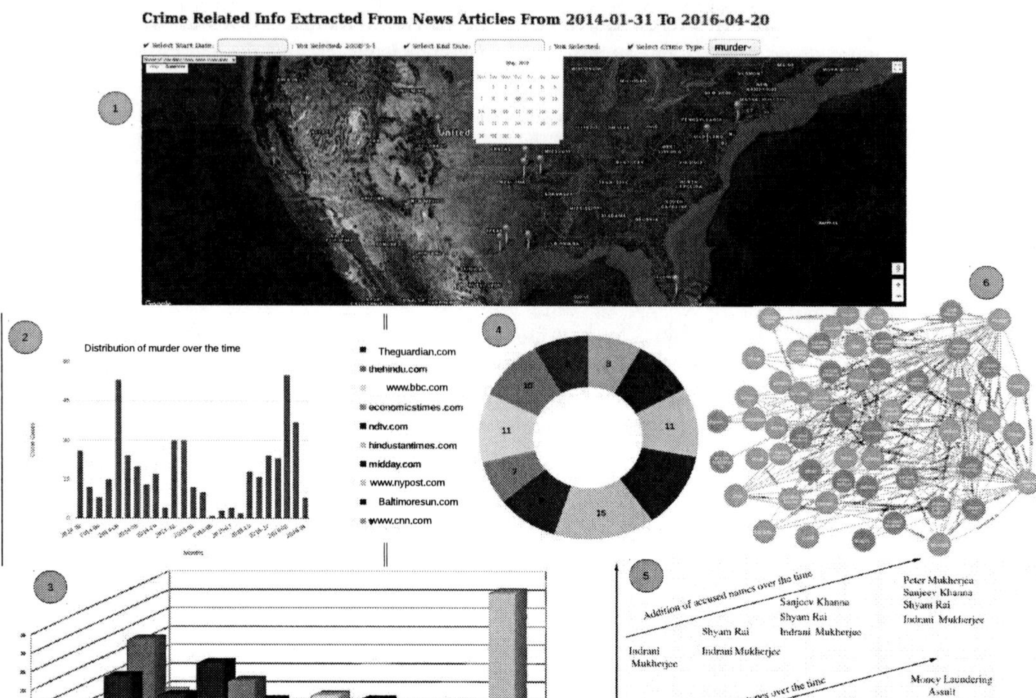

Figure 3: Working of the visualization tool. (1) display a map view that projects distribution of crime across geographical regions. (2) displays distribution of a particular crime over the years (3) shows distribution of crime over geographic region. (5) shows an illustration of a particular news where how crime information changes over time. (6) displays a projection of crime entity knowledge graph constructed from the raw news documents over the past five years.

Table 1: Comparing the F-measure score of different crime entity extraction models.

	Accused	Crime type	Location	Victim	law enforcement	Action taken	Charges
CNN	69	74	68	58	69	59	73
RNN	73	72	63	67	55	62	76
CRNN	77	71	73	67	72	68	81

the CRNN model with respect to other baseline models like, CNN based model, RNN model and our proposed CRNN model. For the sake of space we have reported only the F-measure scores.

References

Rexy Arulanandam, Bastin Tony Roy Savarimuthu, and Maryam A Purvis. 2014. Extracting crime information from online newspaper articles. In *Proceedings of the Second Australasian Web Conference-Volume 155*, pages 31–38. Australian Computer Society, Inc.

Michael Chau, Jennifer J Xu, and Hsinchun Chen. 2002. Extracting meaningful entities from police narrative reports. In *Proceedings of the 2002 annual national conference on Digital government research*, pages 1–5. Digital Government Society of North America.

Vasco Furtado, Leonardo Ayres, Marcos De Oliveira, Eurico Vasconcelos, Carlos Caminha, Johnatas DOrleans, and Mairon Belchior. 2010. Collective intelligence in law enforcement–the wikicrimes system. *Information Sciences*, 180(1):4–17.

Hossein Hassani, Xu Huang, Emmanuel S Silva, and Mansi Ghodsi. 2016. A review of data mining applications in crime. *Statistical Analysis and Data Mining: The ASA Data Science Journal*, 9(3):139–154.

Raymond YK Lau, Peter D Bruza, and Dawei Song. 2008. Towards a belief-revision-based adaptive and context-sensitive information retrieval system. *ACM Transactions on Information Systems (TOIS)*, 26(2):8.

Raymond YK Lau, Dawei Song, Yuefeng Li, Terence CH Cheung, and Jin-Xing Hao. 2009. Toward a fuzzy domain ontology extraction method for adaptive e-learning. *IEEE transactions on knowledge and data engineering*, 21(6):800–813.

Jeffrey Pennington, Richard Socher, and Christopher Manning. 2014. Glove: Global vectors for word representation. In *Empirical Methods in Natural Language Processing (EMNLP)*.

Christopher Westphal. 2008. *Data Mining for Intelligence, Fraud & Criminal Detection: Advanced Analytics & Information Sharing Technologies*. CRC Press.

Lingke: A Fine-grained Multi-turn Chatbot for Customer Service

Pengfei Zhu[1,2,4], Zhuosheng Zhang[1,2], Jiangtong Li[1,2,3], Yafang Huang[1,2], Hai Zhao[1,2,†]
[1]Department of Computer Science and Engineering,
Shanghai Jiao Tong University, China
[2]Key Laboratory of Shanghai Education Commission for Intelligent Interaction
and Cognitive Engineering, Shanghai Jiao Tong University, Shanghai, 200240, China
[3]College of Zhiyuan, Shanghai Jiao Tong University, China
[4]School of Computer Science and Software Engineering, East China Normal University, China
`10152510190@stu.ecnu.edu.cn`, {`zhangzs, keep_moving-lee`}`@sjtu.edu.cn`,
`huangyafang@sjtu.edu.cn`, `zhaohai@cs.sjtu.edu.cn`

Abstract

Traditional chatbots usually need a mass of human dialogue data, especially when using supervised machine learning method. Though they can easily deal with single-turn question answering, for multi-turn the performance is usually unsatisfactory. In this paper, we present Lingke, an information retrieval augmented chatbot which is able to answer questions based on given product introduction document and deal with multi-turn conversations. We will introduce a fine-grained pipeline processing to distill responses based on unstructured documents, and attentive sequential context-response matching for multi-turn conversations.

1 Introduction

Recently, dialogue and interactive systems have been emerging with huge commercial values (Qiu et al., 2017; Yan et al., 2016a; Zhang et al., 2017; Huang et al., 2018; Zhang et al., 2018b; Zhang et al., 2018a), especially in the e-commerce field (Cui et al., 2017; Yan et al., 2016b). Building a chatbot mainly faces two challenges, the lack of dialogue data and poor performance for multi-turn conversations. This paper describes a fine-grained information retrieval (IR) augmented multi-turn chatbot - Lingke. It can learn knowledge without human supervision from conversation records or given product introduction documents and generate proper response, which alleviates the problem of lacking dialogue corpus to train a chatbot. First, by using *Apache Lucene*[1] to select top 2 sentences most relevant to the question and extracting subject-verb-object (SVO) triples from them, a set of candidate responses is generated. With regard to multi-turn conversations, we adopt a dialogue manager, including self-attention strategy to distill significant signal of utterances, and sequential utterance-response matching to connect responses with conversation utterances, which outperforms all other models in multi-turn response selection. An online demo is available via accessing `http://47.96.2.5:8080/ServiceBot/demo/`.

2 Architecture

This section presents the architecture of Lingke, which is overall shown in Figure 1.

The technical components include 1) coreference resolution and document separation, 2) target sentences retrieval, 3) candidate responses generation, followed by a dialouge manager including 4) self-matching attention, 5) response selection and 6) chit-chat response generation.

The first three steps aim at selecting candidate responses, and in the remaining steps, we utilize sentences from previous conversations to select the most proper response. For multi-turn conversation modeling, we develop a dialogue manager which employs self-matching attention strategy and sequential utterance-response matching to distill pivotal information from the redundant context and determine the most proper response from the candidates.

---

† Corresponding author. This paper was partially supported by National Key Research and Development Program of China (No. 2017YFB0304100), National Natural Science Foundation of China (No. 61672343 and No. 61733011), Key Project of National Society Science Foundation of China (No. 15-ZDA041), The Art and Science Interdisciplinary Funds of Shanghai Jiao Tong University (No. 14JCRZ04).

[1]`http://lucene.apache.org`

Proceedings of the 27th International Conference on Computational Linguistics: System Demonstrations, pages 108–112
Santa Fe, New Mexico, USA, August 20-26, 2018.

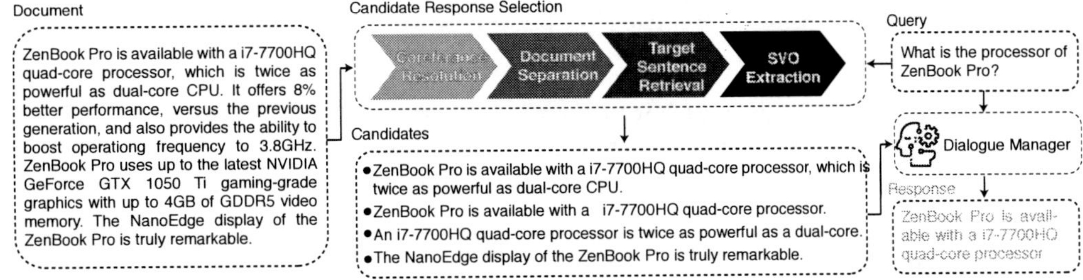

Figure 1: Architecture of Lingke.

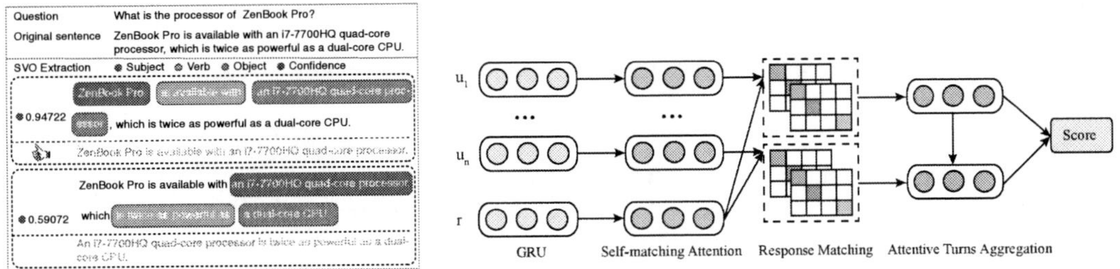

Figure 2: Example of SVO Extraction.

Figure 3: Structure overview of the dialogue manager.

Coreference Resolution and Document Separation   Since the response is usually supposed to be concise and coherent, we first separate a given document into sentences. However, long documents commonly involve complex reference relations. A direct segmentation might result in severe information loss. So before the separation, we used *Stanford CoreNLP* (Manning et al., 2014) [2] to accomplish the coreference resolution. After the resolution, we cut the document into sentences $A = \{A_1, A_2, ..., A_n\}$.

Target Sentences Retrieval   There is abundant information in the whole document, but what current message cares about just exists in some paragraphs or even sentences. So before precise processing, we need to roughly select sentences which are relevant with the current message. We used *Apache Lucene* to accomplish the retrieval. Given sentence collection A from step 1, we retrieve k relevant sentences $E = \{E_1, E_2, ..., E_k\}$. In our system, the value of k is 2.

Candidate Responses Generation   Generally, the response to a conversation can be expressed as a simple sentence, even a few of words. However, sentences from a product introduction document are usually complicated with much information. To extract SVO, we used an open information extraction framework ReVerb (Fader et al., 2011), which is able to recognize more than one group of SVO triples (including triples from the clauses). Figure 2 shows an example. Based on an utterance E_i from E, we extract its SVO triples $E_s = \{E_{s1}, E_{s2}, ..., E_{sn}\}$, $E_v = \{E_{v1}, E_{v2}, ..., E_{vn}\}$, $E_o = \{E_{o1}, E_{o2}, ..., E_{on}\}$, and by concatenating each triple, we obtain multiple of simple sentences $T = \{T_1, T_2, ..., T_n\}$.

The above first three steps generate all sentences and phrases as candidate responses, which are denoted as $R = E \cup T$. What we need to do next is to rerank the candidates for the most proper response.

Dialogue Manager   We combined self-matching attention strategy and sequential utterance-response matching to develop a multi-turn dialogue manager. Figure 3 shows the structure.

(1) Self-matching Attention   Since not all of the information is useful, it is a natural thought that adopts self-matching attention strategy to filter redundant information. Before that, we transform raw dialogue data into word embedding (Mikolov et al., 2013) firstly. Each conversation utterance or candidate

---

[2] https://stanfordnlp.github.io/CoreNLP/index.html

response is fed to the gated recurrent units (GRUs) (Cho et al., 2014). Then, we adopt a self-matching attention strategy (Wang et al., 2017) to directly match each utterance or response against itself to distill the pivotal information and filter irrelevant pieces.

(2) Response Selection   Following Sequential Matching Network (SMN) (Wu et al., 2017), we employ sequential matching for multi-turn response selection. Given the candidate response set, it matches each response with the conversation utterances in chronological order and obtains accumulated matching score of the utterance-response pairs to capture significant information and relations among utterances and each candidate response. The one with highest matching score is selected as final response.

(3) Chit-chat Response Generation   When given a question irrelevant to current introduction document, *Target Sentences Retrieval* may fail, so we adopt a chit-chat engine to give response when the matching scores of all the candidate responses are below the threshold which is empirically set to 0.3. The chit-chat model is an attention-based seq2seq model (Sutskever et al., 2014) achieved by a generic deep learning framework *OpenNMT*[3]. The model is trained on twitter conversation data, which has 370K query-reply pairs, and 300K non-duplicate pairs are selected for training.

3   Experiment

Dataset   We evaluate Lingke on a dataset from our *Taobao*[4] partners, which is a collection of conversation records between customers and customer service staffs. It contains over five kinds of conversations, including chit-chat, product and discount consultation, querying delivery progress and after-sales feedback. We converted it into the structured multi-turn format as in (Lowe et al., 2015; Wu et al., 2017). The training set has 1 million multi-turn dialogues totally, and 10K respectively in validation and test set.

	TF-IDF	RNN	CNN	LSTM	BiLSTM	Multi-View	SMN	Our model
$R_{10}@1$	0.159	0.325	0.328	0.365	0.355	0.421	0.453	**0.476**
$R_{10}@2$	0.256	0.463	0.515	0.536	0.525	0.601	0.654	**0.672**
$R_{10}@5$	0.477	0.775	0.792	0.828	0.825	0.861	0.886	**0.893**

Table 1: Comparison of different models.

Evaluation   Our model is compared with recent single-turn and multi-turn models, of which the former are in (Kadlec et al., 2015; Lowe et al., 2015) including TF-IDF, Convolutional Neural Network (CNN), Recurrent Neural Network (RNN), LSTM and biLSTM. These models concatenate the context utterances together to match a response. Multi-view model (Zhou et al., 2016) models utterance relationships from word sequence view and utterance sequence view, and Sequential Matching Network (Wu et al., 2017) matches a response with each utterance in the context. We implemented all the models following the same hyper-parameters from corresponding literatures (Wu et al., 2017; Lowe et al., 2015). Our evaluation is based on Recall at position k in n candidates ($Rn@k$). Results in Table 1 show that our model outperforms all other models, indicating filtering redundant information within utterances could improve the performance and relationships among utterances and response can not be neglected.

4   Usability and Analysis

In this section, we will discuss the usability of Lingke. In situation of lacking enough dialogue data such as when a new product is put on an online shop, Lingke only needs an introduction document to respond to customers. Because of the chit-chat response generation engine, Lingke can easily deal with any commodity-independent conversations. Thanks to our multi-turn model, Lingke will not get confused when customer gives incomplete questions which need to be understood based on context.

Figure 4-5 show two typical application scenarios of Lingke, namely, *conversation record based* and *document-based* ones, which vary based on the training corpus. Figure 4 shows Linke can effectively respond to the customer shopping consultations. The customer sends a product link and then Lingke

---

[3] http://opennmt.net/OpenNMT
[4] It's the largest e-commerce platform in China. https://www.taobao.com.

Figure 4: A conversation record based example. | Figure 5: A document-based example.

recognizes it, and when the customer asks production specifications Lingke will give responses based on information from the context and the conversation record. Figure 5 shows a typical scenario when a customer consults Lingke about a new product. The customer starts with a greeting, which is answered by chit-chat engine. Then the customer asks certain features of a product. Note that the second response comes from a sentence which has a redundant clause, and main information the customer cares about has been extracted. In the third user utterance, words like "What" and "ZenBook Pro" are omitted, which can be deducted from the prior question. Such pivotal information from the context is distilled and utilized to determine proper response with the merit of self-matching attention and multi-turn modeling.

The user utterances of examples in this paper and our online demo are relatively simple and short, which usually aim at only one feature of the product. In some cases, when the customer utterance becomes more complex, for example, focusing on more than one feature of the product, Lingke may fail to give complete response. A possible solution is to concatenate two relevant candidate responses, but the key to the problem is to determine the intents of the customer.

5   Conclusion

We have presented a fine-grained information retrieval augmented chatbot for multi-turn conversations. In this paper, we took e-commerce product introduction as example, but our solution will not be limited to this domain. In our future work, we will add the mechanism of intent detection, and try to find solutions of how to deal with introduction document that contains more than one object.

References

Kyunghyun Cho, Bart Van Merrienboer, Caglar Gulcehre, Dzmitry Bahdanau, Fethi Bougares, Holger Schwenk, and Yoshua Bengio. 2014. Learning phrase representations using RNN encoder-decoder for statistical machine translation. In *EMNLP 2014*, pages 1724–1734.

Lei Cui, Shaohan Huang, Furu Wei, Chuanqi Tan, Chaoqun Duan, and Ming Zhou. 2017. Superagent: A customer service chatbot for e-commerce websites. In *ACL 2017, Demo*, pages 97–102.

Anthony Fader, Stephen Soderland, and Oren Etzioni. 2011. Identifying relations for open information extraction. In *EMNLP 2011*, Edinburgh, Scotland, UK, July 27-31.

Yafang Huang, Zuchao Li, Zhuosheng Zhang, and Hai Zhao. 2018. Moon IME: neural-based chinese pinyin aided input method with customizable association. In *Proceedings of the 56th Annual Meeting of the Association for Computational Linguistics (ACL 2018), System Demonstration*.

Rudolf Kadlec, Martin Schmid, and Jan Kleindienst. 2015. Improved deep learning baselines for Ubuntu corpus dialogs. *arXiv preprint arXiv:1510.03753*.

Ryan Lowe, Nissan Pow, Iulian Serban, and Joelle Pineau. 2015. The Ubuntu Dialogue Corpus: A large dataset for research in unstructured multi-turn dialogue systems. In *SIGDIAL 2015*, pages 285–294.

Christopher D. Manning, Mihai Surdeanu, John Bauer, Jenny Finkel, Steven J. Bethard, and David McClosky. 2014. The Stanford CoreNLP natural language processing toolkit. In *ACL 2014, Demo*, pages 55–60.

Tomas Mikolov, Kai Chen, Greg Corrado, and Jeffrey Dean. 2013. Efficient estimation of word representations in vector space. *arXiv preprint arXiv:1301.3781*.

Minghui Qiu, Feng Lin Li, Siyu Wang, Xing Gao, Yan Chen, Weipeng Zhao, Haiqing Chen, Jun Huang, and Wei Chu. 2017. Alime chat: A sequence to sequence and rerank based chatbot engine. In *ACL 2017*, pages 498–503.

Ilya Sutskever, Oriol Vinyals, and Quoc V Le. 2014. Sequence to sequence learning with neural networks. In Z. Ghahramani, M. Welling, C. Cortes, N. D. Lawrence, and K. Q. Weinberger, editors, *Advances in Neural Information Processing Systems 27*, pages 3104–3112. Curran Associates, Inc.

Wenhui Wang, Nan Yang, Furu Wei, Baobao Chang, and Ming Zhou. 2017. Gated self-matching networks for reading comprehension and question answering. In *ACL 2017*, pages 189–198.

Yu Wu, Wei Wu, Chen Xing, Ming Zhou, and Zhoujun Li. 2017. Sequential matching network: A new architecture for multi-turn response selection in retrieval-based chatbots. In *ACL 2017*, pages 496–505.

Zhao Yan, Nan Duan, Junwei Bao, Peng Chen, Ming Zhou, Zhoujun Li, and Jianshe Zhou. 2016a. Docchat: An information retrieval approach for chatbot engines using unstructured documents. In *ACL 2016*, pages 516–525.

Zhao Yan, Nan Duan, Peng Chen, Ming Zhou, Jianshe Zhou, and Zhoujun Li. 2016b. Building task-oriented dialogue systems for online shopping. In *AAAI-17*, pages 516–525.

Wei Nan Zhang, Ting Liu, Bing Qin, Yu Zhang, Wanxiang Che, Yanyan Zhao, and Xiao Ding. 2017. Benben: A Chinese intelligent conversational robot. In *ACL 2017, Demo*, pages 13–18.

Zhuosheng Zhang, Yafang Huang, and Hai Zhao. 2018a. Subword-augmented embedding for cloze reading comprehension. In *Proceedings of the 27th International Conference on Computational Linguistics (COLING 2018)*.

Zhuosheng Zhang, Jiangtong Li, Pengfei Zhu, and Hai Zhao. 2018b. Modeling multi-turn conversation with deep utterance aggregation. In *Proceedings of the 27th International Conference on Computational Linguistics (COLING 2018)*.

Xiangyang Zhou, Daxiang Dong, Hua Wu, Shiqi Zhao, Dianhai Yu, Hao Tian, Xuan Liu, and Rui Yan. 2016. Multi-view response selection for human-computer conversation. In *EMNLP 2016*, pages 372–381.

Writing Mentor: Self-Regulated Writing Feedback for Struggling Writers

Nitin Madnani[1]   **Jill Burstein**[1]   **Norbert Elliot**[2]   **Beata Beigman Klebanov**[1]
Diane Napolitano[1]   **Slava Andreyev**[1]   **Maxwell Schwartz**[1]

[1]Educational Testing Service, Princeton, NJ
[2]University of South Florida, Tampa, FL

[1]{nmadnani,jburstein,bbeigmanklebanov,dnapolitano,sandreyev,mschwartz}@ets.org
[2]nelliot3@usf.edu

Abstract

Writing Mentor[TM] is a freely available Google Docs add-on designed to provide feedback to struggling writers and help them improve their writing in a self-paced and self-regulated fashion. Writing Mentor uses natural language processing (NLP) methods and resources to generate feedback in terms of features that research into post-secondary struggling writers has classified as developmental (Burstein et al., 2016b). These features span many writing sub-constructs (use of sources, claims, and evidence; topic development; coherence; and knowledge of English conventions). Preliminary analysis indicates that users have a largely positive impression of Writing Mentor in terms of usability and potential impact on their writing.

1   Motivation

Low literacy is a social challenge that affects all citizens. For example, the Organization for Economic Co-operation and Development (OECD) reports that, on average, about 20% of students in OECD countries do not attain the baseline level of proficiency in reading (OECD, 2016). In the United States (US), we find literacy challenges at K-12 and post-secondary levels. The average National Assessment for Educational Progress (NAEP) reading assessment scores are only marginally proficient for 12th graders in the U.S. (Musu-Gillette et al., 2017). Another important facet of the U.S. literacy challenge is the large number of English language learners (ELLs) enrolled in US K-12 schools (4.8 million in 2014–15). In post-secondary contexts, approximately 20.4 million students in Fall 2017 were expected to be enrolled in 2- and 4-year institutions. Millions of these students lack the prerequisite skills to succeed (Chen, 2016), including lack of preparation in reading and writing (Complete College America, 2012).

We describe *Writing Mentor*, an NLP-based solution to the literacy challenge that is designed to help struggling writers in 2- and 4-year colleges improve their writing at a self-regulated pace. Writing Mentor is a Google Docs add-on[1] that provides automated instructional feedback focused on four key writing skills: credibility of claims, topic development, coherence, and editing. Writing mentor builds on a large body of research in the area of automated writing evaluation (AWE) which has so far primarily been used for scoring standardized assessments (Page, 1966; Burstein et al., 1998; Attali and Burstein, 2006; Zechner et al., 2009; Bernstein et al., 2010). Burstein et al. (2017) examined relationships between NLP-derived linguistic features extracted from college writing samples and broader success indicators (such as, SAT and ACT composite and subject scores). Their findings suggested that AWE can also be useful for generating automated feedback that can help students with their writing.

Writing Mentor has been developed to provide *one-stop-shopping* for writers looking for help with academic writing. Apps such as Grammarly and LanguageTool, cater to individual users but typically focus on English conventions. Applications such as ETS' Criterion (Burstein et al., 2004) and Turnitin's Revision Assistant provide feedback beyond English conventions, but require institutional subscriptions.

[1]Freely available for use with Google Docs at https://mentormywriting.org.

Proceedings of the 27th International Conference on Computational Linguistics: System Demonstrations, pages 113–117
Santa Fe, New Mexico, USA, August 20-26, 2018.

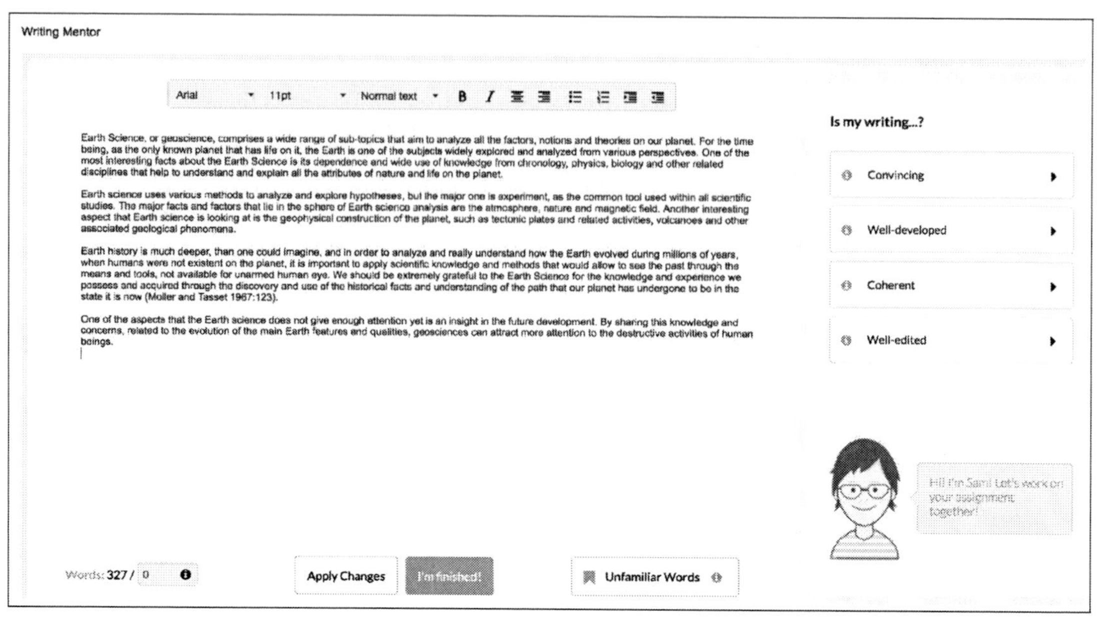

Figure 1: The Writing Mentor interface for categorized, actionable writing feedback.

Convincing	
Claims	Arguing expressions from a lexicon (Burstein et al., 1998) that contains discourse cue terms and relations (e.g., contrast, parallel, summary) and arguing expressions classified by stance (for/against) & type (hedges vs. boosters).
Sources	Rule-based system that detects in-text formal citations consistent with MLA, APA and Chicago styles.
Well-developed	
Topic Development	Detection of topics and their related word sets (Beigman Klebanov and Flor, 2013; Burstein et al., 2016a)
Coherent	
Flow of Ideas	Leverages terms in a document generated for the main topic (as identified by Topic Development above) and their related word sets.
Transition Terms	Identified using the same lexicon as in Claims above.
Long Sentences	Sentences with 1 independent clause & 1+ dependent clauses, identified using a syntactic chunker (Abney, 1996; Burstein and Chodorow, 1999)
Headers	Rule-based system using regular expressions to identify title & section headers.
Use of Anaphora	Pronouns identified using a part-of-speech tagger (Ratnaparkhi, 1996).
Well-Edited	
Grammar, Usage, & Mechanic Errors	9 automatically-detected grammar error feature types, 12 automatically-detected mechanics error feature types, and 10 automatically-detected word usage error feature types (Attali and Burstein, 2006).
Claim Verbs	Verbs denoting claims from the lexicon used in Claims above.
Word Choice	Rule-based system that detects words and expressions related to a set of 13 'unnecessary' words and terms, e.g. *very*, *literally*, *a total of*.
Contractions	Identified using a part-of-speech tagger (Ratnaparkhi, 1996).

Table 1: Inventory of features provided by the NLP backend, grouped by Writing Mentor feedback types.

2 Description

Writing Mentor (WM) can be installed for free from the Google Docs add-on store. The application itself is based on a client-server model with a scalable, micro-service driven backend (Madnani et al., 2018) serving a front-end written in Google Apps Script — a JavaScript-based scripting language used for developing Google Docs extensions and add-ons. Writing Mentor was released on the Google Docs add-on store in November, 2017. Figure 1 shows the main WM interface that users interact with while writing in Google Docs. The panel on the right shows the feedback that WM provides to users – it is categorized

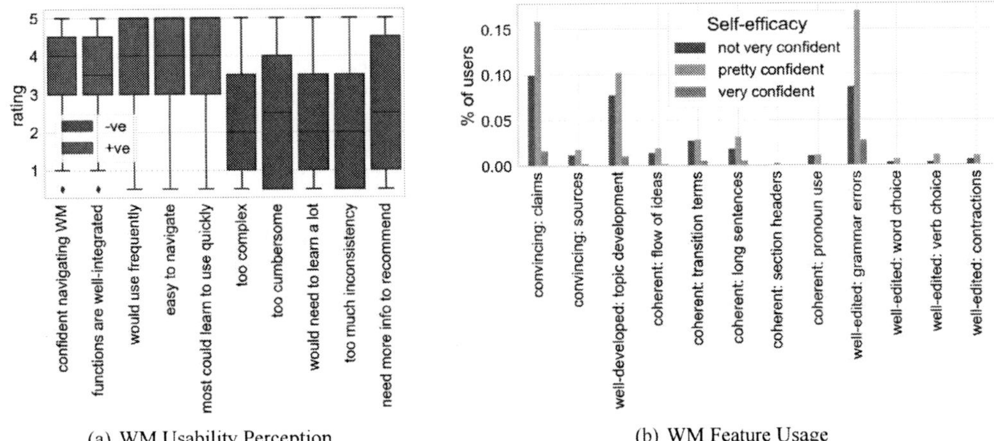

(a) WM Usability Perception   (b) WM Feature Usage

Figure 2: Graphs showing preliminary Writing Mentor evaluations. (a) shows the distribution of ratings provided by users who chose to respond to a survey containing 10 statements (negative ones (-ve) in red, positive ones (+ve) in blue) pertaining to the usability of Writing Mentor (N=301). (b) shows the percentage of users with different levels of reported self-efficacy that preferred to spend the most time (across all documents and sessions) using each Writing Mentor feedback feature (N=1,638).

based on the writing being *Convincing* (e.g., use of claims and citation of sources), *Well-developed* (e.g., adequate topic development), *Coherent* (e.g., a good flow of ideas), and *Well-edited* (e.g., no grammatical or spelling errors). Users can receive feedback on these four aspects of their writing by clicking on the appropriate category and choosing a feedback type. For example, one could click on the *Convincing* category, and then click on "Claims" to see claims identified and highlighted in their text.

Table 1 shows an inventory of the NLP features computed by the backend and the corresponding Writing Mentor feedback type they are used for (in bold). We refer the readers to a detailed video illustrating all feedback types at https://vimeo.com/238406360.

3   Evaluation

We report evaluation results based on demographic and usability surveys that users voluntarily filled out and on additional information potentially correlated with the popularity of the various feedback types captured in WM's usage logs.[2]

As of May 2018, Writing Mentor has 1,960 unique users. Of these, 84% reported English being their first language. In terms of self-efficacy, 8% of all users described themselves as "very confident" writers, 40% as "pretty confident", and 52% as "not very confident". We also asked the users to rate 10 statements pertaining to WM's usability, taken from the Standard Usability Survey (Brooke, 1996). For each statement, users provided a rating on a scale of 1–5, with half point ratings also allowed. Figure 2(a) shows a distribution of the ratings users provided for each statement provided. The first five statements (in blue) represent positive impressions, e.g., "I felt confident navigating Writing Mentor" and the last five statements (in red) represent negative impressions, e.g., "I found Writing Mentor too complex".[3] The figure clearly shows that the majority of the users have largely positive impressions when it comes to the usability of Writing Mentor.

We also computed — from the WM usage logs — which of the specific WM features users spent most time in (across all of their documents and sessions) and how that varies based on the level of reported self-efficacy. Figure 2(b) shows that the three most popular features across all groups appear to be the *grammar errors* feature, followed by the *claims* feature, and then the *topic development* feature which

---

[2]No personally identifying information is collected by Writing Mentor. Users, documents, and sessions are assigned randomly generated IDs for logging purposes.

[3]The full text of the statements and their order the usability survey is available at http://bit.ly/sus-usability.

115

are all known to be extremely important for post-secondary writing. It also shows that, overall, users appear to be trying all WM features. From the usage logs, we also computed that approximately 25% of users return to Writing Mentor and use it again with multiple documents. Repeat use likely indicates that a user is actually benefiting from using Writing Mentor.

4 Conclusion

We described Writing Mentor – a freely available Google Docs add-on that can help struggling post-secondary writers improve their academic writing by providing automatically generated, categorized, and actionable feedback on various aspects of their writing using NLP resources and techniques. We conducted some preliminary evaluations and observed that users have a largely positive impression of Writing Mentor's usability, they are spending time using Writing Mentor features that are known to be important for post-secondary academic writing, and that many of them are returning to use Writing Mentor for multiple documents.

References

Steven Abney. 1996. Part-of-Speech Tagging and Partial Parsing. In *Corpus-Based Methods in Language and Speech*, pages 118–136.

Yigal Attali and Jill Burstein. 2006. Automated essay scoring with e-rater [r] v. 2. *Journal of Technology, Learning, and Assessment*, 4(3).

Beata Beigman Klebanov and Michael Flor. 2013. Word Association Profiles and their Use for Automated Scoring of Essays. In *Proceedings of ACL*, pages 1148–1158.

Jared Bernstein, A. Van Moere, and Jian Cheng. 2010. Validating Automated Speaking Tests. *Language Testing*, 27(3):355–377.

John Brooke. 1996. SUS - A Quick and Dirty Usability Scale. *Usability evaluation in industry*, 189(194):4–7.

Jill Burstein and Martin Chodorow. 1999. Automated Essay Scoring for Nonnative English Speakers. In *Proceedings of a Symposium on Computer Mediated Language Assessment and Evaluation in Natural Language Processing*, pages 68–75.

Jill Burstein, Karen Kukich, Susanne Wolff, Chi Lu, Martin Chodorow, Lisa Braden-Harder, and Mary Dee Harris. 1998. Automated Scoring Using A Hybrid Feature Identification Technique. In *Proceedings of ACL/COLING*, pages 206–210.

Jill Burstein, Martin Chodorow, and Claudia Leacock. 2004. Automated Essay Evaluation: The Criterion Online Writing Service. *AI Magazine*, 25(3):27.

Jill Burstein, B Beigman Klebanov, Norbert Elliot, and Hillary Molloy. 2016a. A Left Turn: Automated Feedback & Activity Generation for Student Writers. In *Proceedings of the 3rd Language Teaching, Language & Technology Workshop*.

Jill Burstein, Norbert Elliot, and Hillary Molloy. 2016b. Informing Automated Writing Evaluation Using the Lens of Genre: Two Studies. *CALICO Journal*, 33(1).

Jill Burstein, Dan McCaffrey, Beata Beigman Klebanov, and Guangming Ling. 2017. Exploring Relationships Between Writing & Broader Outcomes With Automated Writing Evaluation. In *Proceedings of the 12th Workshop on Innovative Use of NLP for Building Educational Applications*, pages 101–108, Copenhagen, Denmark, September.

Xianglei Chen. 2016. Remedial Coursetaking at U.S. Public 2- and 4-Year Institutions: Scope, Experiences, and Outcomes. https://nces.ed.gov/pubs2016/2016405.pdf. [Online; accessed 01-May-2018].

Complete College America. 2012. Remediation: Higher Education's Bridge to Nowhere. http://files.eric.ed.gov/fulltext/ED536825.pdf. [Online; accessed 01-May-2018].

Nitin Madnani, Aoife Cahill, Daniel Blanchard, Slava Andreyev, Diane Napolitano, Binod Gyawali, Michael Heilman, Chong Min Lee, Chee Wee Leong, Matthew Mulholland, and Brian Riordan. 2018. A Robust Microservice Architecture for Scaling Automated Scoring Applications. *ETS Research Report Series*, 2018(1).

Lauren Musu-Gillette, Cristobal De Brey, Joel McFarland, William Hussar, William Sonnenberg, and Sidney Wilkinson-Flicker. 2017. Status and Trends in the Education of Racial and Ethnic Groups 2017. https://nces.ed.gov/pubs2017/2017051.pdf. [Online; accessed 01-May-2018].

OECD. 2016. PISA 2015 Results in Focus. https://www.oecd-ilibrary.org/content/paper/aa9237e6-en. [Online; accessed 01-May-2018].

Ellis B. Page. 1966. The Imminence of ... Grading Essays by Computer. *The Phi Delta Kappan*, 47(5):238–243.

Adwait Ratnaparkhi. 1996. A Maximum Entropy Model for Part-of-Speech Tagging. In *Conference on Empirical Methods in Natural Language Processing*.

Klaus Zechner, Derrick Higgins, Xiaoming Xi, and David M. Williamson. 2009. Automatic Scoring of Non-native Spontaneous Speech in Tests of Spoken English. *Speech Communication*, 51(10):883–895.

NLATool: An Application for Enhanced Deep Text Understanding

Markus Gärtner[1], Sven Mayer[2], Valentin Schwind[2], Eric Hämmerle[2],
Emine Turcan[2], Florin Rheinwald[2], Gustav Murawski[2], Lars Lischke[2],
Jonas Kuhn[1]
[1]University of Stuttgart, Institute for Natural Language Processing (IMS)
Pfaffenwaldring 5B, 70569 Stuttgart, Germany
[2]University of Stuttgart, Institute for Visualisation and Interactive Systems (VIS)
Pfaffenwaldring 5A, 70569 Stuttgart, Germany
[1]`{firstname.lastname}@ims.uni-stuttgart.de`
[2]`{firstname.lastname}@vis.uni-stuttgart.de`

Abstract

Today, we see an ever growing number of tools supporting text annotation. Each of these tools is optimized for specific use-cases such as named entity recognition. However, we see large growing knowledge bases such as Wikipedia or the Google Knowledge Graph. In this paper, we introduce NLATool, a web application developed using a human-centered design process. The application combines supporting text annotation and enriching the text with additional information from a number of sources directly within the application. The tool assists users to efficiently recognize named entities, annotate text, and automatically provide users additional information while solving deep text understanding tasks.

1 Introduction

A wide range of subfields in natural language processing (NLP) nowadays see systems emerging that solve their respective tasks with sufficiently high-quality levels. Especially tools for automatic entity recognition, entity linking or coreference resolution have advanced rapidly in recent years. Those tasks are also common sub-problems of general (human) text understanding. Usability and their actual applicability to real-world use cases are however often neglected aspects in the development of NLP tools.

Even analysts can benefit from the hints such an automatic preprocessing might provide. Unfortunately, the majority of NLP applications are tailored to a rather technically skilled user audience of experts and also typically focus on specific singular problems. The absence of widely applied standards for representing linguistic data and annotations further hampers interoperability of said systems. As a result, it is often difficult for technically less skilled users or non-experts in the field or other disciplines such as digital humanities (DH) to employ those tools successfully for assistance in their own work.

In this paper, we present a web application that aims to fill this gap. It is designed to assist users in analysis tasks that require deep text understanding without demanding expert or technical knowledge. It combines automatic predictions for several tasks centered around entity recognition and coreference resolution with information derived from a knowledge base. As a result, the tool offers a rich visualization of texts and the entities mentioned in them through an easy to use web interface.

2 Related Work

The main task performed by our system is comparable to entity linking, that is linking mentions of entities in unstructured data such as raw text to their corresponding entries in a knowledge base. Due to natural ambiguities and variations in the way entities can be referenced or mentioned, entity linking remains a challenging task for automatic systems and even for annotators or analysts. A variety of approaches and implementations thereof exist, and we refer to Shen et al. (2015) for a comprehensive survey of those.

There are several types of systems related to entity linking that are relevant in the context of this contribution: The simplest are entity disambiguation or linking implementations that also subsequently provide a visualization of their output. Most systems belong to this category such as DBPedia Spotlight[1] (Daiber

---

[1]`http://demo.dbpedia-spotlight.org`

Proceedings of the 27th International Conference on Computational Linguistics: System Demonstrations, pages 118–122
Santa Fe, New Mexico, USA, August 20-26, 2018.

et al., 2013) or the YODIE (Gorrell et al., 2015) module for GATE[2]. They rarely provide more than rudimentary highlighting of the found entities and generally are not aimed at more assistive functions or visualizations. Similar to this, tools for wikification (i.e., annotating mentions with the Wikipedia link of the respective entity) include for instance the Illinois Cross-Lingual Wikifier (Tsai and Roth, 2016).

More advanced in terms of visualization, TASTY (Arnold et al., 2016) implements an as-you-type approach to interactive entity linking. It allows users to write a text through the application's own interface and be provided with a live outline of complementary information, such as a picture or article link. Its design is however limited in the scale of how much of this complementary information is visible at once.

3   Design

To determine requirements and desired features of text analysis and information extraction, we performed a qualitative user study with six computational linguistics (CL) experts (23-38 y.) from our faculty. Semi-structured interviews were conducted to determine desired functionality and features. After providing informed consent, participants received in the first phase of the survey four texts in random order (passages from *The Bible*, *Critique of Pure Reason* by Kant, *The Earthquake in Chile* by von Kleist, and excerpts from the *Nuremberg Trials*) to answer questions about comprehension of the texts. No input by the experimenter was provided. Afterward, we asked participants about features that would help to extract the information. In the second phase, we introduced our project and the first prototype mockups. We asked which tools they normally would use and which features they desire for information extraction. All interviews were transcribed and annotated using Atlas.ti[3].

Our results revealed five feature requests: (1) named entity recognition and filtering for information extraction, (2) tools for named entity density analysis, (3) a tool for additional notes and comments, (4) tools for segmenting and structuring text, and (5) fast inquiries based on background web search performed by the application. Data analysis of the interviews revealed four desired named entity main classes: persons, organizations, locations, and misc. For understanding text, participants asked for summaries of content related information outside the text column. Furthermore, participants desired an overview of named entity occurrences (corpus statistics) and a web-based entity search providing top matches and suggestions of named entities from the Google Knowledge Graph or Wikipedia. For named entity analysis, the participants in our study requested additional information with maps, photographs, and additional text. For misc data, the system should determine the closest match and dynamically present extracted information via text, image, or map. The participants also desired a correction feature of named entities. Additionally, we found that with the rise of high resolution screens and multiscreen setups in today's office environments a new tool should support making use of the increased screen space.

The requirement analysis of features for text annotation, and fast information extraction was used to design paper prototypes and mockups of the tool. In a series of design sessions with interaction designers and NLP professionals we found that a web application is best to implement our Natural Language Analysis Tool (NLATool). Furthermore, by using well established interaction patters we can further support the usability.

4   System

The CL community today already offers a quite wide range of very mature tools for numerous specific NLP tasks. This web-based solution is designed in a modular way to make use of existing analysis infrastructure and enable easy integration of other tools. As the main module, we used Stanford dependency parser (CoreNLP) (Manning et al., 2014) and its' features for text analysis. Additionally we used the Google Knowledge Graph to obtain information about the named entities beyond the text itself.

We implemented the NLATool as a web application . The main view is the text view where the user can view, edit, and delete named entities, the *text component*. However, it also presents an overview of all additional information beyond the text, the *research component*. We followed the metaphor of a split screen to enable the user to see both side by side. The *text component* takes up the left side of the screen

---

[2]https://gate.ac.uk
[3]https://atlasti.com

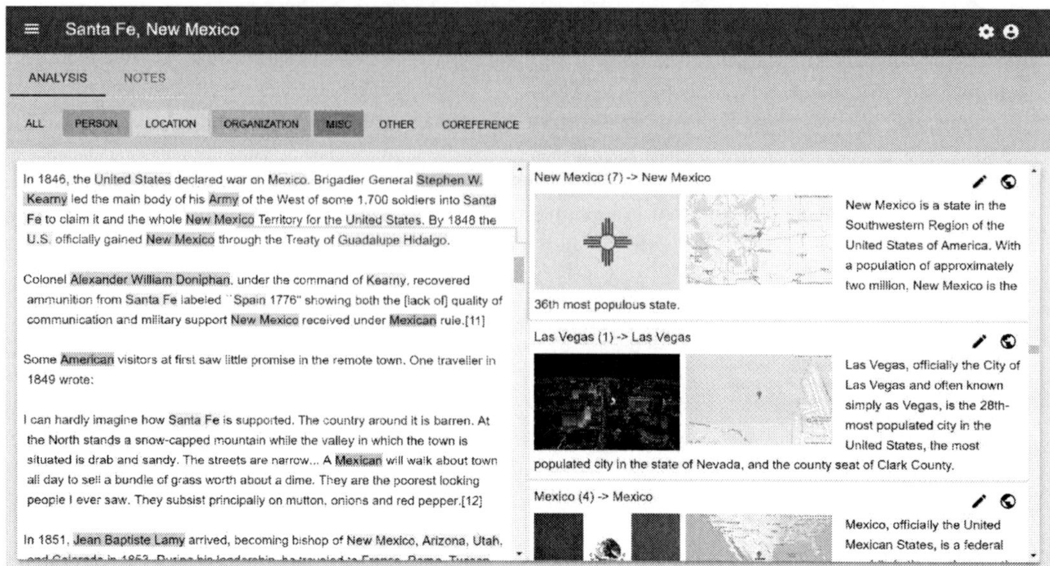

Figure 1: Screenshot of the system showing the menu on top, the text component on the left and the research component on the right. The systems presents the wikipedia article of "Santa Fe, New Mexico", which here is our example text. By hovering over "New Mexico" all related words are highlighted in a more saturated yellow to allow for a fast visual search. The yellow line between the word "New Mexico" and research result fosters spacial relation.

and the *research component* the right side. Additionally, above both views we implemented a menu strip similar to Microsoft Word and Excel. In the menu, the user can turn off and on specific highlighting functions for various named entities classes and enable coreference highlighting. Furthermore, the menu enables the user to switch into *edit mode* and *comment mode*. When switching into one of them the right side, the *research component* gets replaced. In *edit mode*, the user is guided through step by step instruction to add, change, or delete a certain named entity class which corresponds to one or more words. The system internally works with the 7-classes model; however, to not clutter the text we group Date, Time, Duration, Number, Set, and Ordinal into one group named "Other". Additionally, the user can link a different entity to the Google Knowledge Graph in case the previously linked entity is considered incorrect. In *comment mode*, the user can view all comments in a document, and add, change, or delete a comment with is either a global comment or conncted to a span of words.

Beyond the *text view*, the tool offers a view to input plain text which will then be analyzed and presented in the text view. Additionally, as all text and the corresponding comments and edits are stored on the server, the tool also offers to load previous texts. User management is not fully implemented yet as the current intent of the tool is used in a "host your own server" approach as quite often privacy regulations or licenses might not allow to upload text to third-party servers.

The front end of the tool is designed using the material.io framework which delivers the look and feel of a web app. The tool itself uses node.js as the main component and a MySQL database for fast and easy deployment. For the underlying annotation text analysis we use CoreNLP running in a server instance, this allows the node.js server to parse text which was uploaded by the user immediately. For the communication between node.js and the CoreNLP server we build on a free wrapper implementation named node-corenlp[4]. The source code of the system is publicly available under a GNU v3.0 license on GitHub[5]. This allows users to host their own server and enables the community to use the tool more effectively.

---

[4]`https://github.com/gerardobort/node-corenlp`
[5]`https://github.com/interactionlab/NLATool`

4.1 Research Feature

We use CoreNLP to extract all named entities from a given text during initial text setup. Then for each named entity we request the corresponding entry in the Google Knowledge Graph using rest API calls. Each unique result is presented to the user in the *research component* by the comprehensive text given by the Knowledge Graph. If a photo is available, it gets presented alongside the text to further support the user. For Locations and Organizations, an address is also available with the help of the Google Static Map API. For those cases we additionally show a small map directly within the user interface. By clicking on the map a larger interactive version opens in a new tab. For additional information beyond the initial text, the user can click on the text, and third-party content such as the corresponding Wikipedia article opens. As we request further data about every named entity, the Google Knowledge Graph returns the same results for similar requests, such as "Albert Einstein" and "Einstein" both return the same result. We use this property to group all named entities with the same result to reduce the initial clutter of the tool. The user can ungroup them if the initial grouping was incorrect and add new words to a group which was not identified by CoreNLP.

4.2 Highlighting Feature

To foster spacial relation between words and the corresponding research result we first highlight all related words whenever hovering over a word, and second, we add a connection line between the hovered word and the research result (see Figure 1). In case the research result is not in the viewport the elements gets scrolled into the view automatic. When hovering a research element, we use the same approach to foster spacial relationship, the line is drawn, and the words are highlighted.

4.3 Multiscreen Feature

To better support users during text analysis, we implemented a feature to make use of the screen space. Instead, of just having one pair of *text component* and *research component* and scrolling both, we enabled the system to support multiple pairs next to each other in one row. This allows having one pair of the *text* and *research component* per screen. The number of splits can be defined by the user. When using a split view the view changes from a scrolling method to a page flipping implementation. Each *text component* is filled with text but only up to an amount that visually fits into the component.

5 Conclusion

In this paper, we present our new NLATool to support analysis in deep text understanding. In detail, we present a web app based on node.js which combines the established text processing pipeline CoreNLP and the Google Knowledge Graph. We developed the tool using the human-centered design process to better support analysts in their work. Beyond the text, we support the analysts with more insights by presenting additional information gained from the Google Knowledge Graph right within the user interface.

Acknowledgments

This work was in parts funded by the German Research Foundation (DFG) within Cluster of Excellence in Simulation Technology (EXC 310/2) at the University of Stuttgart, the project C04 of SFB/Transregio 161 and project INF of SFB 732.

References

Sebastian Arnold, Robert Dziuba, and Alexander Löser. 2016. Tasty: Interactive entity linking as-you-type. In *Proceedings of COLING 2016, the 26th International Conference on Computational Linguistics: System Demonstrations*.

Joachim Daiber, Max Jakob, Chris Hokamp, and Pablo N. Mendes. 2013. Improving efficiency and accuracy in multilingual entity extraction. In *Proceedings of the 9th International Conference on Semantic Systems*.

Genevieve Gorrell, Johann Petrak, and Kalina Bontcheva. 2015. Using @twitter conventions to improve #lod-based named entity disambiguation. In *Proceedings of the 12th European Semantic Web Conference on The Semantic Web. Latest Advances and New Domains*, New York, NY, USA. Springer-Verlag.

Christopher D. Manning, Mihai Surdeanu, John Bauer, Jenny Finkel, Steven J. Bethard, and David McClosky. 2014. The Stanford CoreNLP natural language processing toolkit. In *Association for Computational Linguistics (ACL) System Demonstrations*.

W. Shen, J. Wang, and J. Han. 2015. Entity linking with a knowledge base: Issues, techniques, and solutions. *Knowledge and Data Engineering, IEEE Transactions on*.

Chen-Tse Tsai and Dan Roth. 2016. Illinois cross-lingual wikifier: Grounding entities in many languages to the english wikipedia. In *Proceedings of COLING 2016, the 26th International Conference on Computational Linguistics: System Demonstrations*.

Sensala: A Dynamic Semantics System for Natural Language Processing

Daniyar Itegulov
Australian National University
ITMO University
daniyar.itegulov@anu.edu.au

Ekaterina Lebedeva
Australian National University
ekaterina.lebedeva@anu.edu.au

Bruno Woltzenlogel Paleo
bruno.wp@gmail.com

Abstract

Here we describe SENSALA, an open source framework for the semantic interpretation of natural language that provides the logical meaning of a given text. The framework's theory is based on a lambda calculus with exception handling and uses contexts, continuations, events and dependent types to handle a wide range of complex linguistic phenomena, such as donkey anaphora, verb phrase anaphora, propositional anaphora, presuppositions and implicatures.

Title and Abstract in Russian

Sensala: Система динамической семантики для обработки естественного языка

В данной статье описывается Sensala – программная система семантической интерпретации естественного языка с открытым исходным кодом, позволяющая получить логический смысл текста. Теоретическим фундаментом для системы послужило лямбда исчисление с обработкой исключений, а использование контекстов, продолжений, событий и зависимых типов позволяет системе интерпретировать широкий спектр таких лингвистических явлений, как «ослиная» анафора, глагольная анафора, пропозициональная анафора, пресуппозиция и импликатура.

1 Introduction

Attempts towards a modern logic-based semantics for natural language can be traced back at least to Montague (1974). He provided a framework for interpreting a fragment of the English language using lambda calculus, giving birth to a new branch of natural language processing, with roots in formal logic. Although Montague's formalisation of the English language is rather limited and serves more as a proof-of-concept, his work was already sufficiently comprehensive to represent quantification and capture the nature of ambiguity.

In the following 40 years Montague's approach was further developed and extended with new techniques for handling various natural language phenomena. Recently, de Groote (2006) showed how to use continuations and contexts to handle dynamic phenomena while still retaining standard mathematical logic constructions (first-order logic on top of a simply typed lambda calculus à la Church (1940)). The lambda calculus of de Groote's framework was extended by Lebedeva (2012) with an exception raising and handling mechanism, which allowed cross-sentential anaphora and presupposition triggers to be formalized. Itegulov and Lebedeva (2018) further combined it with event semantics and dependent type semantics (Bekki, 2014) to represent verb phrase anaphora and propositional anaphora.

SENSALA is based on these recent theoretical advances, which are partly summarized in sections 2 and 3. The linguistic phenomena handled by SENSALA are discussed in section 4 and its architecture is described in section 5. SENSALA has been deployed and can be used through the web interface available at http://sensala.cecs.anu.edu.au.

Proceedings of the 27th International Conference on Computational Linguistics: System Demonstrations, pages 123–127
Santa Fe, New Mexico, USA, August 20-26, 2018.

2 Dynamic Semantics

SENSALA implements the dynamic semantics framework introduced by de Groote (2006) and extended by Lebedeva (2012). The theory is built upon three atomic types: ι, the type of *individuals* (a.k.a. *entities*), o, the type of propositions, and γ, the type of left contexts. The right context is represented as a *continuation* of type $\gamma \to o$. A semantical interpretation of a single sentence has type $\gamma \to (\gamma \to o) \to o$.

de Groote (2006) focused on the representation of anaphora assuming that it has already been solved by some oracle operators, such as $sel_{he}, sel_{she}, sel_{it}$. These operators extract an entity from a left context passed to them and hence have type $\gamma \to \iota$. de Groote and Lebedeva (2010) proposed to view the context as a finite list of entities together with their properties. If c is such a list and $(a, man(a))$ is a new pair, then $(a, male(a)) :: c$ the new list obtained by pre-pending the pair to the list. Consider the following example from (de Groote, 2006):

$$\textit{John loves Mary. He smiles at her.} \tag{1}$$

These two sentences can be individually interpreted as formulae in (2)[1]. Each of these interpretations can be constructed compositionally by interpreting lexical components of the respective sentences. For example, proper name *John* has interpretation $\lambda\psi c.\psi(\mathbf{j}, (\mathbf{j}, m(\mathbf{j})) :: c)$ and pronoun *he* has interpretation $\lambda\psi c.\psi(sel_{he}(c), c)$, where ψ are continuations of type $\iota \to \gamma \to o$.

$$\lambda c\phi.\mathbf{love}(\mathbf{j}, \mathbf{m}) \wedge \phi((\mathbf{m}, f(\mathbf{m})) :: (\mathbf{j}, m(\mathbf{j})) :: c)$$
$$\lambda c\phi.\mathbf{smile}(sel_{he}(c), sel_{she}(c)) \wedge \phi(c) \tag{2}$$

The sequential composition of interpretations in (2) leads to the following normal form:

$$\lambda c\phi.\mathbf{love}(\mathbf{j}, \mathbf{m}) \wedge \mathbf{smiles}(sel_{he}((\mathbf{m}, f(\mathbf{m})) :: (\mathbf{j}, m(\mathbf{j})) :: c), sel_{her}((\mathbf{m}, f(\mathbf{m})) :: (\mathbf{j}, m(\mathbf{j})) :: c))$$
$$\wedge \phi((\mathbf{m}, f(\mathbf{m})) :: (\mathbf{j}, m(\mathbf{j})) :: c)$$

After meta-interpretation of the sel-operators, we obtain the following interpretation of discourse (1):
$$\lambda c\phi.\mathbf{love}(\mathbf{j}, \mathbf{m}) \wedge \mathbf{smiles}(\mathbf{j}, \mathbf{m}) \wedge \phi((\mathbf{m}, f(\mathbf{m})) :: (\mathbf{j}, m(\mathbf{j})) :: c)$$

3 Event Semantics

Event semantics was first described by Davidson (1967) and then extended by Parsons (1990). The resulting neo-Davidsonian event semantics introduces a new atomic type for events e and a few thematic predicates for describing properties of events (e.g. *agent*, *patient*). Consider, for example, the sentence and its interpretation according to neo-Davidsonian event semantics in (3), where predicates *agent* and *patient* indicate the event's participants, while *yesterday* indicates when the event happened:

$$\textit{John met Mary yesterday.}$$
$$\exists e^e.met(e) \wedge agent(e, \mathbf{j}) \wedge patient(e, \mathbf{m}) \wedge yesterday(e) \tag{3}$$

4 Linguistic Phenomena handled by Sensala

Pronominal anaphora are phenomena in which the interpretation of a pronoun depends on an antecedent expression in the left context. Currently, SENSALA can interpret most English personal pronouns. For example, the pronoun *"he"* is interpreted into a selection of an entity with the property $\lambda x.man(x)$ from the left context and the pronoun *"it"* is interpreted into a selection of an entity with the property $\lambda x.\neg person(x)$. Then, after extracting the hypernym relationship, as discussed in section 5.3, SENSALA interprets discourse (4) as (5).

$$\textit{John owns a dog. He loves it.} \tag{4}$$
$$\exists d^{en}.dog(d) \wedge \exists e^{ev}.owns(e) \wedge agent(e, j) \wedge patient(e, d)$$
$$\wedge \exists e'^{ev}.loves(e') \wedge agent(e', j) \wedge patient(e', d) \tag{5}$$

---

[1] $\mathbf{j}$ stands for the entity *John* and $\mathbf{m}$ stands for the entity *Mary*. The predicates f and m represent being female and male.

Propositional anaphora are another type of anaphora, where an anaphoric clause is used to refer to a whole proposition (e.g., a sentence). SENSALA interprets the demonstrative pronoun "that" in, for example, (6) into selection of an event from the left context. Thus, SENSALA interprets (6) as (7):

$$\text{John loves Mary. I heard that from Bob.} \tag{6}$$

$$\exists e^{ev}.loves(e) \wedge agent(e, j) \wedge patient(e, m) \wedge \exists e'^{ev}.heard(e')$$
$$\wedge\, agent(e', speaker) \wedge patient(e', e) \wedge from(e', b) \tag{7}$$

Verb phrase anaphora involve omissions of a full-fledged verb phrase when the ellipsed part can be implicitly derived from the context. The interpretation of verb phrase anaphora is more challenging than the interpretation of propositional and pronominal anaphora: an anaphoric clause in a verb phrase anaphora usually talks about a new event that inherits some properties of another event. For example, the second sentence in (8) talks about an event that inherits the property of being a "leaving" event while also changing the property of being performed by John to the property of being performed by Mary. SENSALA interprets (8) as (9):

$$\text{John left. Mary did too.} \tag{8}$$

$$\exists e^{ev}.left(e) \wedge agent(e, j) \wedge \exists e'^{ev}.left(e') \wedge agent(e, m) \tag{9}$$

Donkey anaphora may occur when the syntactic structure of a sentence does not conform to its meaning. The classical example of donkey anaphora is (10), which SENSALA interprets as (11) using techniques in line with the approach described by de Groote (2006).

$$\text{Every farmer who owns a donkey beats it.} \tag{10}$$

$$\forall f^{en}.farmer(f) \rightarrow \forall d^{en}.donkey(d) \rightarrow$$
$$\forall e^{ev}.owns(e) \wedge agent(e, f) \wedge patient(e, d) \rightarrow \exists e'^{ev}.beats(e') \wedge agent(e', f) \wedge patient(e', d) \tag{11}$$

Implicature is something conveyed in a discourse but not explicitly stated by the discourse. Currently, SENSALA supports deductive implicatures, whose implicit meaning can be derived using classical logic inference rules, but not abductive implicatures, which would require non-monotonic logics. A deductive implicature can be observed in (12), where the implicature is the logically deduced fact "John owns a donkey".

$$\text{Every farmer owns a donkey. John is a farmer.} \tag{12}$$

SENSALA uses the automated theorem prover SCAVENGER (Itegulov et al., 2017) to derive new knowledge from the discourse's interpretation.

5 Software Architecture and Implementation

The architecture of SENSALA has been designed in accordance with software engineering, functional programming and object-oriented programming principles such as immutability, modularity and referential transparency. The adherence to these principles has been facilitated by the use of the hybrid programming language Scala. The source code is available in GitLab at `https://gitlab.com/aossie/Sensala` under a Creative Commons Attribution-NonCommercial-ShareAlike 4.0 International License.

SENSALA has five main modules:

- `core` module contains all basic data structures (e.g. lambda terms, types and left context) and all natural language syntax trees with their interpretation functions.

- `parser` module contains a transformer from a text to its natural language syntax tree.

- `wordnet` module contains an interaction with the WordNet database for extracting relationships between words (e.g. hypernym, synonym).

- `cli` module contains a simple way to interact with SENSALA from the command line.

- web module contains a web server with a user interface (UI) and an application program interface (API) for interacting with SENSALA.

Figure 1 shows SENSALA's execution pipeline, with stages and corresponding modules. The following sections describe three main modules of SENSALA.

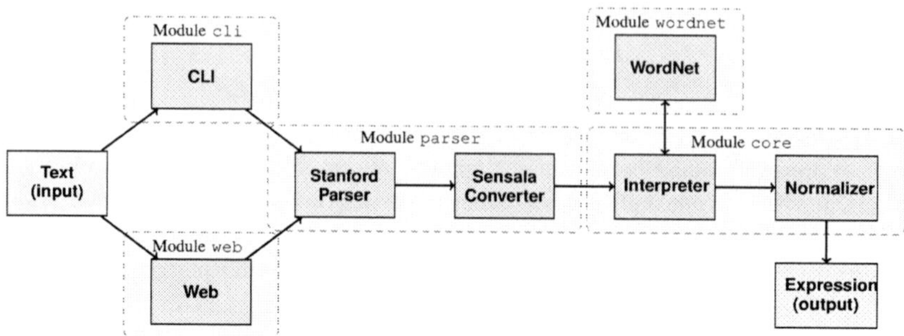

Figure 1: SENSALA execution pipeline

5.1 Core

Every single phrase interpreted in SENSALA is represented by one of the *natural language classes*. The origin trait for all natural language constructions is the NL trait. Second-level traits are English language parts of speech. SENSALA currently supports the interpretation of common nouns, proper nouns, definite and indefinite articles (represented by `QuantNounPhrase` class), pronouns, transitive and intransitive verbs, adjectives, adverbs and some wh phrases. `Discourse` is a class representing a sequential combination of sentences, while a sentence is a noun phrase accompanied by a verb phrase.

5.2 Parser

SENSALA uses the Stanford Parser (Klein and Manning, 2002) to retrieve a Penn-tagged tree from raw text. As the Stanford Parser's output trees differ from the classes described in section 5.1. SENSALA implements a `DiscourseParser` to convert Stanford Parser trees into SENSALA syntax trees.

5.3 WordNet

WordNet (Fellbaum, 1998) is used in SENSALA to extract hypernym relationships (a.k.a. is-a relationships) between common nouns in text. SENSALA uses JWNL library to interface with the WordNet database. The library provides a way to extract hypernym relationship trees from the database. For example, the tree for the word *"farmer"* contains hypernyms *"creator"*,* "person"* and *"organism"*; and the tree for the word *"donkey"* contains hypernyms *"ass"*, *"mammal"* and *"animal"*.

After retrieving all hypernyms of *"farmer"* and *"donkey"*, SENSALA interprets the discourse *"A farmer owns a donkey. He loves it."* successfully. The entity farmer has the property of being a person (according to the WordNet hypernym tree), which is required by *"he"*; and the entity donkey has a property of being an animal, which is one of the satisfying properties for the pronoun *"it"*.

6 Conclusion

SENSALA is a new open source logic-based system for formal semantics of natural language. Although it is still at an early stage of development, SENSALA can already handle various complex linguistic phenomena such as some pronominal anaphora, propositional anaphora, verb phrase anaphora, donkey anaphora, presuppositions and implicatures. It currently supports subsets of English and German. Planned future work includes support of other natural and domain-specific controlled natural languages.

Given that SENSALA is being developed with rigorous software engineering principles in mind and with the ambition of being more than just a prototype, and given the scarcity of tools for formal semantics, we hope SENSALA will become a widely used and useful tool in this research field.

References

Daisuke Bekki. 2014. Representing anaphora with dependent types. In *Logical Aspects of Computational Linguistics*, pages 14–29. Springer Berlin Heidelberg.

Alonzo Church. 1940. A formulation of the simple theory of types. *The Journal of Symbolic Logic*, 5:56–68.

Donald Davidson. 1967. The logical form of action sentences. In *The Logic of Decision and Action*. University of Pittsburgh Press.

Philippe de Groote and Ekaterina Lebedeva. 2010. Presupposition accommodation as exception handling. In *Proceedings of the SIGDIAL 2010 Conference*, Tokyo, Japan, September. Association for Computational Linguistics.

Philippe de Groote. 2006. Towards a montagovian account of dynamics. In *Semantics and Linguistic Theory XVI*.

Christiane Fellbaum. 1998. *WordNet: An Electronic Lexical Database*. MIT Press, Cambridge.

Daniyar Itegulov and Ekaterina Lebedeva. 2018. Handling verb phrase anaphora with dependent types and events. In *Logic, Language, Information, and Computation – WoLLIC 2018*.

Daniyar Itegulov, John Slaney, and Bruno Woltzenlogel Paleo. 2017. Scavenger 0.1: A theorem prover based on conflict resolution. In *Automated Deduction – CADE 26*, pages 344–356. Springer International Publishing.

Dan Klein and Christopher D. Manning. 2002. Fast exact inference with a factored model for natural language parsing. In *Proceedings of the 15th International Conference on Neural Information Processing Systems*, NIPS'02, pages 3–10. MIT Press.

Ekaterina Lebedeva. 2012. *Expression de la dynamique du discours à l'aide de continuations*. Ph.D. thesis, Université de Lorraine.

Richard Montague. 1974. *Formal Philosophy; Selected Papers of Richard Montague*. New Haven: Yale University Press.

Terence Parsons. 1990. *Events in the Semantics of English: A Study in Subatomic Semantics*. MIT Press.

On-Device Neural Language Model based Word Prediction

Seunghak Yu[*]   **Nilesh Kulkarni**[*]   **Haejun Lee**   **Jihie Kim**
Samsung Research, Seoul, Korea
{seunghak.yu, n93.kulkarni, haejun82.lee, jihie.kim}@samsung.com

Abstract

Recent developments in deep learning with application to language modeling have led to success in tasks of text processing, summarizing and machine translation. However, deploying huge language models on mobile devices for on-device keyboards poses computation as a bottle-neck due to their puny computation capacities. In this work, we propose an on-device neural language model based word prediction method that optimizes run-time memory and also provides a real-time prediction environment. Our model size is 7.40MB and has average prediction time of 6.47 ms. The proposed model outperforms existing methods for word prediction in terms of keystroke savings and word prediction rate and has been successfully commercialized.

1 Introduction

Recurrent neural networks (RNNs) have delivered state of the art performance on language modeling (RNN-LM). A major advantage of RNN-LMs is that these models inherit the property of storing and accessing information over arbitrary context lengths from RNNs. The model takes as input a textual context and generates a probability distribution over the words in the vocabulary for the next word in the text. However, the state of the art RNN-LM requires over 50MB of memory (Zoph and Le (2016) contains over 25M parameters; quantized to 2 bytes). This has, in the past, hampered deployment of RNN-LM on mobile devices for word prediction, word completion, and error correction tasks. Even on high-end mobile devices, keyboards have constraints on memory (10MB) and response time (10ms), hence we cannot apply RNN-LM directly without compression.

Various deep model compression methods have been developed. Compression through matrix factorization (Sainath et al., 2013; Xue et al., 2013; Nakkiran et al., 2015; Prabhavalkar et al., 2016; Lu et al., 2016) has shown promising results in model compression but has been applied to the tasks of automatic speech recognition. Network pruning (Han et al., 2015a; Han et al., 2015b) keeps the most the relevant parameters while removing the rest. Weight sharing (Gong et al., 2014; Chen et al., 2015; Ullrich et al., 2017) attempts to quantize the parameters into clusters. Network pruning and weight sharing methods only consider memory constraints while compressing the models. They achieve high compression but do not meet the time constraints of mobile devices and hence none of them are suitable for our application.

To address the constraints of both memory size and computation we propose a word prediction method that optimizes for run-time, and memory to render a smooth performance on embedded devices. We propose shared matrix factorization to compress the model along with using knowledge distillation to compensate the loss in accuracy while compressing. The resulting model is approximately $8\times$ compressed with negligible loss in accuracy and has a response time of 6.47ms per prediction on a high-end mobile devices (e.g. Samsung Galaxy S7). To the best of our knowledge, this is the first approach to use RNN-LMs for word prediction on mobile devices whereas previous approaches used n-gram based statistical language models or unpublished. We achieve better performance than existing approaches in terms of Keystroke Savings (KS) (Fowler et al., 2015) and Word Prediction Rate (WPR). The proposed method has been successfully commercialized.

Proceedings of the 27th International Conference on Computational Linguistics: System Demonstrations, pages 128–131
Santa Fe, New Mexico, USA, August 20-26, 2018.

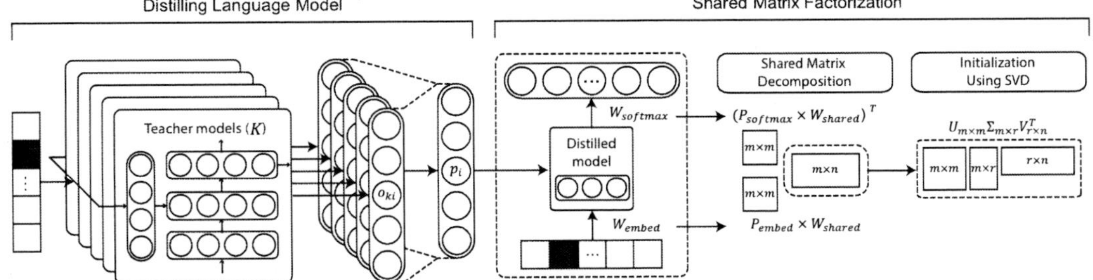

Figure 1: Overview of the proposed method. $\boldsymbol{o_{ki}}$: the i_{th} logits of k_{th} model, $\boldsymbol{p_i}$: the i_{th} softened output of ensemble. $(P_{softmax} \times W_{shared})^T$ and $P_{embed} \times W_{shared}$ substitute $W_{softmax}$ and W_{embed} in the proposed model respectively.

2 Proposed Method

2.1 Baseline Language Model

Figure 1 shows an overview of our approach. All language models in our pipeline mimic the conventional RNN-LM architecture. Each model consists of three parts: word embedding, recurrent hidden layers, and softmax layer. We use the architecture similar to the non-regularized LSTM model by (Zaremba et al., 2014). The hidden state of the LSTM unit h_t is affine-transformed by the softmax function, which is a probability distribution over all the words in the V. We train the model with cross-entropy loss function using Adam optimizer. The initial learning rate is set to 0.001 and decays with roll-back after every epoch with no decrement in perplexity on the validation dataset.

2.2 Distilling Language Model

Knowledge Distillation (KD) (Hinton et al., 2015) uses an ensemble of pre-trained teacher models (typically deep and large) to train a distilled model (typically shallower). Knowledge Distillation helps provide global information to the distilled model, and hence regularizes and requires less iteration for parameter updates. We refer to 'hard targets' as true labels from the data which the baseline model uses, we adapt KD to learn a combined cost function from 'hard targets' and 'soft targets'. 'Soft targets' are generated by adding a temperature T (Eq.1) to averaged logits of teachers' z_i to train distilled model.

$$p_i = \frac{\exp(\frac{z_i}{T})}{\sum_j \exp(\frac{z_j}{T})} \quad \left(\text{where } z_i = \frac{1}{K}\sum_{k=1}^{K} o_{ki}\right) \tag{1}$$

2.3 Shared Matrix Factorization

We present a compression method using shared matrix factorization for embedding and softmax layers of the RNN-LM. We facilitate sharing by W_{shared} for the softmax and embedding layers, allowing for more efficient parameterization of weight matrices. This reduces the total parameters in embedding and softmax layers by half. We introduce two trainable matrices P_{embed} and $P_{softmax}$, called the projection matrices, that adapt the W_{shared} for the individual tasks of embedding and softmax as $W_{embed} = P_{embed}W_{shared}$ and $W_{softmax} = (P_{softmax}W_{shared})^T$. Furthermore, in the layers parametrized by W_{shared} only a few outputs are active for a given input, we suspect that they are probably correlated and the underlying weight matrix has low rank r. For such a weight matrix, W, there exists a factorization of $W_{m\times n} = W^A_{m\times r}W^B_{r\times n}$ where W^A and W^B are full rank. In our low-rank compression strategy, we expect rank of W as r' which leads to factorization as $W_{m\times n} \approx W^A_{m\times r'}W^B_{r'\times n}$.

Moreover, we compress by applying Singular Value Decomposition (SVD) to initialize the decomposed matrices. SVD has been proposed as a promising method to perform factorization for low rank matrices (Nakkiran et al., 2015; Prabhavalkar et al., 2016). We apply SVD on $W_{m\times n}$ to decompose it as $W_{m\times n} = U_{m\times m}\Sigma_{m\times n}V^T_{n\times n}$. U, Σ, V are used to initialize W^A and W^B for the retraining process. We use the top r' singular values from Σ and corresponding r' rows from V^T. Therefore,

Model	PP	Size	CR
Baseline	56.55	56.76	-
+ KD	55.76	56.76	-
+ Shared Matrix	55.07	33.87	1.68×
+ SVD, Retrain	59.78	14.80	3.84×
+ Quantization	∼**59.78**	**7.40**	**7.68×**

Table 1: Evaluation of each model in our pipeline. Baseline uses 'hard targets' and Knowledge Distillation (KD) uses 'soft targets'. Size is in MB and 16-bit quantization is empirically selected for the final model. PP: Word Perplexity, CR: Compression Rate.

$W^A = U_{m \times m} \Sigma_{m \times r'}$ and $W^B = V^T_{r' \times n}$, we replace all the linear transformations using $W_{m \times n}$ with $W^A \times W^B$. Approximation during factorization leads to degradation in model performance but when followed by fine-tuning through retraining it results in restoration of accuracy. This compression scheme without loss of generality is applied to W_{shared}.

3 Experimental Results

3.1 Evaluation of proposed approach

Train data[1] is extracted from resources on the social network services in a raw form it contains 8 billion words. We uniformly sample 10% (196 million) from the dataset. Then we split dataset as 60% for training, 10% for validation and 30% for test. We preprocess raw data to remove noise and filter phrases. We also replace numbers in the dataset with a special symbol, <NUM> and out-of-vocabulary (OOV) words with <UNK>. We append start of sentence token <s> and end of sentence token </s> to every sentence. We convert our dataset to lower-case to increase vocabulary coverage and use top 15K words as the vocabulary. Table 1 shows evaluation result of each step in our pipeline. We empirically select 600 dimensional embedding , a single hidden layer with 600 LSTM hidden units for the baseline model. Word Perplexity is used to evaluate and compare our models. Perplexity over the test set is computed as $\exp(-\frac{1}{N} \sum_{i=1}^{N} \log p(w_i|w_{<i}))$, where N is the number of words in the test set. Our final model is roughly 8× smaller than the baseline (which is huge and slow) with 5% (3.16) loss in perplexity.

3.2 Performance Comparison

We compare our performance with existing word prediction methods using manually curated dataset[2], which covers general keyboard scenarios. Due to lack of access to language modeling engine used in other commercial solutions, we are unable to compare with them on word perplexity metric. To the best of our efforts we try to minimize all the personalization these solutions offer in their prediction engines while performing the human evaluation on the manually curated dataset. We employed three evaluators from the inspection group to cross-validate all the tests in Table 2 to eliminate human errors. We achieve the best performance compared to other solutions in terms of Keystroke Savings (KS) and Word Prediction Rate (WPR) as shown in Table 2. KS is a percentage of keystrokes *not* pressed compared to a keyboard without any prediction or completion capabilities. Every character the user types using the predictions of the language model counts as keystroke saving. WPR is a percentage of correct word predictions in the test set.

4 Conclusions

We have proposed a practical method for training and deploying RNN-LM for a mobile device which can satisfy memory and run-time constraints. Our method utilizes averaged output of teachers to train a distilled model and compresses its weight matrices by applying shared matrix factorization. Our memory

---

[1]The dataset is available at https://github.com/Meinwerk/WordPrediction
[2]The dataset consists of 102 sentences (926 words, 3,746 characters) which are the collection of formal and informal utterances from various sources. It is also available at https://github.com/Meinwerk/WordPrediction

Developer	KS(%)	WPR(%)
Our model	**65.11**	**34.38**
iOS	64.35	33.73
Swiftkey	62.39	31.14
Samsung Galaxy S6	59.81	28.84
G-board	58.89	28.02

Table 2: Performance comparison of our method and other commercialized keyboard solutions by various developers. Higher the better.

footprint is 7.40MB and is well within the run-time constraint of 10ms per prediction (6.47ms). Also, we have compared proposed method to existing commercialized keyboards in terms of keystroke savings and word prediction rate. In our benchmark tests, our method out-performed the others.

References

Wenlin Chen, James T Wilson, Stephen Tyree, Kilian Q Weinberger, and Yixin Chen. 2015. Compressing neural networks with the hashing trick. In *ICML*, pages 2285–2294.

Andrew Fowler, Kurt Partridge, Ciprian Chelba, Xiaojun Bi, Tom Ouyang, and Shumin Zhai. 2015. Effects of language modeling and its personalization on touchscreen typing performance. In *Proceedings of the 33rd Annual ACM Conference on Human Factors in Computing Systems*, pages 649–658. ACM.

Yunchao Gong, Liu Liu, Ming Yang, and Lubomir Bourdev. 2014. Compressing deep convolutional networks using vector quantization. *arXiv preprint arXiv:1412.6115*.

Song Han, Huizi Mao, and William J Dally. 2015a. Deep compression: Compressing deep neural networks with pruning, trained quantization and huffman coding. *arXiv preprint arXiv:1510.00149*.

Song Han, Jeff Pool, John Tran, and William Dally. 2015b. Learning both weights and connections for efficient neural network. In *Advances in Neural Information Processing Systems*, pages 1135–1143.

Geoffrey Hinton, Oriol Vinyals, and Jeff Dean. 2015. Distilling the knowledge in a neural network. *arXiv preprint arXiv:1503.02531*.

Zhiyun Lu, Vikas Sindhwani, and Tara N Sainath. 2016. Learning compact recurrent neural networks. In *Acoustics, Speech and Signal Processing (ICASSP), 2016 IEEE International Conference on*, pages 5960–5964. IEEE.

Preetum Nakkiran, Raziel Alvarez, Rohit Prabhavalkar, and Carolina Parada. 2015. Compressing deep neural networks using a rank-constrained topology. In *INTERSPEECH*, pages 1473–1477.

Rohit Prabhavalkar, Ouais Alsharif, Antoine Bruguier, and Lan McGraw. 2016. On the compression of recurrent neural networks with an application to lvcsr acoustic modeling for embedded speech recognition. In *Acoustics, Speech and Signal Processing (ICASSP), 2016 IEEE International Conference on*, pages 5970–5974. IEEE.

Tara N Sainath, Brian Kingsbury, Vikas Sindhwani, Ebru Arisoy, and Bhuvana Ramabhadran. 2013. Low-rank matrix factorization for deep neural network training with high-dimensional output targets. In *Acoustics, Speech and Signal Processing (ICASSP), 2013 IEEE International Conference on*, pages 6655–6659. IEEE.

Karen Ullrich, Edward Meeds, and Max Welling. 2017. Soft weight-sharing for neural network compression. *arXiv preprint arXiv:1702.04008*.

Jian Xue, Jinyu Li, and Yifan Gong. 2013. Restructuring of deep neural network acoustic models with singular value decomposition. In *Interspeech*, pages 2365–2369.

Wojciech Zaremba, Ilya Sutskever, and Oriol Vinyals. 2014. Recurrent neural network regularization. *arXiv preprint arXiv:1409.2329*.

Barret Zoph and Quoc V Le. 2016. Neural architecture search with reinforcement learning. *arXiv preprint arXiv:1611.01578*.

WARP-Text: A Web-Based Tool for Annotating Relationships Between Pairs of Texts

Venelin Kovatchev[1,3], M. Antònia Martí[1,3], Maria Salamó[2,3]
[1]Facultat de Filología, Universitat de Barcelona
[2] Facultat de Matemàtiques i Informàtica, Universitat de Barcelona
[3]Universitat de Barcelona Institute of Complex Systems
Gran Vía de les Corts Catalanes, 585, 08007 Barcelona, Spain
{vkovatchev, amarti, maria.salamo}@ub.edu

Abstract

We present WARP-Text, an open-source web-based tool for annotating relationships between pairs of texts. WARP-Text supports multi-layer annotation and custom definitions of inter-textual and intra-textual relationships. Annotation can be performed at different granularity levels (such as sentences, phrases, or tokens). WARP-Text has an intuitive user-friendly interface both for project managers and annotators. WARP-Text fills a gap in the currently available NLP toolbox, as open-source alternatives for annotation of pairs of text are not readily available. WARP-Text has already been used in several annotation tasks and can be of interest to the researchers working in the areas of Paraphrasing, Entailment, Simplification, and Summarization, among others.

1 Introduction

Multiple research fields in NLP have pairs of texts as their object of study: Paraphrasing, Textual Entailment, Text Summarization, Text Simplification, Question Answering, and Machine Translation, among others. All these fields benefit from high quality corpora, annotated at different granularity levels. However, existing annotation tools have limited capabilities to process and annotate such corpora. The most popular state-of-the-art open source tools do not natively support detailed pairwise annotation and require significant adaptations and modifications of the code for such tasks.

We present the first version of WARP-Text, an open source[1] web-based annotation tool, created and designed specifically for the annotation of relationships between pairs of texts at multiple layers and at different granularity levels. Our objective was to create a tool that is functional, flexible, intuitive, and easy to use. WARP-Text was built using PHP and MySQL standard implementation.

WARP-Text is highly configurable: the administrator interface manages the number, order, and content of the different annotation layers. The pre-built layers allow for custom definitions of labels and granularity levels. The system architecture is flexible and modular, which allows for the modification of the existing layers and the addition of new ones.

The annotator interface is intuitive and easy to use. It does not require previous knowledge or extensive annotator training. The interface has already been used in the task of annotating atomic paraphrases (Kovatchev et al., 2018) and is currently being used on two annotation tasks in Text Summarization. The learning process of the annotators was quick and the feedback was overwhelmingly positive.

The rest of this article is organized as follows. Section 2 presents the Related Work. Section 3 describes the architecture of the interface, the annotation scheme, the usage cases, and the two interfaces: administrator and annotator. Finally, Section 4 presents the conclusions and the future work.

2 Related Work

In the last several years, the NLP community has shown growing interest in tools that are web-based, open source, and multi-purpose: WebAnno (Yimam and Gurevych, 2013), Inforex (Marcińczuk et al., 2017), and Anafora (Chen and Styler, 2013). Other popular non web-based annotation systems include

[1]The code is available at https://github.com/venelink/WARP under Creative Commons Attribution 4.0 International License.

Proceedings of the 27th International Conference on Computational Linguistics: System Demonstrations, pages 132–136
Santa Fe, New Mexico, USA, August 20-26, 2018.

GATE (Cunningham et al., 2011) and AnCoraPipe (Bertrán et al., 2008). These systems are intended to be feature-rich and multi-purpose. However, in many tasks, it is often preferable to create a specialized annotation tool to address problems that are non-trivial to solve using the multi-purpose annotation tools. One such problem is working with multiple texts in parallel. While multi-purpose annotation tools can be adapted for such use, this often leads to a more complex annotation scheme, complicates the annotation process, requires additional annotator training and post-processing of the annotated corpora. Toledo et al. (2014) and more recently Vivi Nastase and Frank (2018), Vuk Batanovi and Nikoli (2018), and Arase and Tsujii (2018) emphasize the lack of a feature-rich open-source tool for annotation of pairs of texts[2]. Some of these authors develop simple custom-made tools with limited re-usability, designed for for carrying out one specific annotation task. WARP-Text aims to address this gap in the NLP toolbox by providing a feature rich system which could be used in all these annotation scenarios.

To the best of our knowledge, the only existing multi-purpose tool that is designed to work with pairs of text and allows for detailed annotation is CoCo (España Bonet et al., 2009). It has already been used for annotations in paraphrasing (Vila et al., 2015) and plagiarism detection (Barrón-Cedeño et al., 2013). However, CoCo is not open source and is currently not being supported or updated.

3 WARP-Text

By addressing various limitations of existing tools, WARP-Text fills a gap in the state-of-the-art NLP toolbox. It offers project managers and annotators a rich set of functionalities and features: the ability to work with pairs of texts simultaneously; multi-layer annotation; annotation at different granularity levels; annotation of discontinuous scope and long-distance dependencies; and the custom definition of relationships. WARP-Text consists of two separate web interfaces: annotator and administrator. In the *administrator interface* the project manager configures the annotation scheme, defines the relationships and sets all parameters for the annotation process. The annotators work in the *annotator interface*.

WARP-Text is a tool for qualitative document annotation. It provides a wide range of configuration options and can be used for fine-grained annotation. It is best suited to medium sized corpora (containing thousands of small documents) and is not fully optimized for processing, analyzing, searching, and annotating large corpora (containing millions of documents). WARP-Text has full UTF-8 support and is language independent in the sense that it can handle documents in any UTF-8 supported natural language. So far it has been used to annotate texts in English, Bulgarian (Cyrillic), and Arabic.

WARP-Text is a multi-user system and provides two different forms of interaction between the different annotators. In the *collaborative mode*, multiple annotators work on the same text and each annotator can see and modify the annotations of the others. In the *independent mode*, the annotators perform the annotation independently from one another. The different annotations can then be compared in order to calculate inter-annotator agreement.

3.1 Annotation Scheme

The atomic units of the annotation scheme in WARP-Text are *relationships*. The properties of the *relationships* are *label* and *scope*. The *scope* of a *relationship* is a list of continuous or discontinuous *elements* in each of the two texts. The granularity level of the scope determines the *element* type. An *element* can be the whole text, a sentence, a phrase, a token, or can be defined manually. A *layer* in WARP-Text is a set of relationships, whose scopes belong to the same granularity level[3]. The definition of relationships and their grouping into layers is fully configurable through the administrator interface. WARP-Text supports multi-layer annotation. That is, the same pair of texts can be annotated multiple times, at different granularity levels and using different sets of relationships.

---

[2]See also the discussion about looking for tools for annotating pairs of texts in the Corpora Mailing List (May 2017): http://mailman.uib.no/public/corpora/2017-May/026526.html - http://mailman.uib.no/public/corpora/2017-May/026619.html

[3]There is no one-to-one correspondence between granularity level and annotation layer. Each annotation layer is a sub-task in the main annotation task. Multiple annotation layers can work at the same granularity level. For example: at layer (1) the annotator annotates the semantic relations between the tokens in the two texts; at layer (2) the annotator annotates the scope of negation and the negation cues in the two texts. Both layer (1) and layer (2) work at the token granularity level.

3.2 Administrator Interface

The administrator interface has three main modules: a) the *dataset management module*, b) the *user management module*, and c) the *layer management module*. In the *dataset management module* the project manager can: a) import a corpus, in a delimited text format, for annotation; b) monitor the current annotation status and statistics; and c) export the annotated corpus as an SQL file or an XML file. In the *user management module* the project manager creates new users and modifies existing ones. In this module the project manager also distributes the tasks (pairs) among the annotators. In the *layer management module* the project manager configures each of the layers and determines the order of the layers in the annotation process. The project manager configures for each individual layer: 1) the granularity level; 2) the relationships that belong to the layer; 3) the sub-relationships or properties of the relationships; 4) optional parameters such as "sentence lock" and "display previous layers".

3.3 Annotator Interface

The annotator interface has three main modules: a) the *annotation statistics module*, b) the *review annotations module*, and c) the *annotation panel module*. In the *annotation statistics module* the annotator monitors the progress of the annotation and sees statistics such as the number of annotated pairs, and the remaining number of pairs. In the *review annotations module* the annotator reviews the text pairs (s)he already annotated and introduces corrections where necessary. The *annotation panel module* is the core of the annotator interface. One of our main objectives in the creation of WARP-Text was to make it easier to use for the annotators and to optimize the annotation time. For that reason we have made the *annotator panel module* as automated as possible and have limited the intervention of annotators to a minimum. The *annotation panel module* is generated dynamically, based on the user and project configuration. It loads the first text pair, assigned to the current annotator and guides the annotator through the different layers in the order specified by the project manager. Once the text pair has been annotated at all configured layers, the module updates the database, loads the next pair and repeats the process.

We illustrate the annotation process with the interface configuration that was used in the annotation of the Extended Typology Paraphrase Corpus (ETPC) (Kovatchev et al., 2018). The annotation scheme of ETPC consists of two layers: one layer that is configured for annotation at the text granularity level; and one layer that is configured for annotation at the token granularity level.

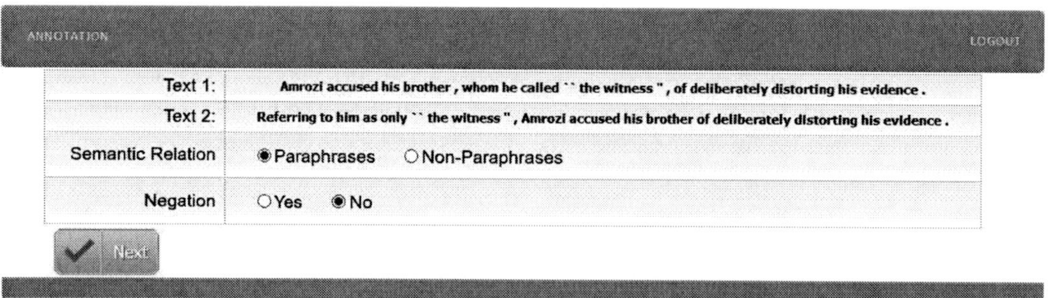

Figure 1: Annotating relationships at textual level.

The textual layer (Figure 1) displays the two texts and allows the annotator to select the values for an arbitrary number of relationships between the texts. In the case of ETPC, the two textual relationships that we were interested in were: 1) "The semantic relationship between the two texts": "Paraphrases" or "Non-paraphrases"; and 2) "The presence of negation in either of the two sentences": "Yes" or "No". In ETPC, both relationships had two possible options, however WARP-Text supports multiple options for each relationship. In this first layer, the scope of the relationship is the whole text.

The second layer (Figure 2) has five functional parts, labeled in the figure with numbers from 1 to 5. The annotator can see the two texts in (1), the annotation at the previous layers in (2), and at the annotation at the current layer in (4). (3) is the navigation panel between the different layers. Finally, (5)

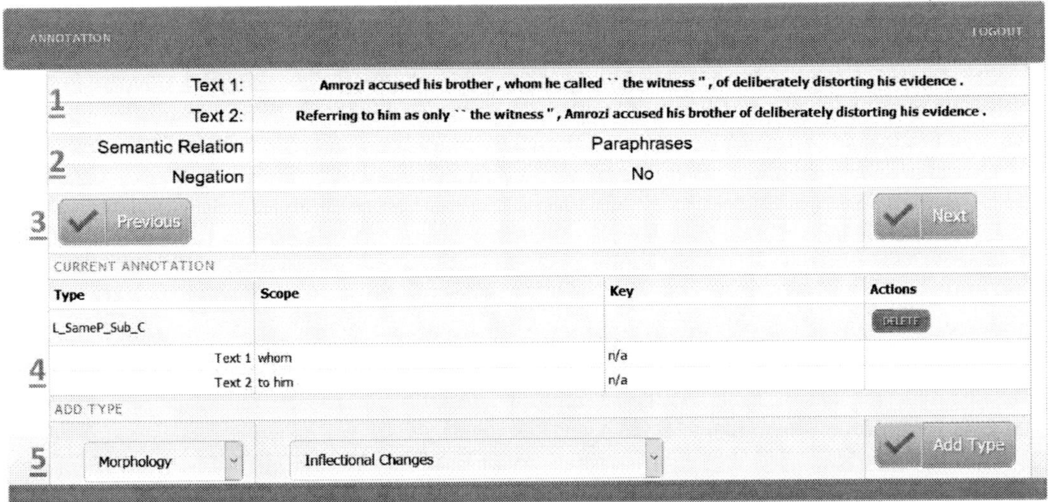

Figure 2: Annotating relationships at token level.

is where the annotator can choose to add a new relationship. The list of possible relationships is defined by the project manager in the administrator interface. In the case of ETPC we organized the relationships in a two-level hierarchical system based on their linguistic meta-category. The token-layer annotation is more complex than the textual-layer annotation as it requires the annotation of scope in addition to the annotation a label[4]. When the annotator chooses a relationship, the "Add Type" button goes to the scope selection page (Figure 3). The scope can be discontinuous and can include elements from one of the texts only or from both. In the case of ETPC, the elements that the annotator can select are tokens. In other configurations, they can be phrases or sentences.

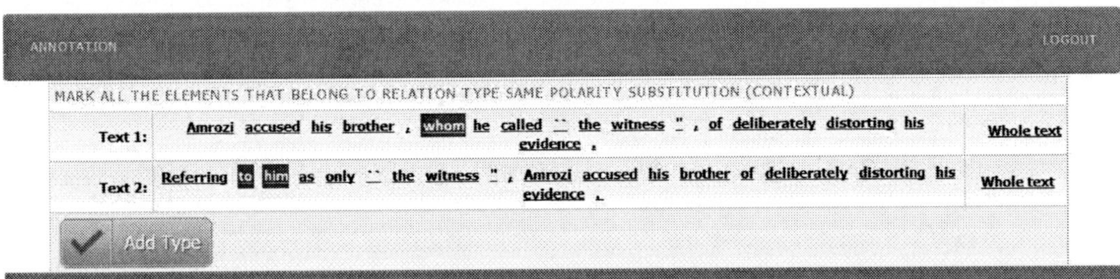

Figure 3: Scope selection page.

The flexibility of WARP-Text makes it easy to adapt for multiple tasks. The textual layer can be used in tasks such as the annotation of textual paraphrases, textual entailment, or semantic similarity. The atomic level annotation layer has even more applications. As we showed in ETPC, it can be used to annotate fine-grained similarities and differences between pairs of texts. It can also be used for tasks such as manual correction of text alignment. Another possible use is, given a summary or a simplified text, to identify in the reference text the exact sentences or phrases which are summarized or simplified.

4 Conclusions and Future Work

In this paper we presented WARP-Text, a web-based tool for annotating relationships between pairs of texts. Our software fills an important gap as the high quality annotation of pairwise corpora at different

---

[4]The token level annotation layer is an instance of the more general "atomic level annotation layer". The organization and work flow described here are the same when the granularity level is "paragraph", "sentence", "phrase", or custom defined.

granularity levels is needed and can benefit multiple fields in NLP. Previously available tools are not well suited for the task, require substantial modification, or are hard to configure. The main advantages of WARP-Text are that it is feature-rich, open source, highly configurable, and intuitive and easy to use.

As future work, we plan to add several functionalities to both interfaces. In the administrator interface, we plan to offer project managers tools for visualization and data analysis, and automatic calculation of inter-annotator agreement. In the annotator interface, we plan to fully explore the advantages of multi-layer architecture. By design, WARP-Text can support parent-child dependencies between layers. However, the pre-built modules available in this first release of the tool use only independent layers. That is, the annotation at one layer does not affect the configuration of the other layers. We also plan to explore the possibility of incorporating external automated pre-processing tools.

Acknowledgements

We would like to thank dr. Irina Temnikova and Ahmed AbuRa'ed for their support and suggestions, and the anonymous reviewers for their feedback and comments.

This work has been funded by Spanish Ministery of Economy Project TIN2015-71147-C2-2, by the CLiC research group (2017 SGR 341), and by the APIF grant of the first author.

References

Yuki Arase and Jun'ichi Tsujii. 2018. Spade: Evaluation dataset for monolingual phrase alignment. In *Proceedings of LREC-2018*.

Alberto Barrón-Cedeño, Marta Vila, M. Antònia Martí, and Paolo Rosso. 2013. Plagiarism meets paraphrasing: Insights for the next generation in automatic plagiarism detection. *Computational Linguistics*, 39(4):917–947.

Manuel Bertrán, Oriol Borrega, Marta Recasens, and Bàrbara Soriano. 2008. Ancorapipe: A tool for multilevel annotation. *Procesamiento del Lenguaje Natural*, 41.

Wei-Te Chen and Will Styler. 2013. Anafora: A web-based general purpose annotation tool. In *HLT-NAACL*.

Hamish Cunningham, Diana Maynard, Kalina Bontcheva, Valentin Tablan, Niraj Aswani, Ian Roberts, Genevieve Gorrell, Adam Funk, Angus Roberts, Danica Damljanovic, Thomas Heitz, Mark A. Greenwood, Horacio Saggion, Johann Petrak, Yaoyong Li, and Wim Peters. 2011. *Text Processing with GATE (Version 6)*.

Cristina España Bonet, Marta Vila Rigat, Horacio Rodríguez, and Antonia Martí. 2009. Coco, a web interface for corpora compilation.

Venelin Kovatchev, M. Antònia Martí, and Maria Salamó. 2018. Etpc - a paraphrase identification corpus annotated with extended paraphrase typology and negation. In *Proceedings of LREC-2018*.

Michał Marcińczuk, Marcin Oleksy, and Jan Kocoń. 2017. Inforex a collaborative system for text corpora annotation and analysis. In *Proceedings of RANLP-2017*, September.

Assaf Toledo, Stavroula Alexandropoupou, Sophie Chesney, Sophia Katrenko, Heidi Klockmann, Pepijn Kokke, Benno Kruit, and Yoad Winter. 2014. Towards a semantic model for textual entailment. In Cleo Condoravdi, Valeria de Paiva, and Annie Zaenen, editors, *Linguistic Issues in Language Technology vol. 9*.

Marta Vila, Manuel Bertran, M. Antònia Martí, and Horacio Rodríguez. 2015. Corpus annotation with paraphrase types: new annotation scheme and inter-annotator agreement measures. *Language Resources and Evaluation*.

Devon Fritz Vivi Nastase and Anette Frank. 2018. Demodify: A dataset for analyzing contextual constraints on modifier deletion. In *Proceedings of LREC-2018*.

Pavel Vondika. 2014. Aligning parallel texts with intertext. In *Proceedings of LREC-2014*, Reykjavik, Iceland, may.

Milo Cvetanovi Vuk Batanovi and Boko Nikoli. 2018. Fine-grained semantic textual similarity for serbian. In *Proceedings of LREC-2018*.

Seid Muhie Yimam and Iryna Gurevych. 2013. Webanno: A flexible, web-based and visually supported system for distributed annotations. In *In Proceedings of ACL-2013 System Demonstrations*, pages 1–6.

A Chinese Writing Correction System for Learning Chinese as a Foreign Language

Yow-Ting Shiue[1], Hen-Hsen Huang[1], and Hsin-Hsi Chen[1,2]

[1]Department of Computer Science and Information Engineering,
National Taiwan University, Taipei, Taiwan
[2]MOST Joint Research Center for AI Technology and All Vista Healthcare, Taiwan
`orina1123@gmail.com, hhhuang@nlg.csie.ntu.edu.tw, hhchen@ntu.edu.tw`

Abstract

We present a Chinese writing correction system for learning Chinese as a foreign language. The system takes a wrong input sentence and generates several correction suggestions. It also retrieves example Chinese sentences with English translations, helping users understand the correct usages of certain grammar patterns. This is the first available Chinese writing error correction system based on the neural machine translation framework. We discuss several design choices and show empirical results to support our decisions.

Title and Abstract in Chinese

爲非母語中文學習者設計的中文寫作更正系統

我們建立了一個爲非母語中文學習者設計的中文寫作更正系統，輸入一個錯誤的句子，此系統可以產生數個建議更正，並查詢附有英文翻譯的相關例句，幫助使用者理解某些文法的正確用法。這是第一個基於神經網路機器翻譯框架的中文寫作錯誤更正系統，在此篇論文中我們討論幾個設計上的選擇，呈現幫助我們做決定的實驗數據。

1 Introduction

Grammatical error correction (GEC) helps users check and correct mistakes in their writing. English GEC has been incorporated in commercial software; in contrast, there is far fewer readily usable writing correction tools for Chinese. Chinese has become a popular foreign language to learn worldwide, motivating the development of Chinese writing correction system targeting second language (L2) learners.

Unlike the classification approach, the translation approach to English GEC does not require exact recognition of error types. With many-to-many mappings handled, it is possible to deal with multiple errors of various types with a single translation model. An open-source statistical machine translation (SMT)-based English GEC system is released by Chollampatt and Ng (2017). More recently, neural machine translation (NMT) is applied to English GEC and improvements over the SMT baseline are shown (Yuan and Briscoe, 2016). With the use of distributional word representations, NMT has better ability to generalize to unseen corrections.

The Shared Task for Chinese Grammatical Error Diagnosis (CGED) (Rao et al., 2017) only evaluates detection but not correction performance until 2017. Some studies focus on certain error types of L2 Chinese, such as word ordering errors (Cheng et al., 2014) and word usage errors (Shiue and Chen, 2016; Shiue et al., 2017). Huang et al. (2016) correct preposition errors. Nevertheless, there has not yet been a general model that handles all types of Chinese writing errors.

Given the promising results of translation approaches in English, it is worth investigating their effectiveness in Chinese. Because the machine translation models need to be trained with parallel corpus of wrong-corrected sentences and there is limited amount of Chinese learner data with annotated corrections, we use NMT models and facilitate them with word embeddings pre-trained on large amount of well-formed Chinese text. To our knowledge, we are the first to apply NMT to Chinese error correction.

Proceedings of the 27th International Conference on Computational Linguistics: System Demonstrations, pages 137–141
Santa Fe, New Mexico, USA, August 20-26, 2018.

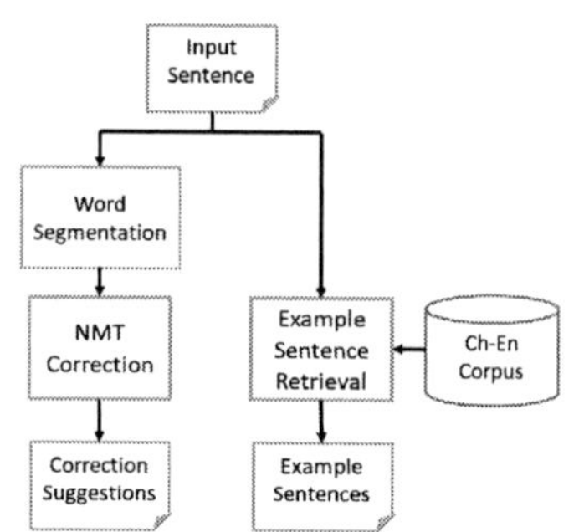

Figure 1: Architecture of our Chinese writing error correction system.

Figure 2: Web-based demonstration of our Chinese error correction system.

To improve writing proficiency, language learners need to know not only how the sentences they wrote are incorrect, but also how to correctly express their intended meanings. Therefore, in addition to correction suggestions, our system provides example sentences related to the input with appropriate level of difficulty. Figure 1 illustrates the overall architecture of our system. The two main components, NMT Correction and Example Sentence Retrieval, will be elaborated in Sections 2 and 3 respectively. All user inputs and system outputs are logged. These records can be utilized to analyze common learner error patterns, and additional training data can be annotated to incrementally improve the system performance. A web-based demonstration of our system is available at `http://nlg6.csie.ntu.edu.tw/CGED-NMT-demo` and a screenshot is shown in Figure 2.

2 Correction with Neural Machine Translation

We treat the error correction task as a translation task from erroneous Chinese to well-formed Chinese. This idea has been widely adopted for English GEC, but we are the first to apply it to the correction of Chinese. A typical NMT model is composed of an encoder and a decoder. The encoder transforms the input sequence into a sequence of hidden states, each of which is calculated with the hidden state of the previous time step and the input of the current time step. The decoder predicts the distribution of words for each time step conditioned on the encoder hidden states and the output of all previous time steps. The encoder-decoder network is trained to maximize the likelihood of the ground-truth translations in the training data. Our system is built on the top of OpenNMT (Klein et al., 2017). We adopt a bidirectional Long-short Term Memory (LSTM) encoder and a two-layer LSTM decoder. Global attention over the sequence of hidden states at the source side is applied. The model generates one to five corrections according to the n-best decoding result. Several design choices will be discussed in Section 2.2.

2.1 Datasets and Evaluation

To train the NMT correction model, we utilize the publicly available datasets of the NLPTEA 14-17 CGED shared tasks[1]. As a whole, there are more simplified Chinese sentences than traditional Chinese ones, so we convert all sentences to simplified Chinese. Each sentence can be completely correct (no correction is needed), or contain one or more errors. The errors are categorized into redundant word, missing word, word selection, and word ordering. However, we build a general correction framework for all types of errors and do not use or predict error type labels. We use the test data of NLPTEA 14 (1,783 sentence) and 15 (1,000 sentences) for validation and testing respectively, and the training data of NLPTEA 14-17 (totally 38,554 sentences) for training. We do not use the test data of NLPTEA 16 and 17 since there are only error type labels but no correction in the datasets.

The correction performance can be evaluated by judging whether a correction is exactly the same as the ground-truth. We report the accuracy as well as hit rates of top candidates. However, hit rates can still be

---

[1]https://sites.google.com/view/nlptea2018/shared-task

somehow strict since a model will not get any scores even if the top candidate it proposes is only slightly different from the answer. Thus, we also report the General Language Evaluation Understanding (GLEU) metric (Napoles et al., 2015), which is a modification of BLEU that rewards correct modifications while penalizing unnecessary changes. We use the publicly released toolkit[2] to calculate GLEU of n-gram order 4. GLEU is calculated only for the top candidate.

2.2 Design Choices

There are several design choices for building the NMT-based correction system. We discuss the reasons for each decision and show experimental results when necessary. In the experiments, we choose the model with the highest validation GLEU and report the performance on the test set. The GLEU of an output that is completely the same as the source can be regarded as a baseline.

Character-based vs. Word-based Models

Although a word is a more meaningful semantic unit, word-based models might suffer from noise induced by segmentation errors, which might occur more frequently in learners' text than in normal well-formed text. On the other hand, character-based models need to handle longer dependencies. We make the fundamental design decision of treating an input sentence as a sequence of characters or a sequence of words based on empirical results. For word segmentation, we use THU Lexical Analyzer for Chinese (THULAC) (Sun et al., 2016)[3], which results in the best correction performance among several Chinese word segmentation tools.

The performance of the two kinds of models is shown in Table 1. We report character-level GLEUs in order to make the metric values of the two models comparable. As can be seen, the word-based model outperforms the character-based model in all evaluation metrics. A possible reason is that the decoder is trained to output well-formed sentences. Though segmentation errors might affect the understanding of the source sentence, the decoder is still possible to "complete" the output sentence based on partial source information. For example, the erroneous sentence "* 我 覺得 他 是 一個 很 好人" (* *I think he is a very good-person*) is corrected to "我 覺得 他 是 一個 很 好 的 人" (*I think he is a very good person*). Based on these results, we decide to use the word-based NMT model in our system.

Pre-trained Word Embeddings

Initializing word representations in NMT models with pre-trained word vectors can be useful when the training data is insufficient. In addition to the standard Word2vec continuous bag-of-words (CBOW) and Skip-gram (SG) embeddings (Mikolov et al., 2013), we also experiment with the continuous window (CWIN) and structured skip-gram (Struct-SG) embeddings (Ling et al., 2015), which consider the relative order of context words during training and are shown to be useful for Chinese error detection (Shiue et al., 2017). We segment the Chinese part of ClueWeb[4] with the THULAC toolkit and train the embeddings with it. The embedding size is fixed to 500 and the context window size is 5 for all kinds of embeddings. The results are summarized in Table 1. All pre-trained word embeddings bring improvement over random embeddings. Generally, the NMT correction model with pre-trained Struct-SG embeddings achieves the best performance. Thus, we use Struct-SG embeddings in our final system.

Model	Features	Accuracy	Hit@3	Hit@5	char. GLEU	word GLEU
(Baseline)	-	-	-	-	0.552	0.411
Character-based	Rand. emb.	0.145	0.293	0.341	0.625	-
Word-based	Rand. emb.	0.190	0.327	0.376	0.650	0.558
Word-based	CBOW	0.210	0.368	0.418	0.655	0.564
Word-based	SG	0.194	0.369	0.414	0.657	0.564
Word-based	CWIN	0.214	0.379	**0.433**	0.658	0.566
Word-based	Struct-SG	**0.232**	**0.387**	0.431	**0.668**	**0.580**

Table 1: Performance of NMT-based correction models

---

[2]https://github.com/cnap/gec-ranking
[3]http://thulac.thunlp.org/
[4]http://lemurproject.org/clueweb09.php

3   Example Sentence Retrieval

Besides giving correction suggestions, our system also shows example sentences to demonstrate how to correctly use the words and grammar patterns in the user input. These example sentences also serve as additional evidence of the correctness of some usage patterns.We adopt UM-Corpus (Tian et al., 2014), a sentence-aligned English-Chinese corpus, as the database of example sentences. We only use sentences in the "Education" domain, which are extracted from online teaching materials. There are 450,000 English-Chinese sentence pairs. We exclude example sentence pairs in which the Chinese sentence is longer than 30 Chinese characters since they usually have complex syntactic structures.

Upon user input, ten example sentences are retrieved. They are ranked by the overlaps of Chinese character bigrams. The more character bigrams an example sentence has in common with the input sentence, the higher score it gets. The score is normalized by the total number of character bigrams. Although more recent retrieval models, such as those based on word embeddings, can handle semantic similarities that are not reflected in the surface form, there is another level of difficulties for foreign language learners to recognize this kind of similarities. Therefore, bigram matching may help to focus on the words and grammar patterns being used in the input sentence.

An example input sentence and the top 3 retrieved example sentences are shown below. As can be seen, the sentences where the phrase "每個月" (*every month*) is used are selected.

Input: * 在泰國每個月天氣都熱 (*In Thailand, the weather is hot every month.*)

Example sentences:

過去十年她每個月都在存錢。　*She had been saving money every month for the last ten years.*
你每個月的食宿費用是多少?　*How much do you charge a month for room and board?*
每個月25元的月租就是白送錢。　*The monthly rent of 25 yuan per month is white money.*

4   Conclusions

We build a writing correction system for learning Chinese as a foreign language. The system not only provides corrections, but also presents example sentences with English translation, illustrating how to correctly use the words and grammar patterns related to the input sentence. The correction is performed with an NMT model enhanced by pre-trained word representations. On the test set of the NLPTEA 15 CGED shared task, the model achieves GLEU 0.67 and 0.58 at the character and the word levels, respectively. Further research can be conducted on top of our framework, and the web interface can facilitate user evaluation of different back-end models.

Acknowledgements

This research was partially supported by Ministry of Science and Technology, Taiwan, under grants MOST-106-2923-E-002-012-MY3, MOST-107-2634-F-002-011- and MOST-107-2634-F-002-019-.

References

Shuk-Man Cheng, Chi-Hsin Yu, and Hsin-Hsi Chen. 2014. Chinese Word Ordering Errors Detection and Correction for Non-Native Chinese Language Learners. In *Proceedings of COLING 2014, the 25th International Conference on Computational Linguistics: Technical Papers*, pages 279–289. Dublin City University and Association for Computational Linguistics.

Shamil Chollampatt and Hwee Tou Ng. 2017. Connecting the Dots: Towards Human-Level Grammatical Error Correction. In *Proceedings of the 12th Workshop on Innovative Use of NLP for Building Educational Applications*, pages 327–333. Association for Computational Linguistics.

Hen-Hsen Huang, Yen-Chi Shao, and Hsin-Hsi Chen. 2016. Chinese Preposition Selection for Grammatical Error Diagnosis. In *Proceedings of COLING 2016, the 26th International Conference on Computational Linguistics: Technical Papers*, pages 888–899. The COLING 2016 Organizing Committee.

Guillaume Klein, Yoon Kim, Yuntian Deng, Jean Senellart, and Alexander Rush. 2017. OpenNMT: Open-Source Toolkit for Neural Machine Translation. In *Proceedings of ACL 2017, System Demonstrations*, pages 67–72. Association for Computational Linguistics.

Wang Ling, Chris Dyer, Alan W Black, and Isabel Trancoso. 2015. Two/Too Simple Adaptations of Word2Vec for Syntax Problems. In *Proceedings of the 2015 Conference of the North American Chapter of the Association for Computational Linguistics: Human Language Technologies*, pages 1299–1304. Association for Computational Linguistics.

Tomas Mikolov, Kai Chen, Greg Corrado, and Jeffrey Dean. 2013. Efficient estimation of word representations in vector space. *arXiv preprint arXiv:1301.3781*.

Courtney Napoles, Keisuke Sakaguchi, Matt Post, and Joel Tetreault. 2015. Ground Truth for Grammatical Error Correction Metrics. In *Proceedings of the 53rd Annual Meeting of the Association for Computational Linguistics and the 7th International Joint Conference on Natural Language Processing (Volume 2: Short Papers)*, pages 588–593. Association for Computational Linguistics.

Gaoqi Rao, Baolin Zhang, Endong Xun, and Lung-Hao Lee. 2017. IJCNLP-2017 Task 1: Chinese Grammatical Error Diagnosis. In *Proceedings of the IJCNLP 2017, Shared Tasks*, pages 1–8. Asian Federation of Natural Language Processing.

Yow-Ting Shiue and Hsin-Hsi Chen. 2016. Detecting Word Usage Errors in Chinese Sentences for Learning Chinese as a Foreign Language. In *Proceedings of the 10th International Conference on Language Resources and Evaluation (LREC 2016)*. European Language Resources Association (ELRA).

Yow-Ting Shiue, Hen-Hsen Huang, and Hsin-Hsi Chen. 2017. Detection of Chinese Word Usage Errors for Non-Native Chinese Learners with Bidirectional LSTM. In *Proceedings of the 55th Annual Meeting of the Association for Computational Linguistics (Volume 2: Short Papers)*, pages 404–410. Association for Computational Linguistics.

Maosong Sun, Xinxiong Chen, Kaixu Zhang, Zhipeng Guo, and Zhiyuan Liu. 2016. THULAC: an efficient lexical analyzer for Chinese. Technical report.

Liang Tian, Derek F. Wong, Lidia S. Chao, Paulo Quaresma, Francisco Oliveira, and Lu Yi. 2014. UM-Corpus: A Large English-Chinese Parallel Corpus for Statistical Machine Translation. In *Proceedings of the 9th International Conference on Language Resources and Evaluation (LREC 2014)*. European Language Resources Association (ELRA).

Zheng Yuan and Ted Briscoe. 2016. Grammatical error correction using neural machine translation. In *Proceedings of the 2016 Conference of the North American Chapter of the Association for Computational Linguistics: Human Language Technologies*, pages 380–386. Association for Computational Linguistics.

LTV: Labeled Topic Vector

Daniel Baumartz　　　　　**Tolga Uslu**　　　　　**Alexander Mehler**

Text Technology Lab
Goethe University Frankfurt
Frankfurt, Germany
`{baumartz,uslu,mehler}@em.uni-frankfurt.de`
`https://www.texttechnologylab.org/`

Abstract

In this paper, we present *LTV*, a website and an API that generate labeled topic classifications based on the *Dewey Decimal Classification* (DDC), an international standard for topic classification in libraries. We introduce *nnDDC*, a largely language-independent neural network-based classifier for DDC-related topic classification, which we optimized using a wide range of linguistic features to achieve an F-score of 87,4%. To show that our approach is language-independent, we evaluate *nnDDC* using up to 40 different languages. We derive a topic model based on *nnDDC*, which generates probability distributions over semantic units for any input on sense-, word- and text-level. Unlike related approaches, however, these probabilities are estimated by means of *nnDDC* so that each dimension of the resulting vector representation is uniquely labeled by a DDC class. In this way, we introduce a neural network-based *Classifier-Induced Semantic Space* (*nnCISS*).

1　Introduction

We present a model for calculating neural network-based *Classifier-Induced Semantic Space*s (*nnCISS*) using the *Dewey Decimal Classification* (DDC), that is, an international standard for topic classification in libraries. Based on this model, input units on the sense-, word-, sentence- or text level can be mapped onto the same feature space to compute, for example, their semantic similarity (Bär et al., 2012; Pilehvar and Navigli, 2015). Such an approach is needed whenever multiresolutional semantic information has to be processed to interrelate, for example, units of different levels of linguistic resolution (e.g., words or phrases to texts).

Contrary to related approaches (Landauer and Dumais, 1997; Blei et al., 2003) we use classifiers to define the dimensions of CISS, which are directly labeled by the underlying target class. This has the advantage that embeddings of linguistic units in semantic spaces can be interpreted directly in relation to the class labels.

In order to demonstrate the expressiveness of *nnCISS*, we conduct two classification tasks and show that using *nnCISS*-based feature vectors improve any of these classifications.

We generate several DDC corpora by exploring information from *Wikidata*, *Wikipedia* and the *Integrated Authority File (Gemeinsame Normdatei – GND)* of the German National Library. Any Wikipedia article in such a corpus is linked to an entry in Wikidata, which contains a property[1] attribute referring to the DDC, or to a GND page containing a corresponding DDC tag[2]. Since many Wikipedia articles refer to Wikidata or the GND, we were able to explore these articles as training examples of the corresponding DDC classes. The DDC includes three levels of thematic resolution: The first level distinguishes 10 main topics, each of which is subdivided into maximally 10 topics on the 2nd level (99 classes), which in turn are subdivided into maximally 10 topics on the 3rd level (915 classes). We use the 2nd and 3rd level of DDC as two alternative classification schemes.

[1] `https://www.wikidata.org/wiki/Property:P1036`
[2] e.g., `https://d-nb.info/gnd/4176546-1`

Proceedings of the 27th International Conference on Computational Linguistics: System Demonstrations, pages 142–145
Santa Fe, New Mexico, USA, August 20-26, 2018.

Wikipedia is offered for a wide range of languages, which allows us to create such corpora for different languages. In addition, translations provided by both Wikipedia and Wikidata enable the creation of language-specific training corpora by evaluating translation relationships between articles assigned to the DDC and articles for which these assignments do not exist. In this paper, we focus on Arabic, English, French, German, Spanish, and Turkish while performing a deeper analysis by example of the German corpus (#articles 15 136, #tokens per article 1 228, #classes 2nd level 98 and #classes 3rd level 641). Additionally we select more Wikipedias from the *List of Wikipedias*[3], where $depth >= 50$ and $\#articles >= 10\,000$, to be available through our *LTV* API.

2   Classification Model

The architecture of the *LTV* framework consists of four steps:

1. We use TextImager (Hemati et al., 2016) for preprocessing (lemmatization, part of speech tagging) the German Wikipedia and perform *Word Sense Disambiguation* (WSD) by means of fastSense (Uslu et al., 2018a), a WSD tool that is trained on the entire German Wikipedia. Our approach is in line with (Pilehvar and Navigli, 2015) and, thus, disambiguates input words to obtain sense representations as input for calculating sense embeddings.

2. The disambiguated Wikipedia corpus is then used to create sense embeddings by means of word2vec (Mikolov et al., 2013) using all sentences as input.

3. The aim is to obtain disambiguated articles and sense embeddings for training a DDC classifier and thus generating *nnDDC*. For this we enrich the disambiguated Wikipedia articles with DDC information using Wikidata/GND. We use (Uslu et al., 2018b) to classify an input on the sense-, word, sentence- or document-level regarding the DDC as the target classification. In this paper, we optimize this classifier with respect to feature selection and extend it by alternatively using sense embeddings combined with a disambiguated corpus.

4. Next we utilize *nnDDC* to generate *nnCISS* for a given input in this way, that each input unit on the sense-, word- or text-level can be mapped onto an n-dimensional feature vector whose dimensions correspond to DDC classes. *nnCISS* generates a probability distribution over the DDC classes (of either the 2nd or 3rd level).

3   Evaluation

3.1   Evaluating *nnDDC*

We evaluate *nnDDC* regarding the question which features are most successful in DDC-oriented text classification.

We have trained and evaluated different document inputs (articles, sections, paragraphs and sentences as well as disambiguations and embeddings) and features like lemmatization of input token, included POS info, removed function words, sub-word units or n-gram features. We have also conducted a parameter study on various training hyperparameters like number of epochs and learning rate. In this way, we have increased the F-score to 87,4%.

Language	DDC 2	DDC 3
German	87,4%	78,1%
English	79,8%	72,6%
Arabic	79,8%	68,8%
Turkish	78,9%	67,5%
French	79,4%	68,1%
Spanish	79,7%	70,5%

Figure 1: F-scores for different languages for 2nd and 3rd level DDC.

Table 1 shows that though *nnDDC* performs worse in the case of the other languages compared to German, the results for the 2nd level of the DDC are nevertheless close to 80%. Evaluating the about 40 more languages we achieve an average score of 71%. Since corpus generation for these languages is straightforward, this also demonstrates that our approach is largely language independent at least what concerns languages that are sufficiently manifested by language specific releases of Wikipedia.

Switching to the 3rd level of DDC, we observe a drop in F-score, while in case of the German Wikipedia we still perform at about 78% and any topic vector is now enriched by providing more detailed information.

3.2 Evaluating *nnCISS*

To show that our DDC-based topic model improves classification, we have performed classification tasks on two data sets: The *DBpedia Ontology Classification Dataset*[4] and the *AG's news corpus*[5]. To be independent of the classifier, this experiment was conducted by means of StarSpace (Wu et al., 2017). Table 2 shows the results and the impact of *nnCISS*, and while the improvements are not very large, with such a high classification quality every percentage is important.

Input	DBpedia	AG News
Text without *nnCISS*	97,89%	89,88%
Text + *nnCISS* (DDC 2)	98,00%	90,18%
Text + *nnCISS* (DDC 3)	98,06%	90,33%

Figure 2: F-Scores in the DBpedia and AG News classification tasks.

4 *LTV* Software Demonstration

We offer the classifier (*nnDDC*) and the DDC topic model (*nnCISS*) for all above mentioned languages on `https://textimager.hucompute.org/DDC/`. It is directly accessible as a REST API or via the UI on the website. We have implemented the classifier for *LTV* as an UIMA annotator, this allows us to seamlessly integrate into TextImager and utilize the pipeline feature to process the input text. In the pipeline we first preprocess the text in exactly the way we prepared our training data and then perform the classification via our annotator. This eliminates the need for the user to preprocess the input and also makes the results reproducible. To use the API one performs a `POST` request which contains the input text to classify as well as some information about the format and the pipeline to use. All available pipelines are listed on the site. For example:

```
{ "inputText": "Beispiel über Angela Dorothea Merkel, ...",
  "inputFormat": "plain", "outputFormat": "ddc_json", "options": [
    { "de": [
      "LanguageToolSegmenter", "ParagraphSplitter",
      "MarMoTLemma", "MarMoTTagger",
      "FastTextDDC2LemmaNoPunctPOSNoFunctionwordsWithCategories
        TextImagerService" ] } ] }
```

This request returns an `JSON` object containing:

```
{ "ddc":[
    {"prob":0.990234,"label":"__label_ddc__320","tags":["ddc2"]},
    ... ],
  "success": true, "language": "de" }
```

The website provides an easy access to the API, requiring no programming skills to use. Users can paste text to classify and select the DDC level and language (it also tries to autodectect the language of the input text and selects a suitable pipeline for you). The UI then displays the results providing the DDC description, see Figure 3.

5 Conclusion

We presented a website and API to access and use a neural network based classifier to categorize DDC classes. For this we have used various features and resources to achieve the best possible classification,

---

[4]`www.wiki.dbpedia.org/data-set-2014`
[5]`www.di.unipi.it/~gulli/AG_corpus_of_news_articles.html`

DDC Classification

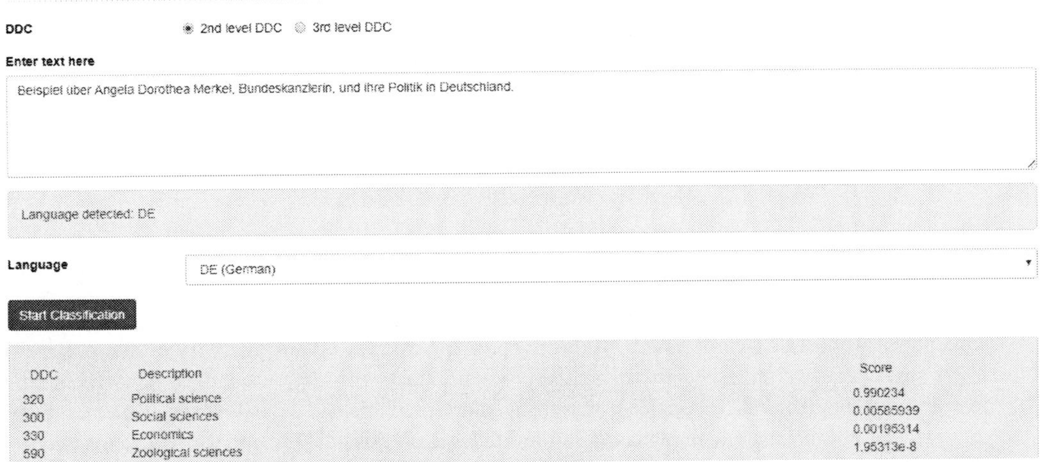

Figure 3: Screenshot of the *LTV* website

managing to achieve a quality of over 87% (and considering the top three classes, we even exceed 96%). For a given text, the classifier generates a probability distribution over the DDC classes and thus a vector. This vector can be used as input for other classification tasks and we have shown that improvements can be achieved.

References

Daniel Bär, Chris Biemann, Iryna Gurevych, and Torsten Zesch. 2012. UKP: Computing semantic textual similarity by combining multiple content similarity measures. In *Proc. of SemEval '12*, pages 435–440, Stroudsburg.

David M Blei, Andrew Y Ng, and Michael I Jordan. 2003. Latent dirichlet allocation. *Journal of machine Learning research*, 3(Jan):993–1022.

Wahed Hemati, Tolga Uslu, and Alexander Mehler. 2016. Textimager: a distributed uima-based system for nlp. In *Proceedings of COLING 2016, the 26th International Conference on Computational Linguistics: System Demonstrations*, pages 59–63.

Thomas K. Landauer and Susan T. Dumais. 1997. A solution to Plato's problem: The latent semantic analysis theory of acquisition, induction, and representation of knowledge. *Psychological Review*, 104(2):211–240.

Tomas Mikolov, Kai Chen, Greg Corrado, and Jeffrey Dean. 2013. Efficient estimation of word representations in vector space. *arXiv preprint arXiv:1301.3781*.

Mohammad Taher Pilehvar and Roberto Navigli. 2015. From senses to texts: An all-in-one graph-based approach for measuring semantic similarity. *Artificial Intelligence*, 228:95–128.

Tolga Uslu, Alexander Mehler, Daniel Baumartz, Alexander Henlein, and Wahed Hemati. 2018a. fastsense: An efficient word sense disambiguation classifier. In *Proceedings of the 11th edition of the Language Resources and Evaluation Conference, May 7 - 12*, LREC 2018, Miyazaki, Japan. accepted.

Tolga Uslu, Alexander Mehler, Andreas Niekler, and Wahed Hemati. 2018b. Towards a DDC-based topic network model of wikipedia. In *Proceedings of 2nd International Workshop on Modeling, Analysis, and Management of Social Networks and their Applications (SOCNET 2018), February 28, 2018*. accepted.

Ledell Wu, Adam Fisch, Sumit Chopra, Keith Adams, Antoine Bordes, and Jason Weston. 2017. Starspace: Embed all the things! *CoRR*, abs/1709.03856.

Interpretable Rationale Augmented Charge Prediction System

[1]**Xin Jiang**[*], [1]**Hai Ye**[*], [2]**Zhunchen Luo**[*], [1]**Wenhan Chao**[†], [1]**Wenjia Ma**
[1]School of Computer Science and Engineering, Beihang University
[2]Information Research Center of Military Science, PLA Academy of Military Science
[1,2]Beijing, China
[1]{xinjiang, yehai, chaowenhan, mawenjia}@buaa.edu.cn
[2]zhunchenluo@gmail.com

Abstract

This paper proposes a neural based system to solve the essential interpretability problem existing in text classification, especially in charge prediction task. First, we use a deep reinforcement learning method to extract rationales which mean short, readable and decisive snippets from input text. Then a rationale augmented classification model is proposed to elevate the prediction accuracy. Naturally, the extracted rationales serve as the introspection explanation for the prediction result of the model, enhancing the transparency of the model. Experimental results demonstrate that our system is able to extract readable rationales in a high consistency with manual annotation and is comparable with the attention model in prediction accuracy.

1 Introduction

Given a case's fact description, charge prediction aims to determine appropriate charge for the criminal suspect mentioned. Existing works generally treat charge prediction as a text classification problem, and have made a series of progress(Liu et al., 2004; Liu and Hsieh, 2006; Lin et al., 2012; Luo et al., 2017). However, in the field of justice, every decision may be a matter of life and death. It is necessary for judges and lawyers to understand the principles of the decisions, since people cannot completely trust the machine-generated judgement results without any interpretation provided.

Interpretability which means the ability of AI systems to explain their predictions, has attracted more and more attention. Hendricks et al. (2016) divide the concept of interpretation into *introspection explanation* which explains how a model determines its final output and *justification explanation* which produces sentences detailing how the evidence is compatible with the system output.

Works have been proposed to enhance the interpretability of AI&Law. From the justification aspect, Ye et al. (2018) consider court views as the explanation for the pre-decided charges. They use a charge-conditioned Seq2Seq model to generate court views based on criminal cases' fact descriptions and the given charge labels. From the introspection aspect, Luo et al. (2017) propose to select supportive law articles and use the articles to enhance the charge prediction accuracy. The supportive law articles is treated as a kind of support for the predicted charge.

In this work, focusing on the introspection explanation of charge prediction, we learn to jointly extract rationales and make charge prediction. The task is not trivial: (1) The granularity of rationales is difficult to grasp – sentence level rationales are not concrete enough while word level rationales lose readability. (2) Corpus with rationale annotation is hard to obtain. (3) Methods of improving the prediction accuracy while having high interpretability are very essential, but have not been well studied. In order to overcome the difficulties above, we propose a hybrid neural framework to (1) extract readable and charge-decisive rationales in the form of key fact snippets from input fact description with the only supervision of charge labels, and (2) elevate charge prediction accuracy by a rationale augmentation mechanism.

---

[*] indicates equal contribution.
[†] Corresponding author.

Proceedings of the 27th International Conference on Computational Linguistics: System Demonstrations, pages 146–151
Santa Fe, New Mexico, USA, August 20-26, 2018.

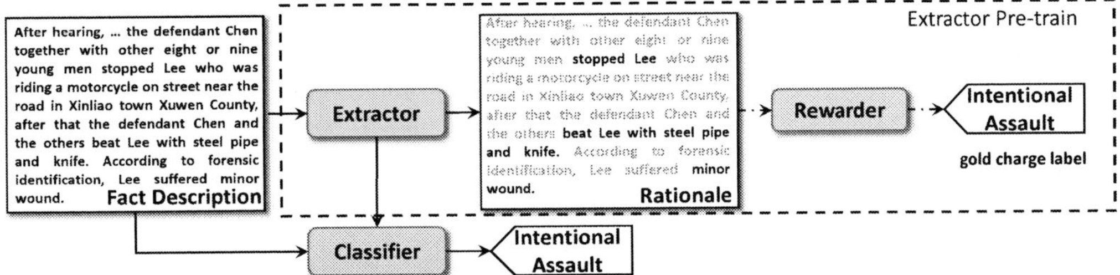

Figure 1: Architecture of Interpretable Rationale Augmented Charge Prediction System

2 Interpretable Rationale Augmented Charge Prediction System

In this section, we will first use mathematical language to define our task and then introduce the proposed Interpretable Rationale Augmented Charge Prediction System. We define the input fact description as word sequence $x = [x_1, x_2, \ldots, x_n]$, and the gold charge label y as a non-negative integer. Given x, we aim to extract rationales $r = \{x_i | z_i = 1, x_i \in x\}$ where $z_i \in \{0, 1\}$, and predict the charge based on x augmented by r. Figure 1 shows the overview of our system. The system takes the fact description in a case as input and outputs the predicted charge as well as the rationales. The rationales play an important role in the predicting process, so they can be seen as an explanation of the charge prediction. The system consists of two main components: **Extractor** and **Classifier**. We train these two components successively.

For the **Extractor** training phase, we apply a deep reinforcement method learning to extract rationales with the only supervision of charge labels. For the **Classifier** training phase, we freeze the parameters of **Extractor**, and the importance of each word is used to make a weighted sum over the RNN hidden states of all words. Then the weighted sum is used to make charge prediction.

2.1 Phrase-level Rationale Extraction

Considering the snippet-like rationales should be more integral in semantics, we propose to represent fact descriptions with phrases (as opposed to words). We split the fact description into phrases with a maximum length of 6. The phrase-level fact x^p is denoted as $[x_1^p, x_2^p, \ldots, x_m^p]$. x_i^p represents the i-th phrase in the fact description. x_i^p's representation is defined as the average word embedding in the phrase.

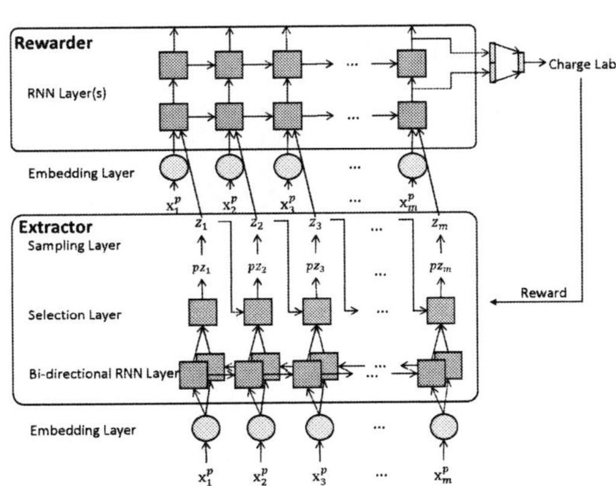

Figure 2: Architecture for Extractor Training

Figure 2 demonstrates the architecture for Extractor training. We introduce a latent variable z ($z \in \{0, 1\}^m$) to define the extraction of phrases. $z_t = 1$ represents the t-th word is chosen as an rationale phrase. The final goal of rationale extraction is to learn a distribution $p(z | x^p)$ over the phrase sequence. At time t, $p(z_t)$ is calculated as follows:

$$p(z_t | x^p, z_{<t}) = sigmoid(W^e[\overrightarrow{h_t}; \overleftarrow{h_t}; z_{t-1}] + b^e)$$
$$\overrightarrow{h_t} = \overrightarrow{f}(x_t^p, \overrightarrow{h_{t-1}}) \quad ; \quad \overleftarrow{h_t} = \overleftarrow{f}(x_t^p, \overleftarrow{h_{t+1}})$$

where $\overrightarrow{f}$ and $\overleftarrow{f}$ are Bi-RNN functions which read the input sequence forward and backward. Here we choose Bi-directional Gated Recurrent Units (Bi-GRU) as the recurrent units. z_t is sampled according to the probability $p(z_t)$. To model the distribution better, at time t, the information from current GRU outputs and the states of $z_{<t}$ are jointly considered to predict the label of x_t^p. The extracted rationales are $r = \{x_i^p | z_i = 1, x_i^p \in x^p\}$. The learning of rationale extraction needs a reward function to guide. Hence, we introduce **Rewarder**, a deep RNN model with 2 layers to model r, generate distribu-

tion over charge labels $\tilde{y}$ and then provide the reward. The final embedding of r is the concatenation of the last states of the two layers. $\tilde{y}$ is calculated as $\tilde{y} = sigmoid(W^r e_r + b^r)$.

To control the quantity of rationales, we introduce a novel penalty over z as $\Phi(z) = |\|z\| - \eta|$ where η is a constant to control $\|z\|$ around η in case of $\|z\|$ being too small or too large. We set η as 7 in this work. We define the loss function as $\mathcal{L}_\theta(r, y) = \|\tilde{y} - y\|_2^2 + \lambda\Phi(z)$. We use the gradient calculation in Lei et al. (2016). Sampling technique (Williams, 1992) is used to approximate the gradient.

2.2 Rationale Augmented Charge Prediction

We move to train **Classifier** utilizing the rationale information generated by **Extractor**. After the previous training, **Extractor** already has the ability to estimate the probabilities of the phrases being rationales. Though the phrase-level representation elevates the rationales' semantic integrality, it causes information loss in the averaging process.

In order to better utilize the information and make charge prediction more accurate, we adopt a RNN model with a rationale augment mechanism. Given the fact description word sequence $x = [x_1, x_2, \ldots, x_n]$, the hidden state at time t in the l-th layer is defined as follow:

$$
h_t^{(l)} = \begin{cases} f(h_t^{(l-1)}, h_{t-1}^{(l)}) & l > 0 \\ f(x_t, h_{t-1}^{(0)}) & l = 0 \end{cases}
$$

where f is a unidirectional RNN function. The representation of fact description in layer l derived from the weighted sum of all the hidden states in layer l. Here, $p(z)$ is treated as the importance distribution on input fact description. And the weights a_t are calculated by a softmax layer based on $p(z_t|x)$, which is provided by the pre-trained **Extractor**. More precisely:

$$
e_{doc}^{(l)} = \sum_1^n a_t h_t^{(l)}
$$

$$
a_t = \frac{\exp(p(z_t|x))}{\sum_{t=1}^n \exp(p(z_t|x))}
$$

The final representation of a fact description is defined as the concatenation of the representation in each RNN layer: $e_{doc} = [e_{doc}^{(0)}; e_{doc}^{(1)}; \cdots; e_{doc}^{(L-1)}]$. Through an activation layer, e_{doc} generates the final distribution $\tilde{y}$ on the charges: $\tilde{y} = sigmoid(W^c e_{doc} + b^c)$. The loss function is defined as: $\mathcal{L}_\theta(x, y) = \|\tilde{y} - y\|_2^2$.

3 Experiments

3.1 Data Preparation

We construct the dataset from China Judgements Online[1]. 80k, 10k and 10k documents are randomly selected as training, validation and test set respectively. We extract the fact description and charge labels using regular expressions. We set up a length threshold of 256. Fact description longer than that will be stripped. We use HanLP[2] to tokenize the Chinese texts. We use CoreNLP (Manning et al., 2014) to parse the syntax tree, and words in a subtree with a max length of 6 make up a phrase. There are 2.8 words in each phrase on average. We also use <name>, <num> and <date> to replace the names, numbers and dates in the corpus. Following Luo et al. (2017), we choose the same charge set involving 50 most common charges and leave the other charges as negative data. To evaluate the rationale extraction performance, we randomly select 1000 documents and ask three legal professionals to annotate the sentences mentioning illegal behaviors. Sentences chosen by at least two professionals are considered as gold rationale sentences. Kappa (Cohen, 1960) between the annotators is 0.773, proving the high consistency of the annotation.

---

[1] http://wenshu.court.gov.cn/
[2] https://github.com/hankcs/HanLP

MODEL	COMPARISON OF RATIONALE EXTRACTION PERFORMANCE
Bi-GRU$_{att}$	… 在 狩猎 过程 中，PP 因地滑 摔跤，导致 其所 持鸟 铳击 发走火，将走 在前面 的 PP 打伤致死… … In the process of hunting, PP fell down due to the slippery ground , leading to the shotgun fire, killing PP who was walking in front …
OURS$^-$	… 在 狩猎 过程 中，PP 因地滑 摔跤，导致 其所 持鸟 铳击 发走火，将走 在前面 的 PP 打伤致死… … In the process of hunting, PP fell down due to the slippery ground , leading to the shotgun fire, killing PP who was walking in front …
OURS	… 在 狩猎 过程 中，PP 因地滑 摔跤，导致 其所 持鸟 铳击 发走火，将走 在前面 的 PP 打伤致死… … In the process of hunting, PP fell down due to the slippery ground , leading to the shotgun fire, killing PP who was walking in front …

MORE DEMONSTRATION OF OUR SYSTEM
CASE 1 [$Official\ Embezzlement$]$_{charge}$ … PP 利用 其 担任 [公司 业务员 的 职务 便利]$_{key\ point}$，从公司 仓库 提走 多部 手机，后将 手机 卖掉，货款 挥霍。… …Using his [position as a company salesman]$_{key\ point}$, PP took phones from the company's warehouse, sold the phones, and squandered the money…
CASE 2 [$Larceny$]$_{charge}$ …PP$_1$ [趁 PP$_2$ 家中 无人 之机]$_{key\ point}$，进入 到 PP$_2$ 家卧室 内 伺机 盗窃。被 PP$_2$ 回家 后 发现，PP$_1$ 翻墙 逃跑… …[When PP$_2$ was not at home]$_{key\ point}$, PP$_1$ went to PP$_2$'s bedroom to steal. When PP$_2$ came home, PP$_1$ fled the wall and ran…
CASE 3 [$Negligently\ Causing\ Fire$]$_{charge}$ …在 焚烧 耕地上 的 杂草 时，[不慎]$_{key\ point}$ 引发 山林 火灾。案发 后，PP 积极 救火，主动 向 上级 说明 失火 情况… … When burning weeds on land, PP [inadvertently]$_{key\ point}$ ignited the mountain fire. PP actively doused the fire and reported the fire situation …
CASE 4 [$Arson$]$_{charge}$ …PP$_1$ 因 生意 竞争 与 PP$_2$ 产生 积怨。PP$_1$ 酒后 [萌生 放火 烧 PP$_2$ 手机店 的 念头]$_{key\ point}$，进入 PP$_2$ 的 店内 将 纸箱 点燃… …PP$_1$ hates PP$_2$ for business competition. After drinking. PP$_1$ [wanted to burn PP$_2$'s shop]$_{key\ point}$. PP$_1$ entered the shop and lighted the carton…
CASE 5 [$Negligent\ Homicide$]$_{charge}$ … PP$_1$ 驾驶 货车 在 倒车 过程 中，[因 疏忽人意]$_{key\ point}$ 将 负责 指挥 倒车 的 PP$_2$ 挤伤，后 PP$_2$ 抢救 无效 死亡… …When reserving the truck, PP$_1$ [inadvertently]$_{key\ point}$ injured PP$_2$, who was in charge of commanding PP$_1$. PP$_2$ died later. …
CASE 6 [$Intentional\ Homicide$]$_{charge}$ …PP$_1$ 从 家中 携带 匕首 出门 寻找 PP$_2$ [进行 报复]$_{key\ point}$，将 PP$_2$ 捅倒 后，在 颈部 来回 割，致 PP$_2$ 当场 死亡… …PP$_1$ took the dagger and looked for PP$_2$ [for revenge]$_{key\ point}$. He stabbed PP$_2$ and cut the neck back and forth, causing PP$_2$ to die on the spot…

Table 1: Examples of extracted rationales. The highlighted words are rationales extracted by models. Different colors are used to align Chinese original text and corresponding English translation. The cores which can directly influence the charges are artificially marked as "key point".

MODEL	CHARGE PREDICTION						RATIONALE EXTRACTION			
	MICRO			MACRO			MACRO			ACC
	P	R	F	P	R	F	P	R	F	
Bi-GRU	89.64	90.60	90.12	81.84	76.25	78.08	–	–	–	–
Bi-GRU$_{att}$	**90.22**	**91.16**	**90.68**	83.97	77.78	79.70	74.6	73.7	68.5	76.3
OURS$^-$	86.25	87.29	86.77	77.08	72.79	73.78	**78.5**	75.7	72.2	79.7
OURS	89.84	91.06	90.45	**84.28**	**77.99**	**80.34†**	70.5	**90.75**	**75.9‡**	**79.8‡**

Table 2: Charge prediction and rationale extraction results. "‡": significantly better than Bi-GRU$_{att}$ (p<0.01). "†": better than Bi-GRU$_{att}$ (p<0.05).

3.2 Baselines

We choose three types of baselines: Bi-GRU, Bi-GRU$_{att}$ and OURS$^-$. Bi-GRU reads the input sequence forward and backward. The final fact representation used for charge prediction is the average of the hidden states. Bi-GRU$_{att}$ is the base Bi-GRU model with an attention mechanism followed. We adopt similar attention calculation in Yang et al. (2016). OURS$^-$ consists of **Extractor** and the **Rewarder** used for training. That is, only the extracted rationales are used to make charge prediction. Additionally, it discards the concept of phrase. It can be seen as a modified version of Lei et al. (2016): simpler structure in $p(z|x)$ modeling, but almost the same classification performance.

3.3 Experimental Results and Case Study

Rationale Extraction We choose 20 most heavily weighted words in each document as extracted rationale words (almost equal to the rationale word count extracted by OURS). The result in Table 2 proves that our model significantly outperforms the attention model on rationale extraction. Table 1 presents the models' performance on rationale extraction. The first three same sentences are selected from a case with a charge of *negligent homicide* which is suitable for people causing one's death due to negligence. Only our model notices the fact that the shotgun fire was due to the slippery fall, which is a key point distinguishing the case from *intentional homicide*.

In addition, in the lower part of Table 1, we further present the rationale extraction performance of our system on several pairs of example with different but confusing charges. These examples demonstrate that our system can capture key points to distinguish the similar charges. In case 1, our system observes the fact "his position as a company salesman" which is the key point of distinguishing *Official Embezzle-men* from *Larceny*. For the remaining cases, our system also seizes a series of key details such as "When PP_2 was not at home", "inadvertently", and "for revenge", and correctly predicts the charges.

Charge Prediction   We evaluate charge prediction performance using precision, recall and F1, in both micro and macro level. As shown in Table 2, Bi-GRU proves to be a strong baseline and the effect of attention mechanisms is obvious. Interestingly, though Bi-GRU$_{att}$ ranks first on all micro metrics, our model has better performance on macro metrics. This proves our method's competitive ability on subtle differences capturing, especially when making decision among infrequent but confusing charges. The huge gap between OURS$^-$ and OURS on charge prediction proves that our two-step rationale augmented base strategy fully utilizes the information contained in non-rationale text.

4   Conclusion

We propose a neural based system to jointly extract readable rationales and elevate charge prediction accuracy by a rationale augment mechanism. Sufficient experiments demonstrate that our model outperforms the attention based model on rationale capturing while having comparable classification accuracy.

Acknowledgements

We would like to appreciate the comments from anonymous reviewers and the data annotation from the the legal professionals. This work is supported by National Key Research and Development Program of China (Grant No. 2017YFB1402400) and National Natural Science Foundation of China (No. 61602490).

References

Jacob Cohen. 1960. A coefficient of agreement for nominal scales. *Educational and psychological measurement*, 20(1):37–46.

Lisa Anne Hendricks, Zeynep Akata, Marcus Rohrbach, Jeff Donahue, Bernt Schiele, and Trevor Darrell. 2016. Generating visual explanations. In *ECCV (4)*, volume 9908 of *Lecture Notes in Computer Science*, pages 3–19. Springer.

Tao Lei, Regina Barzilay, and Tommi S. Jaakkola. 2016. Rationalizing neural predictions. In *Proceedings of the 2016 Conference on Empirical Methods in Natural Language Processing, EMNLP 2016, Austin, Texas, USA, November 1-4, 2016*, pages 107–117.

Wan-Chen Lin, Tsung-Ting Kuo, Tung-Jia Chang, Chueh-An Yen, Chao-Ju Chen, and Shou-de Lin. 2012. Exploiting machine learning models for chinese legal documents labeling, case classification, and sentencing prediction. volume 17.

Chao-Lin Liu and Chwen-Dar Hsieh. 2006. Exploring phrase-based classification of judicial documents for criminal charges in chinese. In *ISMIS*, volume 4203 of *Lecture Notes in Computer Science*, pages 681–690. Springer.

Chao-Lin Liu, Cheng-Tsung Chang, and Jim-How Ho. 2004. Case instance generation and refinement for case-based criminal summary judgments in chinese. *J. Inf. Sci. Eng.*, 20(4):783–800.

Bingfeng Luo, Yansong Feng, Jianbo Xu, Xiang Zhang, and Dongyan Zhao. 2017. Learning to predict charges for criminal cases with legal basis. In *Proceedings of the 2017 Conference on Empirical Methods in Natural Language Processing, EMNLP 2017, Copenhagen, Denmark, September 9-11, 2017*, pages 2727–2736.

Christopher D. Manning, Mihai Surdeanu, John Bauer, Jenny Rose Finkel, Steven Bethard, and David McClosky. 2014. The stanford corenlp natural language processing toolkit. In *ACL (System Demonstrations)*, pages 55–60. The Association for Computer Linguistics.

Ronald J. Williams. 1992. Simple statistical gradient-following algorithms for connectionist reinforcement learning. *Machine Learning*, 8:229–256.

Zichao Yang, Diyi Yang, Chris Dyer, Xiaodong He, Alexander J. Smola, and Eduard H. Hovy. 2016. Hierarchical attention networks for document classification. In *HLT-NAACL*, pages 1480–1489. The Association for Computational Linguistics.

Hai Ye, Xin Jiang, Zhunchen Luo, and Wenhan Chao. 2018. Interpretable charge predictions for criminal cases: Learning to generate court views from fact descriptions. In *Proceedings of the 2018 Conference of the North American Chapter of the Association for Computational Linguistics: Human Language Technologies, NAACL-HLT 2018, New Orleans, Louisiana, USA, June 1-6, 2018, Volume 1 (Long Papers)*, pages 1854–1864.

A Cross-lingual Messenger with Keyword Searchable Phrases
for the Travel Domain

Shehroze Khan, Jihyun Kim, Tarik Zulfikarpasic, Peter Chen, Nizar Habash
New York University Abu Dhabi
{shehroze,jihyun,tz638,peter.wei.chen,nizar.habash}@nyu.edu

Abstract

We present Qutr (Query Translator), a smart cross-lingual communication application for the travel domain. Qutr is a real-time messaging app that automatically translates conversations while supporting keyword-to-sentence matching. Qutr relies on querying a database that holds commonly used pre-translated travel-domain phrases and phrase templates in different languages with the use of keywords. The query matching supports paraphrases, incomplete keywords and some input spelling errors. The application addresses common cross-lingual communication issues such as translation accuracy, speed, privacy, and personalization.

1 Introduction

The increasing mobility of today's world population naturally leads to the need for easier and more accurate cross-lingual communication tools. Solutions to help transcend language barriers range from using body language, travel phrasebooks and, more recently, machine translation software and hardware devices. However, these methods come with different limitations. Traditional travel phrasebooks, while useful for looking up travel-specific vocabulary, require tedious effort to flip through pages and only allows one-way communication. Recent advancements in machine translation, such as using Google's neural machine translation (Wu et al., 2016), has enabled fast, accurate translations between numerous language pairs, but has limitations for travelers since most machine translation systems are trained on the news domain, and are not optimized for conversational or travel domain language. In this demo paper, we present Qutr (Query Translator), a real-time cross-lingual messaging app. Qutr relies on querying a database that holds commonly used pre-translated travel-domain phrases with the use of keywords. While both users need to have the app downloaded, each user only needs the database for their language of preference, since Qutr internally uses an interlingual representation. As such, a Qutr user need not know what the other user's language is. Qutr addresses the two limitations mentioned above by providing an easily searchable phrasebook that focuses on travel domain conversational language.

We next present some related work (Section 2), followed by system description (Section 3). After concluding and discussing future directions (Section4), we summarize the demo plan (Section 5).

2 Related Work

The mobile application Yochina aimed to aid cross-lingual and cross-cultural understanding by supporting dialogues between English and Chinese, and German and Chinese (Xu et al., 2014). This app addressed many of the problems of existing apps for cross-lingual communication in travel, but still faced issues of operating on a single device and relying on a more manual input of phrase selection, which reduced the speed of communication. Finch et al. (2011) suggest the use of picture icons as input sequences to speed up the communication process. Other translation apps, such as Speak&Translate, support bidirectional and speech-to-text conversation, but all require sharing of a single device, which travelers might find uncomfortable when communicating with a stranger in a completely new environment. Furthermore, apps that rely on speech-to-text interfaces suffer from reduced conversational privacy, lowered quality in noisy environments and diminished accessibility for deaf and hard-of-hearing individuals.

Proceedings of the 27th International Conference on Computational Linguistics: System Demonstrations, pages 152–156
Santa Fe, New Mexico, USA, August 20-26, 2018.

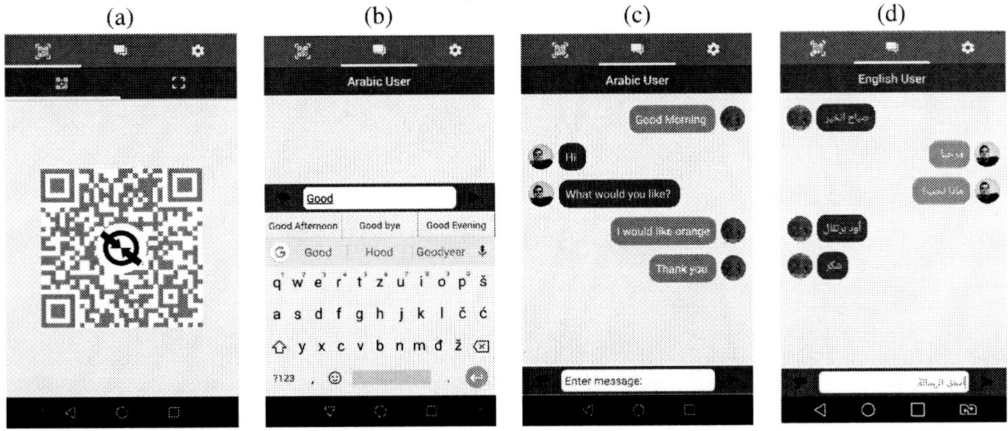

Figure 1: Qutr User Interface screens: (a) QR code, (b) Phrase Suggestions (c) English user side conversation, (d) Arabic user side conversation

3 System Description

Our system, Qutr, tackles the abovementioned issues with a real-time messenger app that enables users to communicate on their individual devices in a fast, highly-accurate and user friendly manner. Qutr models a modern form of a travel phrasebook that is easily searchable by natural language querying and that operates on separate devices. Our phrasal database is queried with users' keywords in order to retrieve suggestions for best matches, which are then matched to existing, high-quality translations. Unlike other translation apps that require databases for the source and target languages to be pre-downloaded, Qutr only expects databases for the individual user's language, which relate it to the Qutr interlingua representation. This allows one Qutr user to communicate with any other user regardless of their preferred language. While the prerequisite of having the app installed on both users' end could be a potential drawback, it addresses the discomfort and risks of sharing a single device. Qutr users establish instant connection using QR code scanning, thus preventing delay or disruption in the flow of real-life communication. The QR code 'handshake' supports privacy as the two users do not need to share any information about themselves. The text input and output interface also supports privacy and overcomes the challenges faced when one or both users are deaf or hard-of-hearing. To maximize the usability of Qutr, we have built fully functioning versions in both Android and iOS. We imagine that Qutr can be first rolled out to airport information desks and hotel front desks where travelers are likely to use it more. Next, we present the various Qutr system components.

3.1 User Interface

Our application interface follows a very intuitive schema. Upon opening the application, users are directed to a screen displaying their unique QR code which they will scan to setup a connection with the other user, as shown in Figure 1 (a). When one of the users scans the other's QR code, they are both redirected to a private chat screen. They begin by inputting keywords and selecting one of the shown suggestions in the suggestion bar that best matches what they wish to communicate – Figure 1 (b). Users have to select from at least one of the suggestions (or concepts) before sending it, ensuring that the translated version exists on the other side. A sample conversation between an Arabic-speaking user and an English-speaking user is shown in Figure 1 (c,d).

3.2 Phrase Corpus Design

The phrases that users select and communicate with are queried from our pre-translated phrase database. The current version contains translation triples of 3,500 iconic phrases in Arabic, Chinese and English. Each of these triples is associated with a Concept ID and a Phrase Structure tag. The *Concept ID* is a

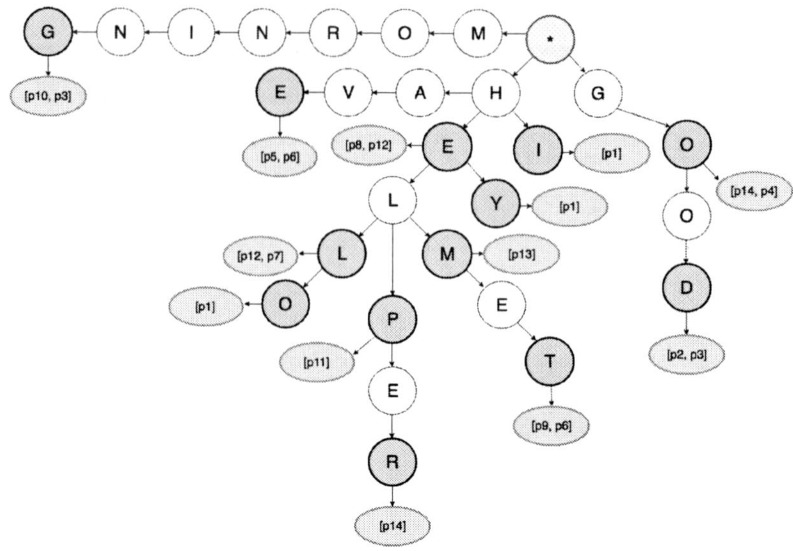

Figure 2: Sample English word trie to identify phrases from query words

unique index that points to the iconic version of the phrase. Alternative phrases in some languages may exist and will point to the same unique index. This index is the only information that is passed between users' interfaces when communicating. The *non-iconic* phrases (or *paraphrases*) are used to increase the possibility of matching a concept. The *iconic* version is the one that is presented to the user. The *Phrase Structure Tag* is inspired by the Universal Part-of-Speech (POS) Tagset (Petrov et al., 2012), but also includes phrase-level tags such as "sentence," "noun phrase," and "verb phrase," in addition to POS tags such as "particle," "adjective" and "adverb."

Having a large and accurate database of colloquial and alternative paraphrases in all three languages was key to improving the system's usability and coverage. Since there was no existing corpus available for travel-specific paraphrases, we created our own by scraping translated phrases from a wide range of websites, such as Wikitravel and educational English as Second Language (ESL) resources. This approach came with challenges such as language-specific formatting or missing and/or inaccurate translations in the third language (e.g., Arabic when using Chinese sources), which we accounted for by using multiple open-source Natural Language Processing tools. For example, we used a Chinese Segmentation library Jieba (Sun, 2017) to split Chinese phrases into semantic tokens, a necessary step for suggesting accurate phrase matches. For abnormalities that were too ambiguous or hard to find and change using code, we relied on human translators.

Most of the original scraped phrases were context-specific and pre-filled with named entities, such as "I want a flight to Tokyo." We used a pre-trained named entity recognition model from the SpaCy[1] to replace such named entities with the template placeholder, denoted by asterisk (*). Template phrases refer to near-complete sentences with subject or object noun placeholders. An example template phrase is "I want *" which can have any noun phrases replace the asterisk, but not a verb phrase such as "buy apples." To handle the latter case, we have another phrase "I want to buy *." By allowing noun phrases but not verb phrases, we restrict the possibility of recursive sentence construction due to subordinate clauses and compound sentences.

3.3 Query to Phrase Mapping

Dynamic parsing of user input to retrieve closely matching phrase suggestions is cardinal for guiding user conversation. Kumar et al. (2018) have demonstrated that the problem of composing well-formed natural

---

[1] `https://spacy.io/`

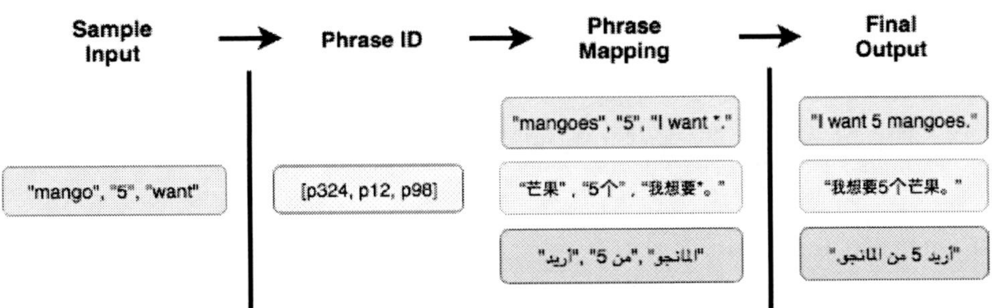

Figure 3: Sentence Generation Process

language questions from user input queries has many useful applications, not only for web search engines, question answering systems and bot communication systems, but also for digital assistants where guiding users to their exact needs is paramount. While they reduce this query-to-question conversion to a translation problem, we utilize the same idea to navigate our users' conversations through suggesting phrases from our database that match an input query.

Ortega et al. (2003) suggest the use of a trie to rapidly search autocompletion strings from user input queries; autocompletion terms stored along the trie are dynamically scored higher if they match user input every time they enter a new character. The authors encourage tagging these terms, enabling efficient searching due to the added filtering and contextualizing. Following a similar implementation scheme, we stored our phrases (iconic and paraphrases) in a trie, where each of the constituent words in a particular phrase are stored with the corresponding concept ID of that phrase. Figure 2 depicts a possible English phrase trie. Note how the paraphrase words *Hello*, *Hi*, and *Hey* will all return the same concept ID [p1].

The phrase suggestion algorithm iterates over the input characters, traversing the trie from the root node. If an exact match is found, we return the corresponding list of concepts. Otherwise, we *auto-complete* by traversing from the last reached node to all possible completion nodes. The concepts are ranked with preference for exact match and minimal edit distance from the input word. The trie also tolerates one character error per word. Imperfect word matches and autocompletions are ranked lower in the identified set of phrases. If users input custom words that are not in our database, we send the words themselves as foreign words. Digit sequences and emoji are also sent as is.

3.4 Paraphrase to Iconic Phrase Mapping

It is not always possible to have one-to-one mapping of paraphrases between languages since many colloquial expressions are language and culture specific. We therefore handle paraphrases at language-specific levels by adding extra information to the concept IDs of each paraphrase. For example, "Hello" may have a concept ID of [p1] while "Hey," its paraphrase, would be linked to [p1.en.00] to indicate that it is the first paraphrase of concept [p1] in our database. This additional paraphrase marking scheme can easily scale not only to cover synonyms, but also gender and other inflections of an iconic phrase. For example, in Arabic, the phrase "Would you like coffee?" would have two forms depending on gender of the second person. In this case, we would append extra information to its concept ID to resemble [p500.ar.00.sf] and [p500.ar.00.sm] to differentiate between singular female and singular male versions of a phrase depending on the other user's profile. This is a possible solution for correctly personalizing machine translated conversations based on the user's profile-specified gender, which no existing translation systems do to our knowledge. The current prototype version does not yet support translations that account for inflections in our existing phrases, but we plan on adding it in the future.

3.5 Cross-lingual Sentence Generation

Sentence generation in Qutr happens twice per message: once to the user's source language (from selected concepts) and once to the target language (from received concepts). The former serves to map into the iconic phrase from the query which may have a typo or is a non-iconic paraphrase. The generation function takes in an unordered array of concept IDs and target language as two parameters and returns the full sentence as an output (Figure 3). The algorithm relies on a set of language-agnostic generation rules that order phrases by looking at the phrase structure tags of each phrase. The parallel phrase translations, which maintain the same syntactic roles and template structure for each concept ID, guarantee consistency and universal applicability of the rules. The nature of task-driven communication between different native speakers also means that the *sentences* can be very succinct, informal or even incomplete.

4   Conclusion and Future Work

We presented Qutr, a cross-lingual messenger app for the travel domain with support for English, Chinese and Arabic. Qutr's interface relies on users in one language utilizing query words to find and construct phrases that are sent as concept IDs to users speaking a different language. In the future, we plan to further improve on coverage and conversation flow. We plan to add not only more iconic phrases, but also paraphrases. We plan to complete gender inflections for existing phrases to fully support the correct inflection in conversations. Furthermore, while we have conducted limited pilot tests, we plan a large multi-user evaluation to test the quality of Qutr compared to using phrasebooks or Google Translate. We also plan to add new language phrase databases for wider multilingual support. With the addition of more languages, we envision that Qutr could be used as a language learning tool by giving users an option to view the translated versions of the phrases they wish to communicate on the other side.

5   Demo Plan

In the demo of this work, we will provide six mobile phones (three iOS and three Android), with two phones for each of the three supported languages: Arabic, English and Chinese. We will also provide a laptop showing an instructional video demonstrating how to use the Qutr app, and provide some specific scenarios to guide conference attendees interested in this app to role play use cases with the demo presenters and with each other. An example of the demo video is shown here: `https://vimeo.com/262015667`.

Acknowledgments

This effort has been supported by the New York University Abu Dhabi Science Capstone Project Fund. We would like to thank Ms. Ella Noll and Professor Sebti Foufou for helpful discussions.

References

Andrew Finch, Wei Song, Kumiko Tanaka-Ishii, and Eiichiro Sumita. 2011. picoTrans: Using pictures as input for machine translation on mobile devices. In *Proceedings of the International Joint Conference on Artificial Intelligence*.

Adarsh Kumar, Sandipan Dandapat, and Sushil Chordia. 2018. Translating web search queries into natural language questions. In *Proceedings of the Language Resources and Evaluation Conference, Miyazaki, Japan*.

Ruben E Ortega, John W Avery, and Robert Frederick. 2003. Search query autocompletion. US Patent 6,564,213.

Slav Petrov, Dipanjan Das, and Ryan McDonald. 2012. A universal part-of-speech tagset. In *Proceedings of the Language Resources and Evaluation Conference, Istanbul, Turkey*.

Junyi Sun. 2017. Jieba - Chinese text segmentation module.

Yonghui Wu, Mike Schuster, Zhifeng Chen, Quoc V Le, Mohammad Norouzi, Wolfgang Macherey, Maxim Krikun, Yuan Cao, Qin Gao, Klaus Macherey, et al. 2016. Google's neural machine translation system: Bridging the gap between human and machine translation. *arXiv preprint arXiv:1609.08144*.

Feiyu Xu, Sven Schmeier, Renlong Ai, and Hans Uszkoreit. 2014. Yochina: Mobile multimedia and multimodal crosslingual dialogue system. In *Natural Interaction with Robots, Knowbots and Smartphones*, pages 51–57. Springer.

Towards Automated Extraction of Business Constraints
from Unstructured Regulatory Text

Rahul Nair and **Killian Levacher** and **Martin Stephenson**
IBM Research - Ireland
`rahul.nair@ie.ibm.com`
`killian.levacher@ibm.com`
`martin_stephenson@ie.ibm.com`

Abstract

Large organizations spend considerable resources in reviewing regulations and ensuring that their business processes are compliant with the law. To make compliance workflows more efficient and responsive, we present a system for machine-driven annotations of legal documents. A set of natural language processing pipelines are designed and aimed at addressing some key questions in this domain: (a) is this (new) regulation relevant for me? (b) what set of requirements does this law impose?, and (c) what is the regulatory intent of a law? The system is currently undergoing user trials within our organization.

1   Setting

Large organizations spend considerable resources on reviewing regulations and ensuring that their operations, policies and procedures are compliant with the law. There has been a rapid growth in the number of regulations globally with more than 12,000 enacted/pending in 2016 compared to roughly 4,000 in 2008 (Compliance and Risks, 2016). In response, organizations are looking to make their compliance processes more responsive and efficient.

To better understand the existing workflows, we undertook a series of 14 interviews with compliance experts within our organization. Each expert is responsible for a certain class of legal requirements within a particular jurisdiction. For example, one of the experts was responsible for labeling requirements in North America, another for battery regulations in Chile etc.

Most experts have access to services that provide periodic briefs on regulatory changes. Once a new regulation is received, a legal review is conducted to broadly classify the document into the business categories that it most likely impacts. Many documents require translation before this legal review, since they originate from non-English speaking countries. Based on the labels, a more detailed review is carried out by each specific department. The review results in a list of requirements that need to be addressed. Compliance experts then map the requirements to current policies and evaluate if changes are needed for compliance. Changes recommended are handled by implementation teams.

The main pain points uncovered during the interviews where (a) too much (irrelevant) information from services that alert the experts on regulations, (b) lengthy and time consuming processes to determine whether specific products are relevant to the legislation (e.g. translation), (c) diverse set of regulations, some short (2 pages) and some long (~800 pages) with no way to prioritize them. The experts indicated interest in tools to help them "get from the law to 'action required' status," quickly, and distill requirements to "likely to impact us".

Natural language processing (NLP) applications in this domain are not new. Previous efforts have shown obligation extraction using semantic annotations (Kiyavitskaya et al., 2008), use of deep question answering architecture to evaluate compliance (Pasetto et al., 2013) and perform entity extraction using a domain ontology (Sapkota et al., 2012). We limit our review due to space restrictions.

Proceedings of the 27th International Conference on Computational Linguistics: System Demonstrations, pages 157–160
Santa Fe, New Mexico, USA, August 20-26, 2018.

In this paper, we present a system to extract business constraints from regulatory text[1]. We design three NLP pipelines aimed at addressing some of the challenges identified in the interviews. The pipelines address the questions (a) what set of requirements does a law impose (Section 2.2)? (b) what is the regulatory scope/intent of a law (Section 2.3)?, and (c) is this (new) regulation relevant for me (Section 2.4)?

2 Models

We focus on global regulations in the import-export area, which consists of laws related to batteries, labeling, electronic waste/product take back, emissions, energy efficiency, chemical and environmental legislation. Figure 1 shows the three pipelines. These are described next with the data used to train the system.

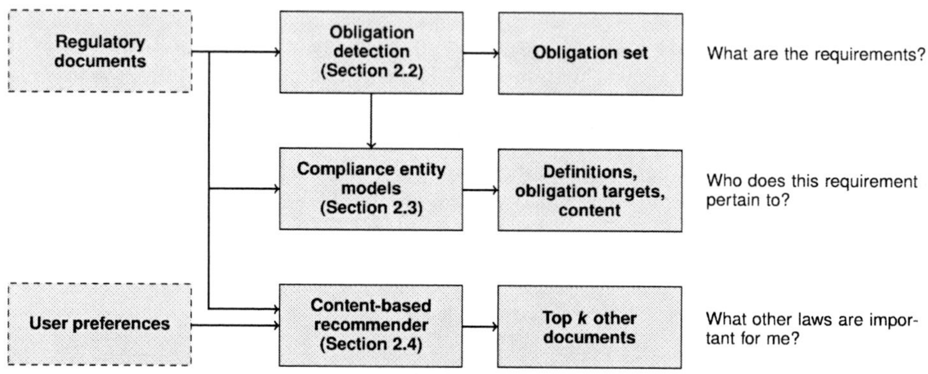

Figure 1: Overview of pipelines

2.1 Data

Our analysis is based on two primary data sources, as well as one semi-automatically annotated dataset. The primary source is an internal dataset, containing several thousand regulations from 168 jurisdictions, curated by legal experts since 2008. The dataset contains translations into English where necessary, along with manually generated summaries and product classifications. A second primary source is a set of requirements that have been manually extracted from these laws that impact one specific division within IBM. While this represents positive examples, we sampled from unrelated documents to generate negative samples for our classification task in Section 2.2.

Based on these primary sources, using a semi-automatic annotation process, the set of 129,313 obligations was parsed with a set of patterns. Patterns were manually extracted from a sample of obligations. The annotation process generated regulatory entity annotations (see Section 2.3) iteratively generating a corpus of 100,831 annotations covering 54,632 obligations.

2.2 Obligation detection

The *obligation detection* task seeks to classify input sentences into binary classes representing requirements or not.

Classical approaches involve using handcrafted features following by a supervised classification model. Features could include one hot encoding of words, distributed word representations, or TF-IDF vectors. More recently, deep learning architectures, such as LSTM's and CNN's have been shown to give good results. We experimented with these approaches. Of all the features, character n-grams performed the best along with TF-IDF vectors. Features derived from distributed word representations did the worst. Table 1 shows accuracy scores for the top performing pipelines. We chose to implement the random forest model with TF-IDF features and bigrams of character n-grams ($n = 3$). Character

---

[1]A video of the system can be viewed at `https://www.youtube.com/watch?v=Xt9j0qb_yT0`

n-grams improved classification scores over simply using TF-IDF vectors presumably by accounting for spelling variations.

Model	Features	Mean Acc.	Min Acc.	Max Acc.
Random forest	TFIDF-bigrams	0.930	0.912	0.943
Linear SVM - L1	TFIDF-bigrams	0.920	0.908	0.943
Random forest	TFIDF	0.919	0.885	0.941
Passive-Aggressive	TFIDF-bigrams	0.911	0.889	0.939

Table 1: Accuracy of top-4 pipelines for the obligation classification task (5-fold cross validation)

In our corpus, we found that obligation clauses tend to be longer than general descriptive text, on average roughly $\sim 50\%$. The system gathers user feedback on obligations clauses to improve classification scores over time.

2.3 Compliance Entity Extraction

The *compliance entity extraction* task seeks to determine to whom specific requirements pertain to. We distinguish two broad classes of entities (figure 2), (a) definition entities - within clauses that represent stakeholders or specific equipment, and (b) obligation entities - that are the legislative target of a specific clause. Within each class of entities, we further extract *targets* that is the specific entity, and *content* which describes the target. Taken together, the definitions and obligation targets, allows the system to determine if a specific obligation has a material impact on a business.

Extracting definitions is challenging for several reasons. Definition entities can be located in a dedicated section of laws, or scattered across different sections. This makes it difficult to assess the relevancy of a document. Definitions may be inconsistent across documents or even sections. For example, *manufacturers of batteries* in one document might be referring specifically to *manufacturers of zinc-carbon batteries*, while another document might be referring to *manufacturers of batteries located in the European Union*.

Extraction of obligation targets within clauses is challenging using traditional information retrieval approaches. These approaches can, at best, only return whether business entities are mentioned or not. This is usually insufficient to determine the legislative target. For example, consider the case of *manufacturers of batteries* in the following clause *"Distributors of lithium batteries should provide consumers with recycling services depending upon the recycling requirement stated by manufacturers of batteries"* where it is not the target.

The model consists of a perceptron algorithm trained using as an input, the sentences previously classified as an obligation (section 2.2). For each of the tokens in these obligation sentences, the entity extraction model is provided with, as an input, features consisting of each token's original string, lemma, part of speech, lower case string and shape (whether the token is a number, abbreviation, legal article number etc.). The algorithm was trained using a mini-batch approach with the semi-automatic annotated dataset described in Section 2.1 and produces labels in IOB format for each of the four possible annotation outputs described in figure 2. The model achieves a token-level accuracy of 0.95 across labels. An example of the four entities extracted by the model are shown in Figure 2.

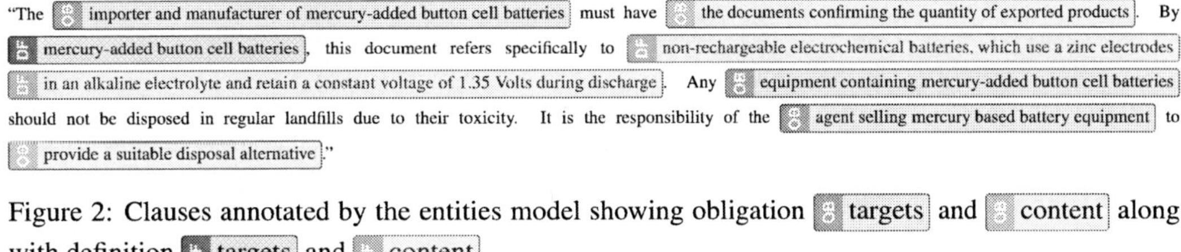

Figure 2: Clauses annotated by the entities model showing obligation targets and content along with definition targets and content

2.4 Content-based legislation recommender

Given (a) a corpus of regulatory documents and (b) user preferences for regulatory topics, the *recommendation* task seeks to determine the top k documents that best match user preferences. The purpose of this task is to aid compliance experts in regulation discovery.

The approach is driven by a simple domain insight gleaned during one of our interviews. Large legislative initiatives happen infrequently and result in large framework type documents. Over time, legislative bodies then issue amendments to fix issues with law or close loop holes. Compliance experts in turn reference a handful of these 'framework' type regulations often.

We therefore define a user profile as a set of documents, called a *user library*. For each document in the corpus, we generate a feature vector X based on TD-IDF vectors along with additional hand crafted features of one hot encoding of jurisdictions. Based on positive samples from the user library, and negative samples randomly sampled to have balanced classes, we train a user-specific linear SVM $y = f_u(X)$ to determine the separating hyperplane for a user. Given a set of new documents, the recommendation procedure sorts them by distance to the hyperplane and reports the top k documents.

We do not present a formal evaluation of this pipeline, since user trials are ongoing. However, we report on preliminary experiments with two 'framework' agreements, the REACH legislation (chemical restriction laws) passed in 2006, and the WEEE directives (waste electronics laws) passed in 2003 both in the EU. Using a set of documents that represent a hypothetical user library (the regulation along with guidance and explainer documents), the system recommended all the amendments to these laws within the top 20 recommended documents.

3 Architecture

The implemented system does a web crawl of authoritative sources for 8 jurisdictions and continuously updates the corpus. The platform relies on a mix of open and proprietary components to implement these pipelines. It is deployed for internal use on a kubernetes cluster on IBM Cloud, and scales easily on demand. The system is undergoing user trials with a panel of compliance experts within IBM. Feedback on annotation quality, document recommendation value and other user focused metrics are being gathered as part of this. Early feedback suggests improved ways to present information on the extracted entities and their definitions across documents.

4 Challenges and future work

Several technical challenges remain. Parsing of text from some document formats is unreliable, notably PDFs. Legislative documents come in varied formats, and occasionally are multi-lingual. Sentence structures of obligations are complex and it is unclear if pipelines, such as those presented here, readily transfer across various regulatory domains. Lastly, obligation clauses are open to interpretation.[2]

References

Compliance and Risks. 2016. Global growth of regulations. `https://www.complianceandrisks.com/ /public/growth_of_regulations_jan_2016.pdf`. Accessed: 2018-05-08.

Nadzeya Kiyavitskaya, Nicola Zeni, Travis D Breaux, Annie I Antón, James R Cordy, Luisa Mich, and John Mylopoulos. 2008. Automating the extraction of rights and obligations for regulatory compliance. In *International Conference on Conceptual Modeling*, pages 154–168. Springer.

Davide Pasetto, Hubertus Franke, Weihong Qian, Zhili Guo, Honglei Guo, Dongxu Duan, Yuan Ni, Yingxin Pan, Shenghua Bao, Feng Cao, et al. 2013. Rts-an integrated analytic solution for managing regulation changes and their impact on business compliance. In *Proceedings of the ACM International Conference on Computing Frontiers*, page 24. ACM.

Krishna Sapkota, Arantza Aldea, Muhammad Younas, David A Duce, and Rene Banares-Alcantara. 2012. Extracting meaningful entities from regulatory text: Towards automating regulatory compliance. In *Requirements Engineering and Law (RELAW), 2012 Fifth International Workshop on*, pages 29–32. IEEE.

---

[2]The authors thank Léa Deleris and Yufang Hou for reviews of an earlier draft.

A flexible and easy-to-use semantic role labeling framework
for different languages

Quynh Ngoc Thi Do   Artuur Leeuwenberg   Geert Heyman   Marie-Francine Moens
Department of Computer Science, KU Leuven, Belgium
{quynhngocthi.do,tuur.leeuwenberg,geert.heyman,sien.moens}@cs.kuleuven.be

Abstract

This paper presents *DAMESRL*[1], a flexible and open source framework for deep semantic role labeling (SRL). DAMESRL aims to facilitate easy exploration of model structures for multiple languages with different characteristics. It provides flexibility in its model construction in terms of word representation, sequence representation, output modeling, and inference styles and comes with clear output visualization. Additionally, it handles various input and output formats and comes with clear output visualization. The framework is available under the Apache 2.0 license.

1   Introduction

During the first decade of the 21st century, mapping from the syntactic analysis of a sentence to its semantic representation has received a central interest in the natural language processing (NLP) community. Semantic role labeling, which is a sentence-level semantic task aimed at identifying "Who did What to Whom, and How, When and Where?" (Palmer et al., 2010), has strengthened this focus. Recently, several neural mechanisms have been used to train end-to-end SRL models that do not require task-specific feature engineering as the traditional SRL models do. Zhou and Xu (2015) introduced the first deep end-to-end model for SRL using a stacked Bi-LSTM network with a conditional random field (CRF) as the top layer. He et al. (2017) simplified their architecture using a highway Bi-LSTM network. More recently, Tan et al. (2018) replaced the common recurrent architecture with a self-attention network, directly capturing relationships between tokens regardless of their distance, resulting in better results and faster training. The work in deep end-to-end SRL has focused heavily on applying deep learning advances without considering the multilingual aspect. However, language-specific characteristics and the available amount of training data highly influence the optimal model structure.

DAMESRL facilitates exploration and fair evaluation of new SRL models for different languages by providing flexible neural model construction on different modeling levels, the handling of various input and output formats, and clear output visualization. Beyond the existing state-of-the-art models (Zhou and Xu, 2015; He et al., 2017; Tan et al., 2018), we exploit character-level modeling, beneficial when considering multiple languages. To demonstrate the merits of easy cross-lingual exploration and evaluation of model structures for SRL provided by DAMESRL, we report performance of several distinct models integrated into our framework for English, German and Arabic, as they have very different linguistic characteristics.

2   Task Definition

Formally, the goal of end-to-end SRL is to predict a sequence $(l_1, l_2, \ldots, l_n)$ of semantic labels given a sentence $(w_1, w_2, \ldots, w_n)$, and its predicate w_p as input. Each l_i, which belongs to a discrete set of PropBank BIO tags, is the semantic tag corresponding to the word w_i in the semantic frame evoked

---

[1]The source code can be found at: https://liir.cs.kuleuven.be/software_pages/damesrl.php.

Proceedings of the 27th International Conference on Computational Linguistics: System Demonstrations, pages 161–165
Santa Fe, New Mexico, USA, August 20-26, 2018.

by w_p. Here, words outside argument spans have the tag **O**, and words at the beginning and inside of argument spans with role r have the tags $\mathbf{B_r}$ and $\mathbf{I_r}$, respectively. For example, the sentence "the cat chases the dog ." should be annotated as "the$_{\mathbf{B-A0}}$ cat$_{\mathbf{I-A0}}$ chases$_{\mathbf{B-V}}$ the$_{\mathbf{B-A1}}$ dog$_{\mathbf{I-A1}}$.$_{\mathbf{O}}$".

3 System Architecture

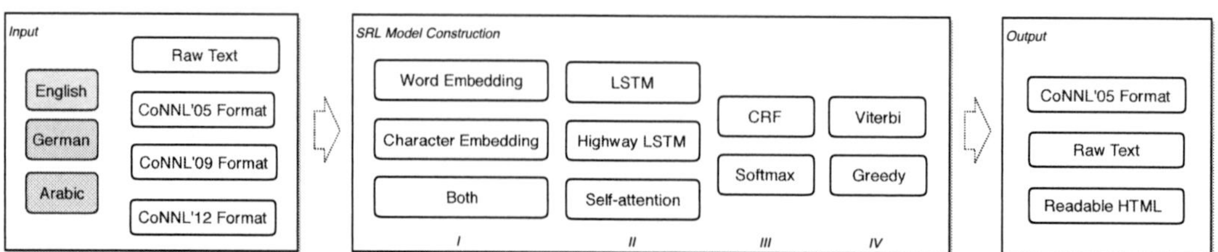

Figure 1: Schematic overview of the DAMESRL architecture from input to output.

DAMESRL's architecture (see Fig. 1) facilitates the construction of models that prioritize certain language-dependent linguistic properties, such as the importance of word order and inflection, or that adapt to the amount of available training data. The framework, implemented in Python 3.5 using Tensor-Flow, can be used to train new models, or make predictions with the provided pre-trained models.

3.1 Input and Output

The input/output format of DAMESRL is a shortened version of the CoNLL'05 format, which only contains the Words, Targets and (possibly) Props columns[2]. DAMESRL also provides an HTML format that can be directly visualized in the web browser (as in Fig. 2).

3.2 Model Construction Modules

As can be seen in Fig. 1, the framework divides model construction in four phases: (I) word representation, (II) sentence representation, (III) output modeling, and (IV) inference.

Phase I:　The word representation of a word w_i consist of three optional concatenated components: a word-embedding, a Boolean indicating if w_i is the predicate of the semantic frame (w_p), and a character representation. DAMESRL provides a Bi-LSTM network to learn character-level word representations helping for languages where important SRL cues are given through inflections, such as case markings in German and Arabic. Despite the foreseen importance, character-level embeddings have not been used in previous work (Zhou and Xu, 2015; He et al., 2017; Tan et al., 2018).

Phase II:　As core sequence representation component, users can choose between a self-attention encoding (Tan et al., 2018), a regular Bi-LSTM (Hochreiter and Schmidhuber, 1997) or a highway Bi-LSTM (Zhang et al., 2016; He et al., 2017).

Phase III:　To compute model probabilities, users can choose a regular softmax, or a linear chain CRF as proposed by (Zhou and Xu, 2015), which can be useful for languages where word order is an important SRL cue, such as English, or when less training data is available (shown in Section 4).

---

[2]http://www.lsi.upc.edu/ṡrlconll/conll05st-release/README

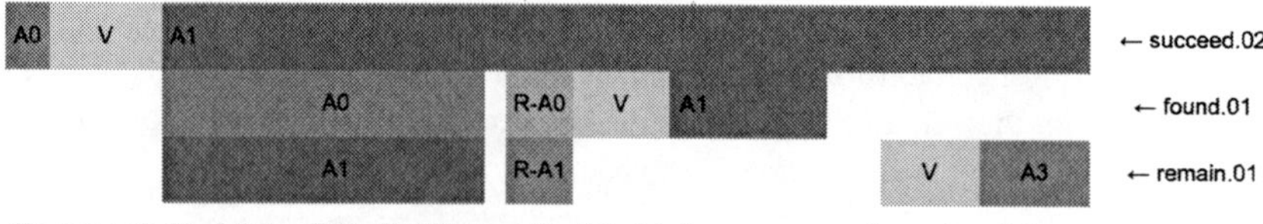

Figure 2: Screen-shot of the HTML Output

Phase IV: The inference phase provides two options for label inference from the computed model probabilities including greedy prediction and Viterbi decoding.

4 Experiments

4.1 Settings

To evaluate our framework, and show the benefits of choosing certain model components, we construct five models: HLstm, Char, CRFm, Att, and CharAtt, whose configurations are shown in Tab. 1. The

Table 1: Configurations of experimental models.

	HLstm	Char	CRFm	Att	CharAtt
Word Emb.	✓		✓	✓	
Word + Character Emb.		✓			✓
Highway LSTM	✓	✓	✓		
Self-Attention				✓	✓
Softmax	✓	✓		✓	✓
CRF			✓		

Table 2: Training data.

	English	German	Arabic
Source	CoNLL'05	CoNLL'09	CoNLL'12
# Sentences	39832	36020	7422
Vocab. size	35094	67495	45683
# Predicates	90750	17400	20001

selected models are evaluated in three languages: English, German and Arabic (see Tab. 2) using the standard CoNLL'05 metrics. Information about the used SRL data is shown in Tab. 2. We initialize the weights of all sub-layers as random orthogonal matrices. The learning rate is fixed in the first N_1 training epochs, and halved after every next N_2 epochs. Detailed settings and the word embeddings used to initialize the word representation layer used per language are found in Tab. 3.

Table 3: Experimental settings.

Setting	Model	Value
Optimizer	All	AdaDelta, $\epsilon = 1e{-}06$
Learning rate	All	1.0
Dropout probability	All	0.1
Label smoothing value	All	0.1
Word-emb size	All	100
Word-emb type	All	GloVe
Batch size	All	80 predicates
Early stopping patience	All	100
N_1	HLstm, Char, Att, CharAtt	400
N_2	HLstm, Char, Att, CharAtt	100
N_1	CRFm	100
N_2	CRFm	30
# Max. training epochs	Att, CharAtt	800
# Hidden layers	Att, CharAtt	10
# Max. training epochs	HLstm, Char, CRFm	500
# Hidden layers	HLstm, Char, CRFm	8
Hidden layer size	HLstm, Char, CRFm	300
Character-emb. size	Char, CharAtt	100
Position Encoding	Att, CharAtt	Timing
Word-emb. data	English	Wikipedia+Gigaword[3]
Word-emb. data	German	Wikipedia
Word-emb. data	Arabic	None

Table 4: Training (Tr.) and prediction (Pr.) times (greedy) for English.

	Tr. time / epoch	Pr. time / predicate
HLstm	10 mins	8.5 ms
Char	12 mins	15.5 ms
CRFm	8 mins	11.4 ms
Att	2 mins	3.4 ms
CharAtt	5 mins	4.2 ms

---

[3]From: https://nlp.stanford.edu/projects/glove/

Table 5: Results on CoNLL'12 Arabic and CoNLL'09 German data: precision (P), recall (R), and F1.[4]

| Model | Arabic | | | | | | German | | | | | | | | |
| | Development | | | Evaluation | | | Development | | | Out-Of-Domain | | | Evaluation | | |
	P	R	F1	P	R	F1	P	R	F1	P	R	F1	P	R	F1
HLstm	46.2	45.2	45.7	47.4	45.3	46.3	67.9	66.4	67.1	55.6	57.2	56.4	68.2	67.1	67.6
Char	51.2	50.2	50.7	47.5	46.0	46.7	69.1	66.5	67.8	54.0	55.2	54.6	68.2	67.0	67.6
CRFm	50.8	47.7	49.2	51.9	48.0	49.9	68.7	66.0	67.3	55.3	53.8	54.6	65.8	64.4	65.1
Att	50.4	48.0	49.2	50.0	46.7	48.3	71.6	70.8	71.2	54.7	56.8	55.7	71.9	71.5	71.7
CharAtt	56.9	56.0	**56.5**	56.0	54.5	**55.2**	74.8	73.8	**74.3**	57.2	57.3	**57.3**	73.4	73.6	**73.5**

Table 6: Results on CoNLL'05 English data: precision (P), recall (R), and F1. We compare our results with other state-of-the-art deep *single* models.

| Model | Development | | | Out-Of-Domain | | | Evaluation | | |
	P	R	F1	P	R	F1	P	R	F1
Lstm + CRF (Zhou and Xu, 2015)	79.7	79.4	79.6	70.7	68.2	69.4	82.9	82.8	82.8
HLstm (He et al., 2017)	81.6	81.6	81.6	72.9	71.4	72.1	83.1	83.0	83.1
Att (Tan et al., 2018)	82.6	83.6	83.1	73.5	74.6	**74.1**	84.5	85.2	84.8
HLstm-ours	82.2	81.9	82.0	72.6	71.2	71.9	83.4	82.8	83.1
Char	82.3	82.1	82.2	73.3	71.7	72.5	83.8	82.9	83.4
CRFm	81.9	81.5	81.7	72.0	69.6	70.9	84.0	83.1	83.5
Att-ours	83.0	83.4	83.2	74.5	72.9	*73.7*	84.8	84.7	84.8
CharAtt	83.6	83.5	**83.5**	73.5	72.6	73.0	85.0	84.8	**84.9**

Table 7: F1 scores on CoNLL'05 English data, CoNLL'09 German data and CoNLL'12 Arabic data using 2000 random training sentences: Dev (Development), Eval (Evaluation), and Ood (Out of Domain).

| Model | English | | | German | | | Arabic | |
	Dev	Eval	Ood	Dev	Eval	Ood	Dev	Eval
HLstm-ours	62.8	54.3	64.9	42.34	45.58	40.44	35.12	34.42
Char	64.8	55.2	65.8	**43.99**	**47.64**	**42.39**	36.52	37.01
CRFm	**65.8**	**57.5**	**67.0**	43.42	44.06	40.73	**38.91**	**38.36**
Att-ours	57.4	51.7	59.6	32.48	37.13	31.45	23.38	23.32
CharAtt	58.2	52.4	60.7	33.35	38.49	31.91	35.10	34.70

4.2 Results and Discussion

In Tab. 5-6, we compare the five models on English, German and Arabic. The proposed CharAtt out-performs all other models in almost all cases except the English out-of-domain setting. As can be seen in Tab. 6, our implementation achieves competitive performance to other state-of-the-art systems for English. To the best of our knowledge, we report the first SRL results (in CoNLL'05 metrics) for German and Arabic without using linguistic features.

In general, we find that using character embeddings improves the performance of HLstm and Att, although at a cost of increased processing time. Interestingly, using character embeddings is particularly effective for the Att model. One explanation could be that character embeddings are important for learning good attention masks as they encode information about the syntax of words and the sentence, e.g., it facilitates the system in learning that the number (singular/plural) of a subject and its verb should match.

Among the three languages, the performance gain by character-level representations is larger for German and Arabic than for English. This can be explained by the much larger vocabularies for German and Arabic combined with the smaller training datasets (#sentences, and #predicates) for these languages. Moreover, many grammatical cases, which are very strong predictors for semantic roles, are explicitly

---

[4]Note that the CoNLL'09 data is automatically converted to CoNLL'05 format using the script by Björkelund et al. (2009).

marked through use of inflection in German and Arabic.

To evaluate the influence of the training size on model performance, we train the models on a random sample of 2000 sentences for each language (see Tab. 7). Intriguingly, the attention models perform worst in this setting, indicating their need of large datasets. A reason for this could be that the attention models consider the sequential dependency between hidden states to a lesser degree than recurrent models do. In contrast, CRFm achieves the best results for English and Arabic, and the second best result for German. In fact, CRFm exploits not only the input sequence – using the LSTM – but also the sequential output dependencies, to compute output probabilities. We can see that this is very beneficial when less training data is available, especially when word order is a strong cue for SRL, which applies well for a strict word order language like English. For such cases the output dependencies can be learned even from less training data, which results in the CRFm model to excel. As can be seen in Tab. 7, when comparing Char with HLstm-ours and CharAtt with Att-ours, the benefit of using character embeddings is demonstrated on small datasets as well.

5 Conclusions

We introduced an open source SRL framework, DAMESRL, which provides flexible model construction, using state-of-the-art model components, handles various input and output formats, and which comes with clear output visualization. Using our framework, we slightly improve the state-of-the-art results of single end-to-end deep systems on the English CoNLL'05, and report the first experimental end-to-end deep SRL results for German[5] and Arabic[5]. We have shown that the flexible model construction provided by the framework is crucial for exploring good model structures when considering different languages with different characteristics, especially when training data is limited. DAMESRL is made available under the Apache 2.0 license.

References

Anders Björkelund, Love Hafdell, and Pierre Nugues. 2009. Multilingual semantic role labeling. In *Proceedings of CoNLL: Shared Task*, CoNLL '09. ACL.

Luheng He, Kenton Lee, Mike Lewis, and Luke Zettlemoyer. 2017. Deep semantic role labeling: What works and whats next. In *Proceedings of ACL*, volume 1. ACL.

Sepp Hochreiter and Jrgen Schmidhuber. 1997. Long short-term memory. *Neural Computation*, 9(8).

Martha Palmer, Daniel Gildea, and Nianwen Xue. 2010. *Semantic role labeling*, volume 3. Morgan & Claypool Publishers.

Gabriel Pereyra, George Tucker, Jan Chorowski, Lukasz Kaiser, and Geoffrey E. Hinton. 2017. Regularizing neural networks by penalizing confident output distributions. In *Proceedings of the ICLR Workshop*.

Zhixing Tan, Mingxuan Wang, Jun Xie, Yidong Chen, and Xiaodong Shi. 2018. Deep semantic role labeling with self-attention.

Yu Zhang, Guoguo Chen, Dong Yu, Kaisheng Yaco, Sanjeev Khudanpur, and James Glass. 2016. Highway long short-term memory RNNs for distant speech recognition. In *Proceedings of ICASSP*. IEEE.

Jie Zhou and Wei Xu. 2015. End-to-end learning of semantic role labeling using recurrent neural networks. In *Proceedings of ACL-IJCNLP*, volume 1. ACL.

---

[5]To the best of our knowledge, no results have been reported using CoNLL'05 metrics on these data. Pereyra et al. (2017) only report precision for argument classification for Arabic instead of using the standard CoNLL'05 metrics.

Author Index

Association for Computational Linguistics
209 N. Eighth Street
Stroudsburg, Pennsylvania 18360